LESLEY RIDDOCH is an award-winning broadcaster, writer and journalist. She writes weekly columns for *The Scotsman* and *Sunday Post* and is a regular contributor to *The Guardian*, *Newsnight Scotland*, *Scotland Tonight* and *Any Questions*. She is founder and Director of Nordic Horizons, a policy group that brings Nordic experts to the Scottish Parliament.

Lesley presented *You and Yours* on BBC Radio 4, *The Midnight Hour* on BBC2 and *The People's Parliament* and *Powerhouse* on Channel 4. She founded the Scottish feminist magazine *Harpies and Quines*, won two Sony awards for her daily Radio Scotland show and edited *The Scotswoman* – a 1995 edition of *The Scotsman* written and edited by its female staff. She lives in Fife and is married to an Englishman who grew up in Canada.

Reading Lesley Riddoch's Blossom *is like inhaling fjord air after being trapped in a sweaty backroom. Just brilliant.*
PAT KANE, singer and columnist

Inspiring, galvanising analysis of the untapped potential of Scottish people power.
KARINE POLWART, singer/songwriter

Blossom *confirms Lesley Riddoch's reputation as one of our top campaigning journalists.*
PAUL HUTCHEON, Herald

Luath Press is an independently owned and managed book publishing company based in Scotland and is not aligned to any political party or grouping. *Viewpoints* is an occasional series exploring issues of current and future relevance.

Cracking. A hopeful antidote to so much empty nastiness in politics. Read!
ALYN SMITH MEP

It's brilliant – every politician in the land should be made to read the chapter on inequality. I love the human stories in the book, but it's rich with evidence too. The most engaging social policy book I've read in ages (ever?).
JENNY KEMP, Zero Tolerance Campaign

Every Scot should read Blossom *by Lesley Riddoch before they vote. I'm reading* Blossom *right now and every paragraph crystallises the nebulous sensations of deep divide inequality and snobbery I have experienced my whole life.*
DES DILLON, writer

Blossom *is something we should all be reading. This is the book William Power and Edwin Muir should have written ... on a fine work.*
ELSPETH KING, Director, Stirling Smith Art Gallery and Museum

To all undecideds in Scotland, and all progressives – just to everyone... read Lesley Riddoch's Blossom. *She just gets it.*
DAVID GREIG, playwright

Blossom *reveals a Scotland full of promise, whose richest resource – her people – remains untapped. Riddoch's belief in Scotland's countrymen and women is the lifeblood of* Blossom.
NEWSNET SCOTLAND

A hard-hitting condition of Scotland tour-de-force and a characteristically feisty contribution to (and beyond) the present constitutional debate.
PADDY BORT, Product Magazine

Blossom

What Scotland Needs To Flourish

LESLEY RIDDOCH

Luath Press Limited
EDINBURGH
www.luath.co.uk

Dedicated to Chris Smith – my constant support.

First published 2013
Reprinted 2013

ISBN: 978-1-9083736-69-4

The paper used in this book is recyclable. It is made from
low chlorine pulps produced in a low energy, low emissions manner
from renewable forests.

Printed and bound by
Martins the Printers, Berwick upon Tweed

Typeset in 11.5 point Sabon

Contents

Acknowledgements

Muriel Alcorn
Bella Caledonia
Øivind Bratberg
Paddy Bort
Professor David McCrone
Hannah Derbyshire
Development Trusts Association Scotland
Prof Tom Devine
Foster Evans
Maggie Fyffe
Jim Harvey
Mary Hepburn
Luath Press, Kirsten Graham and Louise Hutcheson
Cathy McCormack
Prof Catriona MacDonald
Rosemarie MacEachen
Cailean MacLean
Robin McAlpine
Prof Charles McKean
Mark Perryman
Perspectives magazine, especially Davie Laing
Tommy Riley
Mona Røhne
The Scotsman
Tore Tanum
Ann Soutar
Phil Welsh
Andy Wightman
Raymond Young

All the above have saved me from errors in fields where they are expert and the faults or misjudgements that survive their amendments are mine alone.

Introduction

IDENTITY OR BAGGAGE? Scotland is currently on a quest for one, weighed down by the other. Can independence resolve long-standing problems and create fresh momentum for change? Certainly a new home, job or even a divorce can improve a bad situation all on its own. Sometimes though, a change of circumstance just shifts old problems to pastures new – unpacked baggage and all. Nations are no different.

This book suggests a change of constitutional control will not be enough to transform Scotland. That's not meant to be gloomy or defeatist – it's actually a vote of confidence in the capacity of Scots to handle more power in real, reinvigorated communities than any politicians are currently offering.

Social inequality clashes with every idea Scots have about themselves – and yet it's accepted as normal together with top-down governance, weak local democracy, disempowerment, bad health and sporting estates the size of small countries. Of course Scotland also boasts the Tartan Army, whisky exports, a social democratic consensus, Andy Murray, a wheen of best-selling authors, stunning scenery and energy resources. Life is great for some and not at all bad for others so we turn away from an inconvenient truth.

In international terms, Scotland is more often exceptional for all the wrong reasons.

We have sub-east European health outcomes, ghettoes of near unemployable people, an indoors culture and high rates of addiction and self harming behaviour. Scotland also has the smallest number of people owning the largest amounts of land, the lowest proportion standing for election and the largest local authorities with the least genuinely local control of tax and resources in Europe. We have one of the biggest income gaps between rich and poor. And although no-one has done the research, I'd also guess we have the least outdoorsy population, the smallest number of boat owners per mile of coastline and a high number of children who aren't sure eggs come from hens. But arguably we also have the most popular cities, varied landscape,

magnificent scenery, valuable energy resources, richest inventive tradition and most diverse linguistic heritage in the UK.

So is Scotland's enduring ability to punch beneath its weight caused
by our lack of statehood – or is it the other way around?

I appreciate that is not the way those closely involved with the
independence referendum would frame the question. I was brought up
in Belfast during the 'Troubles' when even a Buddhist was asked, 'Aye,
but are you a Catholic or a Protestant?'

And yet without structural change this misunderstood, unequal,
stoic and feisty country may be much the same for generations, regardless of the referendum outcome. The gardener may have a wider
range of tools available but fundamentals like soil, fertility, aspect
and shelter will remain unchanged. Perhaps these structural problems
need more attention than the contents of the garden shed.

I think deep down, Scots know it's time to stop celebrating just
because we occasionally sit a performance point above England at the
bottom of almost every international health and wellbeing league table.
We've been badly served by political debate which is often sloganeering,
simplistic and scaremongering and by a media which has become a collective echo chamber for suspicion, pessimism and despair.

There is a way out for Scotland – a way for this country to truly
blossom. But it needs us to question what we currently regard as
normal and inevitable. And that, by definition, is very hard.

Our working knowledge of the way other countries operate is
limited. Likewise our real understanding of how the other half lives
in Scotland itself. So we can't believe inequality can really cause the
shameful, premature mortality of the 'Scottish Effect'. We can't imagine having a wee bit of land, or a forest hut for weekend escapes. We
can't conceive that a shift of investment from later life to early years
could improve Scotland's social problems within a generation. We can't
visualise a country where young people come first, good health is not
delivered by doctors or guaranteed by the presence of a nearby A&E
department, speculators aren't allowed to push up housing prices and
genuine communities raise taxes and run their own services. We can't
envisage how life and democracy would be improved if Scotland hit
the North European average of 70 per cent turnout at local elections
not nearly bottom with 38 per cent.

Most Scots simply haven't experienced life in healthier democracies where entitlement is not the preserve of an elite, co-operation is in with the bricks and equality is a shared policy goal. But nor has the average Scot sampled the other extreme – life on benefits in our own 'deserts wi windaes' – as Billy Connolly called Scotland's massive, peripheral housing estates. So we just don't know that some of those 'hopeless' communities have managed to create profound social change virtually unaided. Nor do we feel the pain personally when some bold pioneers are broken by a top-down system of governance, designed and run by fellow Scots. Betwixt and between the average Scot does not know the best of times or the worst of times. So we settle too readily for something in between.

This is not to blame anyone. Social segregation means we almost all live in ghettos – quite unaware of how other people live across the great divides of class, gender, geography, occupation and sometimes religion. Successive generations have picked up fragments of Scottish history from John Prebble, films and libraries – not school. And international comparisons have always followed blood ties and emigration patterns to distant English-speaking nations larger than our own instead of successful, like-sized neighbours.

This book attempts to plug some of those knowledge gaps – abroad and at home – with stories, statistics, theories and solutions – and each chapter focuses on a real situation in a problematic area of Scottish life.

Blossom unashamedly draws its inspiration from the exceptional 'ordinary' Scots I've met over 30 years as a journalist, broadcaster, feminist and supporter of community action, makes comparisons with other nations, especially the Nordics, and tends to see the same life lesson in each exceptional story and successful democracy. People generally 'fix' and maintain themselves if they control local resources and have genuinely equal chances in a country that understands the importance of hope and social solidarity.

Academic work and the views of fellow commentators are quoted throughout, but the book is driven by the evidence, inspiration and practical solutions of particularly determined and insightful Scots who've acted to improve their lives – often despite the authorities and in advance of politicians.

Blossom is an account of Scotland at the grassroots through the stories of people I've had the good fortune to know – the most stubborn, talented and resilient people on the planet. They've had to be. Some have transformed their parts of Scotland. Some have tried and failed. But all have something in common – they know what it takes for Scotland to blossom.

We should know too.

So this book poses a question as important as the one Scots must answer on 18 September 2014. Why is Scotland still one of the most unequal societies and sickest man (and woman) of Europe despite an abundance of natural resources and a long history of human endeavour? In answering that question there is no mention of Devo Max or Section 30 powers. There is no great effort to come down on one 'side' or the other. But there is copious mention of the power possessed by 'ordinary' Scots and the top-down, overbearing approach to governance (Scots built and made from girders) which has left that collective human capacity largely untapped and Scotland's rivers, land, sea, lochs, forests and other natural assets underused and largely beyond democratic control.

Facts and figures are a vital part of any story. But they don't bring Scotland's dilemma alive. They don't explain why people with choices act as if they had none. They don't explain why Scots over the centuries have put on weight, not democratic muscle. They don't explain why cash and socialist tradition have failed to shift poverty. They don't explain why some Scots trash Scotland while others tiptoe around like the place is only rented for the weekend. Why don't ordinary Scots behave like the permanent, responsible owners of this beautiful country? Is it because we are not the owners – and never have been?

For all the talk about being Jock Tamson's bairns, Scotland is a surprisingly elitist society where a relatively small number of people own land, run businesses, possess wealth, stand for election and run government. The result is a deep-seated belief that ordinary Scots cannot own and run things, don't want to own and run things and indeed that it hardly matters who does.

It matters. It matters so much that talented folk still leave Scotland instead of pushing for fundamental change. Well-intentioned public servants scour the universe for an explanation of the Scottish Effect (where Scots health is consistently worse than English counterparts in areas with similar levels of deprivation).[1] Perhaps the answer is simple. Perhaps the sheer stultifying burden of disempowerment has finally caught up with us all.

Imagine Scottish culture as a beautifully knitted, warmth-providing, well-constructed and substantial jumper snagged on a bit of barbed wire. Its wearer tries to move forward – but cannot. A pause is needed to lift the garment clear. Scotland is thus snagged. And no amount of pulling away at the problem will get us off this stubborn, progress-inhibiting hook.

Devolved or independent, Scotland must belong to all its people – to have, hold, inhabit, farm, walk, plant, hunt, develop, mine, explore and even accidentally damage – not to small, self-selecting social groups. The bad news is that such change runs counter to some inherited outlooks. The good news is that it can be done.

This is my own view of a country I have always regarded as home thanks to Highland parents who avidly read the *Sunday Post* and *The Scots Magazine*, faithfully watched *The White Heather Club* and listened to Robbie Shepherd during long expatriate years in Woverhampton (where I was born) and Belfast (where I grew up). We moved to Glasgow when I was 13 but I headed to university in England and Wales and a BBC training course in London before coming back for good at the tender age of 24. What puzzled me when we first 'crossed the water' in 1973 puzzles me still. Scotland quite obviously isn't England or Ireland. But so often Scots ignore what's truly distinctive and successful about their culture, hero worship the very long dead (Wallace and Bruce spring to mind), skip the intervening period and despair about the future. Why is that? I once wrote and produced a BBC Scotland programme with the comedian Frankie Boyle. He played the Ghost of Christmas Past taking a mythical First Minister Jock O'Donnell through 25 years of Scottish politics with all its promises, false starts and new dawns. I had written most of the script but the last growling line was all his own.

'We're brought so low because we aim so high.' He was right. A

---

1 Glasgow Centre for Population Health's report 'Investigating a Glasgow Effect' found the current deprivation profiles of Glasgow, Liverpool and Manchester are almost identical. Despite this, premature deaths in Glasgow 2003–2007 were more than 30 per cent higher, with all deaths around 15 per cent higher. This 'excess' mortality was seen across virtually the whole population: all ages (except the very young), males and females, in deprived and non-deprived neighbourhoods.

nation with lower aspirations would feel less pain faced with the fact of its stubborn underachievement. But somewhere in our heads – or hearts – we aim to create the ultimate nation. A country as equal as the Nordics but as passionate as the Irish. As well organised as the Swedes but as personally connected as the Broons. As energy rich as Saudi Arabia but as green as Denmark. As confident as the crazy Icelanders but as prudent as our (former) selves.

With a heck of a lot of work – it's entirely possible. But somehow Scots don't believe their fantasy can ever become a reality. Why not? Perhaps because our political leaders believe we aren't up for the challenge. They doubt us and we see it. So we doubt them and ourselves. Of course politicians deliver warm words about change, equality and community involvement – but in the end voters judge governments by actions, not slogans. A state that really believed in the capacity of its people wouldn't infantilise or micromanage them. A government that understood the potential of communities wouldn't stifle them with top-down control. Political leaders who backed long term change wouldn't fund a plethora of short term projects. Professionals who truly valued active communities would hand out resources and power instead of hanging onto them. A long term shift of resources from the centre to empowered communities would be the 'settled will' of the Scottish people. Is it?

Does such a mature and mutually respectful country sound like Scotland?

Call me old fashioned but perhaps this 'national question' needs ventilating as much as 'the special one'.

This is a personal and doubtless highly opinionated account of Scotland's long journey towards self-awareness and greater self-governance. It could be dismissed as a rant. It is certainly a polemic. The connections made, arguments developed and trains of thought could be wrong and simplistic – or spot on and needing said. *Blossom* proceeds in the hope that at least some observations fall into the latter category. All too often society pays attention only to what it can measure, describe and prove. With problems that have endured changes of government, century and council boundary – we must look beyond that.

I am first to admit that the journalist is often a jack-of-all-trades and mistress of none. Perhaps that's led me to venture between academic disciplines – into areas where wiser heads fear to tread. A smart economist will not venture an opinion on crime patterns. A respected historian will hesitate to comment on child wellbeing. A coronary specialist will not give advice on thyroid disorders. And yet they are all related.

Perhaps what's needed is a new discipline of generalist. Or perhaps that's what journalists were always meant to be before they went off ambulance chasing instead. This is not a comprehensive work – there's little mention of subjects that could (and have) consumed entire volumes – particularly religion, economics and law. I have tried not to duplicate existing work but to focus on areas of Scottish life and perspectives that seem overlooked.

Nothing written here is intended to be personally critical, anti-English or pro-Scots. My aim is to examine the larger currents in which most of us are mere flotsam and jetsam, doing what's possible, least difficult or expected in our various worlds.

My world has included Norway since 2010 when I started to research a PhD in Oslo and set up a policy group called Nordic Horizons, which brings specialists from all Nordic nations to address MSPs, civil servants and members of the public in the Scottish Parliament. So I make a lot of Nordic comparisons which may suggest I see Scotland as a mini Norway. Actually, that wouldn't be so bad. But Scotland's destiny is to become more fully herself – not a pale version of any other nation, no matter how well they do at the Winter Olympics. The recessionary times we currently inhabit are fearful yet also eye-opening. The widespread use of English across the world allows international comparison as never before. So basing policy on what's ae been isn't good enough.

I've been encouraged to write what I can pending ultimate enlightenment by Welsh writer and academic Gwyn Jones, Iceland's principle chronicler in the English language, who once observed:

> There is a longstanding theory that by the time an actress is equipped to play Juliet she is too old for the part. The Viking historian may equally fear that before he acquires all the languages, reads all the books and passes all the covers of all the periodicals, he will have reached the blameless haven of senility without a word rendered. Patently to wait on definitive knowledge is to wait on eternity.

This of course was written by a man who performed a forensic exami-
nation of Celtic, Anglo-Welsh, Nordic and Icelandic cultures before he
lifted a pen. But in the spirit of a man whose own inspiration was this
quote from the Icelandic scholar Sigurður Nordal, I will soldier on.

'It is very pleasant to be a little drunk, on a little pony, in a little rain.'
Or as Borders poet Ian McFadyen reinvisaged those words in a new Scots
haiku after the first edition of *Blossom*:

> It's lichtsome
> oan a wee pownie
> in jist a wee smirr o rain,
> wi a wee bleeze oan.

Amen to both.

CHAPTER ONE

Scottish Identity

LET'S LAY THIS ONE to rest straight away – Scotland has a more distinctive personality than many independent neighbours. We have massive oil resources – Ireland has next to none. We have a better wind resource than Denmark and more wave energy potential than Portugal. We have a strategic location the Vikings once killed for, we land more fish than Sweden and Finland combined[1] and have a natural scenic splendour that makes other Europeans weep. We have more viable and internationally ranked cities than the rest of the UK[2] and Europe's highest ranked research university.[3] We have more coastline than Germany, a richer folk tradition than the Spanish (OK, we could argue over that one) a list of inventors proportionately longer than any other nation on earth and world-renowned whisky, energy and engineering firms.

We have natural and cultural assets other countries would give their eye teeth to possess – but somehow the overall result is not a healthy nation with affordable energy, comfortable homes, cutting edge technology as standard and creative lives spent guddling around in nature.

We could spend a lot of time arguing about who's to blame for what we already know – Scotland has some of the worst health, employment and social outcomes in Europe and one of the biggest income gaps. Take a look at Figure 1 below which vividly demonstrates the link between income and outcomes in Scotland today.[4] If you live in one of the ten per cent poorest neighbourhoods you are five times more likely to experience crime, twice as likely to have chronic

---

1   Scottish catches in 2011 were 363,800 tonnes – Sweden 212,000 Finland 151,000 http://epp.eurostat.ec.europa.eu.

2   Edinburgh was voted 'Best UK City' 2012 for the 13th year in a row by *Guardian* and *Observer* readers, 'Favourite UK City' by *Conde Naste* readers in 2012 (2010 Award Winner for Best City), 'most desirable UK city in which to live' in YouGov poll 2009 and one of the world's top ten cities by a travel magazine in 2008 – *Lonely Planet* guide rated Glasgow as one of the world's top ten cities the same year.

3   The University of Dundee was voted Europe's 'Best Place to Work in Academia' in an annual worldwide survey compiled by *The Scientist* magazine, 2012.

4   Each cohort represents the ten per cent of neighbourhoods which contain the most and least income-deprived people. These two groups (of the least and most income deprived) each represent over 700 neighbourhoods

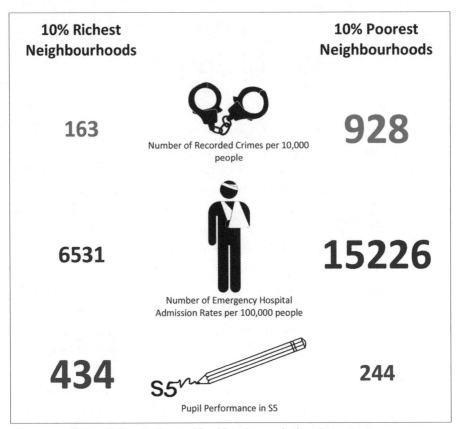

Figure 1: Deprivation and health, crime and education outcomes

or serious health problems that result in emergency hospital admission
and your kids will score only half the combined academic results of
their most affluent s6 peers in the ten per cent richest neighbourhoods.
These are dramatically unequal outcomes.

The picture of income inequality is equally stark. In 2010–11 the
poorest 30 per cent of Scots received 14 per cent of national income
and there's been very little change in this income inequality since
1998–99.[5]

(there are 6,505 'neighbourhoods' and 500 to 1000 people per neighbourhood. So each of the two ten per cent
groups represents over 350,000 people living in Scotland) Figure 1 shows health, education and crime outcomes
for the two 'poorest' and 'richest' ten per cent of neighbourhoods in Scotland. Emergency Hospital Admissions
per 100,000 people Pupil Performance measured by 'average tariff' scores from pupils sqa exam results from
2010/11. ucas use these scores to establish entry into higher education. Crime rates recorded by the Scottish
Index of Multiple Deprivation (simd), 2012 and only show police recorded crime. The 'richest' and 'poorest'
neighbourhoods have been selected by the percentage of their population who are income deprived. Compiled
from 2011 government statistics by researchers at the Improvement Service.

5   http://www.scotland.gov.uk/Resource/0041/00416632.pdf.

Scotland's assets are like familiar, family heirlooms for the few and untouchable, almost imaginary treasures for the many. Inequality has nipped Scotland in the bud.

So let's not spend too much time arguing. Income and health, education and employment outcomes in Scotland are very unequal – even by the unequal standards of Britain. The only real question is why.

Scots currently inhabit a large, overgrown garden where monocultures run riot, dominant plants stifle diversity, native species grow in the shade, climbers are unsupported, soil is exhausted, seeds are blown elsewhere, weeds run unchecked and litter fills corners. Passers-by admire the backdrop and spot the potential but puzzle over the general lack of care. Somewhere under the weeds the little white rose of Scotland is still alive – growing, budding but never quite flowering for more than a few precious days.

How can it? A competent gardener is needed to restructure the garden from the grassroots upwards. But the best candidates are always overlooked – the Scottish people themselves. We could inhabit a well-tended, diverse garden, home to foreign exotica, hardy hybrids and flowering, reproductive and distinctively Scottish plants. But it would take a collective and united commitment of time and effort.

And we are divided.

Some believe Scotland is already a viable proposition, whilst others think the country has large, sick, hopeless urban populations and dispersed rural communities inhabiting barren (looking) land fit only for grouse moors. Can both 'sides' be right? Is there a single verdict upon which a majority can agree?

Scotland is a distinctive nation. But its identity may not derive from the commonly accepted symbols of nationhood. And that's a paradox worth exploring.

It's more than 300 years since the Treaty of Union. Britain PLC has partly de-merged its acquisitions. Scotland has regained a parliament, is set to vote on independence, and feelings of Scottishness abound. No wonder. It would be hard to think of a nation with more visible, durable and internationally accepted calling cards of identity – tartan, bagpipes, Auld Lang Syne, haggis, Burns whisky, golf.

And yet.

Do all Scots identify with these tartanised symbols of nationhood?

Disconnected from the environment that created them, kilt-wearing, single-malt quaffing, Pringle-wearing, golf-mad Scots seem strangely inauthentic. Like an identikit picture on a Wanted poster – each piece may be accurate but the whole face doesn't look like anyone real.

Nonetheless, at some point all Scots have tried to pour themselves into the part. Like 90-minute-Christians who appear in church for marriages and funerals, 90-minute-Scots 'turn out' for Burns Nights, Rugby matches, Tartan Army events, weddings and funerals. When identity is demanded or ritual is required, the kilt appears, a few poems or songs are dusted down and serious drinking helps lads focus on the only point of Scottish identity that seems to matter.

Not being English.

Not indulging in pedantry, moderation, village greens, David Cameron, New Labour, house price discussions, real ale, cricket or morris dancing.

It's easy to sneer. But if this describes the English – what does it make the Scots?

Immoderate, excessive, concrete-jungle tolerating, Old Labour, lager-drinking, football-worshipping, hard men? The current working definition of Scottishness is male to the core and ties a nation psychologically and symbiotically to a neighbour über Scots would rather not emulate.

If anyone hadn't noticed, the English are currently on a quest of their own – driven to self-discovery by the apparently resurgent Celts. Jeremy Paxman, Kate Fox, David Starkey, Simon Schama – the bookshelves are groaning with attempts to create a DNA of the English that does not rely on Empire, Good Queen Bess, 1966, Dunkirk and *EastEnders*.

If being English is currently a puzzle, being not English is an absolute nonsense, a sentiment expressed succinctly in Renton's speech in *Trainspotting*:

> I hate being Scottish. We're the lowest of the fucking low, the scum of the earth, the most wretched, servile, miserable, pathetic trash that was ever shat into civilization. Some people hate the English, but I don't. They're just wankers. We, on the other hand, are colonised by wankers. We can't even pick a decent culture to be colonised by. We are ruled by effete arseholes. It's a shite state of affairs and all the fresh air is ever going to change that.

It's no wonder young Scots want out – into a bigger or smaller world where identity can be defined by sex, drugs, music, hairstyle, Facebook friends – anything other than the dull, outdated straitjacket that accompanies the geographical accident of being Scottish.

And yet.

Try believing Scots are not a distinctive group but just self-deluded northern Brits surfing the net and watching MTV in a globalised world devoid of local cultural reference. Andy does. This earnest Scottish TV researcher came over to chat after a BBC discussion programme in which I was the only person to think Scottish independence was a perfectly reasonable political choice. The comment seemed to bother him. Like I had otherwise been on or near his wavelength but with one apparent endorsement of Scotland as a meaningful entity, had jumped straight onto another planet.

Looking at this well-meaning, naïve product of modern Britain, it seemed like time for mischief.

Was Andy watching MTV in a terraced house – the traditional unit of 'British' housing?

Nope – he lived in a tenement.

Did he take A-levels like most British students?

Nope – he took Highers. A more rounded education, according to his mum.

Did his parents own their house, like the average Briton?

Nope, and unlike most English students he stayed in their council flat during university. Cheaper.

After MTV, would he stay in to watch the Ashes followed perhaps by *The Vicar of Dibley*?

Nope. Unlike anyone south of the border, he'd listen to a witheringly sarcastic phone-in about the day's football (*Off the Ball*) watch a sitcom about two auld geezers on a bleak housing estate (*Still Game*) and stay in with a lager because he had no cash to buy a round.

Ever thought of going out and just buying a pint for yourself, Andy?

Dinnae be daft.

Aye – Andy disnae quite speak proper English when he disnae huv tae either.

With Scotland's best fishing on the doorstep, does Andy own a fishing rod, or a boat, perhaps?

Naw – and he disnae dae 'country' dancing or shoot deer either.

Do any of his family own land?

C'mon, we live in a council house.

OK Andy.

Did you vote for Britain's favourite painting in 2005 – Turner's *Fighting Temeraire* (The Battle of Trafalgar)? Or Britain's favourite poem in 2009 – Rudyard Kipling's 'If'?

Nope – Andy's top marks would go to Dali's *Christ of St John of the Cross* (a picture he knows in great detail because unlike many English galleries, access to Scottish public art has always been free). And on best poem he'd be torn between Burns' 'Tam O'Shanter', MacDiarmid's 'Drunk Man Looks at the Thistle' and MacCaig's lines about his best poem being two fags long.

And yes, before I ask, Andy's dad did work in the shipyards, refused to buy his council flat on principle, voted Labour until the shipyards closed, switched to the SNP, decided they were Tartan Tories and then supported Tommy Sheridan until the Parliament building costs overran – at which point he stopped voting altogether and died (prematurely) from lung disease five years ago.

Andy – how did your mum vote?

D'you know, her son never actually asked.

Andy, catch a grip.

The Scots are not just what happens when you vary England's default settings – more rain, less winter daylight, more poverty, more hills, more cloud, less sun, fewer people, less ethnic diversity. Though these basic physical and social truths have certainly helped shape identity and behaviour.

Scots are not just intemperate versions of our more measured southern cousins. We don't live in the same houses, laugh at the same jokes, read the same books, or share the same life expectancy. We don't have the same capacity to commercialise ideas. We don't have the same informal rules about collective behaviour. We don't speak quite the same language and we don't (publicly) aspire to the same social goals. We don't have the same history, weather, geology, bank notes, education system, legal system or tradition of ownership. We don't vote the same way and we don't die at the same rate or from the same diseases.

Scots are no more northern variants of the English than the Irish are western ones.

The Scottish identity is not just a bundle of remnants – a set of random behaviours by mindless contrarians welded together into a dangerously unstable and unpredictable personality. Scots are quite obviously and consistently different from their neighbours – English, Irish or Norwegian. But different enough?

Scots are (characteristically) in two minds. Most folk believe national difference must be enormous before policy or governance arrangements need pay the blindest bit of attention. Thus Scotland must be as unlike England as Brazil is unlike Denmark before difference is worth recognising or nurturing. National difference must be as stark as two primary colours and as non-negotiable as the old Iron Curtain before it can hope to justify 'nationhood'. In practice, this 'high bar' of distinction is not louped by many independent European states. And yet, perversely, the Scots demand it of themselves.

The Nordic nations differ by only a few shades of grey. The Low Countries have pastel coloured borders. And yet try suggesting Spain and Portugal, the Netherlands and Belgium, Norway and Sweden should merge. Try it and stand well back. In mainland Europe, slight but important points of cultural distinction form the cornerstone of each nation state. I remember interviewing the Sinn Fein leader and former IRA man Martin McGuinness for Channel Four's *People's Parliament* during that bizarre period in the '80s when his voice was 'banned' on TV and radio. If Sinn Fein got their wish and Northern Ireland became part of the Irish Republic, I asked, what would be visibly different to the casual onlooker?

He thought for a while and said: 'The street signs would be in Irish Gaelic.'

The same thought occurred to every member of the production team – is that all? Could such a tiny change possibly justify those long decades of struggle, death, grief and violence?

And yet, travel from Germany to the Netherlands and street signs are often the only visible evidence of border crossing. In fact, Scotland does look different – there are mostly terraced houses in English cities and mostly tenements in Scottish ones (though I'll grant you Newcastle stretches the point). And yet we speak mostly the same language, share institutions and recent centuries of history with our southern cousins. So the Martin McGuinness question arises again. Does a very different history once upon a time justify change today? Do real social and cultural differences justify full political independence?

Look around. Some distinctive nations choose to go it alone, others opt to remain within larger states. Former parts of Denmark are now within the Federal Republic of Germany, the population of the United States of America contains more Spanish speakers than Spain, Russia straddles five time zones and the single state of Brazil is physically larger than the 50 states of Europe. Enormous diversity can remain within some single states (though usually with more devolution than Britain has tolerated) whilst other nations depart from remarkably similar states as soon as war, occupation or revolution permits.

Of course Scotland is a sufficiently distinctive nation to consider political independence. But Scotland has more than cultural distinctiveness. The secret ingredient is what Benedict Anderson called the Imagined Community 'because the members of even the smallest nation will never know most of their fellow-members, meet them, or even hear of them, yet in the minds of each lives the image of their communion.'[6]

You could call it a form of love. That warm, mutual feeling of confidence and trust between independent people that encourages them to join forces, share resources and change living arrangements to face the future together.

But hey – love? In a debate about Scottish identity?

That's a toughie for a nation that doesn't do emotion (without a large skelp of drink).

So the constitutional debate focuses on detail, process, money and currency – like a divorce where hurt, betrayal and despair cannot be discussed and practicalities assume paramount and disproportionate importance. Who will have the stereo – and can its future be sensibly discussed in isolation from the CDs?

Here's the thing. National self-determination isn't about technicalities; it's about identity, confidence and trust. That's not to say the technical questions are trivial. Almost everything written about Scottish

---

6   Benedict Anderson, *Imagined Communities: Reflections on the Origins and Spread of Nationalism* (London: Verso, 1983).

independence eventually touches on the Black Gold. Will oil sustain a new Scottish state or does recent banking collapse suggest Scotland cannot rely on its own resources to stand alone? Can Alex Salmond guarantee Scots will be better off in an independent Scotland?

Of course he can't.

If Scots need guarantees and cast-iron certainty, the country will remain a grudging and grumbling part of the UK forever. None of our small, independent neighbours broke away from larger states to be better off. Far from it. When Norway announced independence from Sweden in 1905 it immediately became the second poorest nation in Europe. The tiny independent nation of Iceland which boasted the world's first parliament reluctantly returned to Norwegian control in the 13th century after tree-felling turned the island into a northern desert. Still its tiny population (smaller than Dundee) seized the chance for independence without a moment's hesitation when the Germans occupied Stepmother Denmark in 1944.

Back then, Iceland had no geo-thermal power, had not fought and won the Cod Wars, nor gambled and lost everything thanks to a bunch of cocky young bankers. What it did have, was a sudden influx of American soldiers at the Keflavik airbase, radiating confidence, driving jeeps and promising to stick around. And then Iceland took a leap in the dark.

So it goes. The urge to break away from an existing union – political, marital or financial – is rarely totally rational, or economically prudent. There may be preparation, debate and plans – but eventually caution becomes an anchor and the voyage must begin.

Mind you, Scotland approaches the independence question with yet another current running – localism. It may not be necessary for Scotland to prove its people are dramatically different or guaranteed to have short-term economic success or even part of an imagined community to argue that 5 not 55 million people is a better size for democracy and effective governance – especially with a public sector dismantling government at Westminster.

Culture, oil, politics, history and size. Scotland has as many reasons for seeking independence as any other restless nation – although currently the argument convinces more voters south of the border than north of it. A majority of English people has consistently supported

Scottish independence since the 2007 SNP victory raised the question. Some – like English socialist Mark Perryman – think the departure of the collectivist Scots would provide a long overdue jolt to the complacent English left. Others – like ex-*Sun* editor Kelvin McKenzie – think Scots are whingeing subsidy junkies and cannot wait to halt the 'gravy train' heading north. Mind you, I'm sure he thinks the same about Yorkshire.

Such strong southern support for Scottish independence could have been harnessed to prompt a UK-wide debate about federalism, devolution and democratic change right across the paternalistic, top-down United Kingdom. It could – but it hasn't.

It's been far easier to portray Scotland's endless agonising over constitutional status as a right royal pain. We do want more powers, don't we? A bit... no a bit more... no that's too much... no maybe it's fine... What about a referendum with one question... Or two... no, wait...

It's been far easier to mock northern indecision, view Scottish independence as Alex Salmond's personal obsession and his party's landslide majority in 2011 as a form of mass hypnosis. It's not so easy to regard the plodding Scots as a revolutionary vanguard destined to challenge Britain's centralised, class-riven, unequal society until something better emerges. But who else will? The conservative English? Or the Welsh? Gubbed by their neighbours in 1283, our Celtic cousins were forced to dance to an English tune in education, health, local government, housing and even political outlook, despite devolution. In the last Westminster elections just 1.7 per cent of Scottish MPs were Conservative compared to 20 per cent of Welsh MPs and 56 per cent of English MPs with the Northern Irish water muddied by different political loyalties – as is their prerogative.

1.7 per cent, 20 per cent and 56 per cent. Those figures tell us something.

The distinctiveness of Wales is largely cultural, not political or institutional. Welshness is kept alive by male voice choirs, Welsh language schools, S4C, the Methodist Chapel and (once upon a time) by campaigns against holiday homes. No-one can be in any doubt the Welsh are culturally distinct from the English. But has that been enough to create feelings of nationhood or a drive towards a new Welsh state? Like defiant prisoners whistling 'Home of our Fathers' as the firing squad take aim, Welsh culture has been the last defence against economic and social domination. The Scots have always had more – we've had unique, long-lasting institutions.

No offence to speakers of Welsh, Gaelic or Scots, but language alone does not sustain nor fully define a nation – at least not this one. Law abiding, rational, dour old souls that we are, Scots are defined by outlooks created by institutions that predate (and have survived) the Union. By an education system that seeks breadth, not specialism. By a legal system based on statute, not precedent. By a Kirk not led by the Head of State. By a housing policy not historically based on sale and inheritance, but (for better and worse) on tenancy and rent. By an economy based (recently) on state activity not private enterprise. And by an endless and hopeless quest for kinship and connection in lieu of the social democratic state, Scots have lacked the opportunity (and determination) to build.

All that most Britons notice about Scots is that we wear kilts – but who doesn't these days – and have two public holidays at Hogmanay.

In fact, we do many things differently north of the border but since we don't quite understand why any more, there's no reason anyone else should. As a result Scots are often propping up what doesn't matter and ignoring what does.

Occasionally we catch the scent of a blossom that has been taken from the room – like Hugh MacDiarmid's little white rose of Scotland that 'smells so sweet and breaks the heart'.

What is it then? What is Scottishness?

It isn't the Scottish football team – however convenient a repository that is for outpourings of male emotion.

It isn't – sadly – organised communitarian endeavour. Most Scots don't do credit unions, local energy companies, or local asset ownership (at least not on the scale of our European neighbours although we are catching up). We don't do local governance – perversely in a tiny country we do extremely large.

It isn't a tradition of healthy living. We don't do the body as a temple, exercise, eating vegetables or getting outdoors. We don't live in nature. We don't build in wood.

Our 'ither' national dish is probably chicken tikka masala washed down with Irn-Bru or super lager.

We reassert our collective proletarian identity with every curry we order, every sun-bed we occupy, every triple voddie we demolish in the name of a 'good time' and every year of life expectancy we thereby lose. All to prove we are Scottish – the underdogs against the British Bulldogs. David against Goliath. Wee, tough Billy Bremner against louche, decadent David Beckham.

We cling to a tough-talking, self-mocking, cynical world outlook instead of recognising such gallows humour for what it is – a coping mechanism created in days of appalling poverty and maintained by affluent descendants out of guilt and solidarity with those still mired in near-permanent inequality. A world we dare not fully acknowledge, tackle or fix.

So Scots generally ignore the paradox of an empty rural land-scape in which there is somehow no affordable space for us to live. We blame the resulting high rural property prices on wealthy incomers seeking second homes instead of an absurd land scarcity tolerated by successive Scottish governments. We allow city to remain divided from country and therefore – uniquely at our latitude – have no weekend hut or cabin culture. We are at home in the pub, on the terracing, in the DIY store or on the couch – not in nature. We live indoors like trog-lodytes amongst the finest natural scenery in northern Europe. Land remains over-priced and under-used – people-free thanks to planning preference, economic difficulty and landowner diktat. Empty, man-made desolation is now 'Natural Scotland'.

We tell ourselves it doesn't matter. Modern Scots are predominantly urban Scots, after all, with gyms for exercise, parks for dog walking, some of Europe's most popular cities for leisure and trips abroad for guaranteed sunshine. What happens in run-down rural areas is not our problem. What goes wrong in wrecked urban communities is not our fault.

Life is good – by and large. Scotland bumps along. Most of the nation's health problems are concentrated in a few postcodes the rest don't visit. Successive studies – including David Cameron's Happiness Index – suggest Scots are generally happier than folk down south.[7] And

---

7   http://www.scotsman.com/news/odd/scotland-revealed-as-one-of-happiest-parts-of-britain-1-2644565
    http://www.theguardian.com/commentisfree/2012/feb/29/ons-happy-scots-northern-irish

when the economy improves / Labour gets back into power/ Scotland votes for independence, everything will get better.

These at least are the 'classic' outlooks still favoured by many of our politicians. Scots are currently being asked to define Scottishness through the constitutional prism of independence alone. But perhaps that isn't a wide, searching or engaging enough perspective. Polls consistently show Scots want more economic control and tax-raising based here – but maybe not total independence. Not yet. Desire for the 'Full Monty' is being blocked, perhaps by satisfaction with being British, perhaps by 300 years as a junior partner but possibly by something that's been around longer. Chronic disempowerment. The kind that arises from centuries living on land we could not own, piers we could not use, rivers we could not fish and forests we could not enter. Centuries inhabiting homes we could not (till recently) own, improve or inherit and cities, towns and villages whose shape we (still) cannot really determine. Centuries speaking in dialects and languages we could not use in official situations and thinking about realities, histories and people we would never hear on the radio or TV channels of our own public broadcasting services.

The Scots' much discussed 'lack of confidence' cannot be remedied by simply 'pulling ourselves together', developing 'positive self-talk' or 'thinking big.' Our disempowerment arises from several centuries of 'get out' and 'keep off' signs – many erected by fellow Scots. A sense of engagement can't just be switched on – especially when involvement in Scottish democracy has historically been so limited.

Awash with credit, homes, cars, flat-screen televisions, patios, fridge-freezers and leather three piece suites – most modern Scots are leading lives of relative comfort compared to our forebears. But are we in control of this country? Are Scots actively shaping Scotland or are we still passively shaped by it – absent experts, distant officials, old choices, old loyalties, old divisions, old money and all?

This may seem a harsh, even alarmist critique of a country that's evidently not on its collective knees. The blight of inequality affects only some. The fear of 'falling behind' encourages just as strong and self-improving a reflex amongst others. On a good day, no symptoms of general malaise are visible. But look closely. Just as disease spreads when herd immunity falls below 90 per cent, just as a barrel is soured by one badly bruised apple – so the whole of Scotland is impacted by the acute problems of the few.

Look closer still. Our collective response contains symptoms of low-grade damage – hesitation, poor self-esteem and chronic fear of making mistakes.

No matter how few are truly crippled by 'the Scottish Effect', we all experience and pay for it. In cash terms, of course, but in the more important matter of outlook too. Trust in the capacity of others, belief there is such a thing as society and our very identity as equality-loving Scots – all these precious social goods are threatened by the existence of no-go zones, jobless, loan shark patrolled, drug dependent ghettoes, fear of others and the corrosive cynicism of the dispossessed. Aye right. We are the only nation who could turn a double positive into a negative and bestow that withering outlook on a leading Book Festival (it's still a good title, mind).

Above all though, inequality eats away at leadership. Who knows what pace of change can reasonably be sustained when some can run marathons whilst others can hardly walk to the chippy? How can such an unevenly empowered group cross the road together when one person's uncertainty causes everyone else to falter? Blight on healthy plants doesn't arise by mistake or coincidence. It's the fairly predictable outcome of difficult climate, poor soil conditions, a lack of protection, shelter and nourishment. As with gardens so with nations.

Of course Scotland is not doing too badly. Of course there are successful Scots. Of course there always will be exceptions – but few as powerful as the rule. This book contends that the expectation of exclusion is at the core of Scottish identity. Even though the children and great-grand children of the dispossessed now have some wealth and material goods they don't have and don't expect to have the collective power to shape their local lives or feel Scotland is unequivocally their country and their responsibility to use well. Such chronic disempowerment disappeared in large parts of Europe when feudalism was abolished thanks in part to the Napoleonic Code which ended privilege based on birth.[8] It didn't happen here. That single fact

---

8   The Code was adopted in many countries occupied by the French during the Napoleonic Wars, and thus formed the basis of private property law in Italy, the Netherlands, Belgium, Spain, Portugal (and their former colonies), Poland and many German regions .

has allowed exclusion to become normalised and privilege to thrive –
even as Scots try to entrench their broadly social-democratic values at
Holyrood. The Scottish Establishment has used wealth, brass-neck,
cultural confidence and long experience of controlling valuable assets
to keep a grip on Scotland's institutions and collective expectations.
That grip weakened with devolution and weakened further with
the surprise election of two SNP governments. The move towards a
more equal, Nordic-style society has begun. But the move is hesitant
– as progressive Scots are divided by the all-consuming battle over
independence.

There's no doubt Scotland has a distinct, national identity. Not all
good. But not all bad either.

The task for Scots is to let that flower blossom – to dismantle
shade-creating, top-down structures of governance and weed out the
negativity and self-doubt caused by the persistent blight of inequality. This book aims to show that among ordinary Scots, far from the
chattering classes and against incredible odds, that process has already
begun. And nowhere is community action more urgently needed – and
the Scottish way of life more sadly distinctive – than in the realm of
health.

CHAPTER TWO

The Scottish Effect – Inequality Kills

I SEARCH:

Tommy Riley, men's health.

Nothing.

Tommy Riley, Drumchapel.

Wikipedia comes up.

Drumchapel – a huge housing estate built in 1953. The housing is now 72 per cent post-war tenement and six per cent multi-storey flats. The current population is estimated at 15,000, split into 6,000 house-holds.

And that's it. Mass deprivation, bad housing, poverty, three gener-ations of unemployment, violence, despair – not a mention.

Perhaps this forgotten housing scheme on the periphery of Glasgow defies easy description. Perhaps no-one familiar with the workings of Wikipedia knows enough about the Drum to embellish, and vice versa. In the world's largest online repository of knowledge, such oversight is almost an achievement.

This search is proving harder than I'd imagined.

Maybe I've misspelled his name.

Tommy Reilly, Glasgow.

Something.

Tommy Reilly… folk singer and winner of the Orange Unsigned prize in 2009. I don't need to click on the image to know this is not my man.

OK: *Drumchapel Men's Health Group.*

Absolutely nothing.

This can't be right. I stop to rummage in the boxes by my desk. Twenty minutes later I have the *Scotsman* article I wrote about Tommy Riley's ground-breaking project 17 years ago, complete with my notes, the group picture, date and the precise project name.

Danny Morrison Men's Health Centre, Drumchapel, Glasgow 1996.

Nothing.

I google the other names listed in the article.

Davie Best, Richard Booth, Martin Coyle, Alan Kemp, Terry Forey, James McConnell, Drumchapel.

A big fat howling nothing.

The internet does not know these men. Or their project. Or the outcome of funding battles they had with Glasgow Health Board and the Scottish Office. Or the struggles they had with themselves. Or the lives they lived afterwards.

These men are not on Facebook or Twitter. They have not written peer-reviewed reports about the identity crisis of the working-class male, half a lifetime's unemployment or their uniquely bad health outcomes. They have not been invited to symposia of the great and good to explain the superhuman effort needed daily not to sink back, sign on, tune out and give up. These men were walking experts on how to survive in Scotland's toughest urban environment. Now, they have simply disappeared.

Drumchapel Men's Health Group. Courtesy of *The Scotsman*.

I look at the guys, defensive but purposeful, eyes narrowed to challenge the reader just as the act of being framed, recorded and judged once challenged them.

But the photograph proves it. They were there. I was there. These were the founders of the Drumchapel Men's Health Group in 1993 – architects of a minor social revolution in one of the hardest, most macho parts of Glasgow with the highest rates of chronic illness, suicide and premature death amongst men in Europe. How can that not be recorded in some version of Scotland's digital story?

Finally I find two other articles written when the project opened in 1996. After that... nothing.

I can't remember when I first met Tommy Riley, but thanks to my notes I do remember his story.

He was born in 1949 in Whiteinch on the Clyde. His dad was a safety officer at the nearby Yarrow's shipyard.

'In our old house I used to sleep with granny and granddad. I had three older sisters who slept with my parents and two grown-up older brothers. It was my grandparents' house. Everything was spotless – scrubbed stairs and an inside loo.'

With his early experience of overcrowding, lack of basic amenities and the struggle to maintain 'decent' standards, Tommy's upbringing was probably fairly typical. When he was four, Tommy's parents got their own flat in the newly opened suburban estate of Drumchapel.

'It was a huge adventure at first. The number nine bus stopped at the supermarket and beyond it was just a massive construction site and mud. It was great fun for us weans. We were given a top floor flat – I remember it seemed so high. We had much more space – and a veranda! We used to take a wee picnic table and sit out there. The bathroom was enormous but we didn't use the bath unless the fire was on and the water was heated by the back boiler. There was a lovely big sink and we had baths in it instead.'

At 15 Tommy started work as a grocer's message boy in the neighbouring affluent suburb of Bearsden.

'I remember the hills. Imagine taking a heavy grocer's bike full of shopping up the Boclair Road hill. None of the folk who lived up there gave me a tip, though. Not even at Christmas.'

Then Tommy's dad gave up his job because of bronchial problems.

'He smoked Woodbine. He would light the Woodbine, take three draws, nip it and put it in a tin. There were stacks of tins in a cupboard. That's how I started smoking.'

Tommy changed jobs to earn more cash and worked as a binman. Then at building sites. Then at a whisky bond.

'I caught hepatitis while I was working there. One of the symptoms was an enlarged liver, so the doctor asked, "Do you drink?" I said no. My job was to dilute the alcohol from 100 per cent to 70 per cent for customs by adding water and turning on rousers to churn it aw thegither. I also changed the filters. So I was basically breathing in pure alcohol all day. There was no other job at Chivas, so I left to work at the Goodyear Tyre factory... it closed a couple of years later.'

Disappointment and health problems – all related quite matter-of-factly. Unemployed at the age of 29, Tommy tried to find a new job, without success. Worse, he was still struggling with hepatitis-induced chronic fatigue.

'I slowly realised I wasn't going to work again – not proper work, not the work I was put on this planet to do. I wouldn't let my wife work. We were surviving on benefits, but the bills kept coming in. It wasn't until I was ill and flat on my back that she got a job. And she's never looked back. When my wife started work as a home help and started to get a salary, I could see she was becoming more secure as a person, and I was becoming more insecure. Then she got the chance to go full-time. That was the straw that broke the camel's back, because I was never going to work again. For a year I lay in my bed. I just couldn't handle it. At the end I thought, if I lie here any longer I will die.'

Tommy's wife became the breadwinner, supporting their four children while Tommy became distant and depressed over his inability to earn a living. He tried to kill himself, twice.

Then he became a patient of Danny Morrison. According to Tommy, the former workmate from Goodyear saved his life.

'Danny used to mix the carbon black [a pigment and reinforcing filler in rubber products, especially tyres]. Afterwards it was accepted the stuff is carcinogenic. Aw the other guys in that section are dead. He got ill – it wiz cancer – so they moved him tae the packaging line. That's how I knew him. I used tae trim tyres next to him.'

Danny Morrison received a good redundancy payment – compensation, perhaps, for acquiring an industrial disease. But he drank most of it. He became an alcoholic and was admitted to hospital where a cancerous tumour was discovered in one of his lungs. Somehow he managed to kick the booze, came home and was treated by a young doctor who put him on experimental cancer treatment.

'He got 20 times the usual dose of radiation. His skin flaked aff and he looked like he'd had massive sunburn. His natural defences were knackered.'

But Danny's health improved.

The tumour shrivelled to the size of a pea and Danny could breathe properly for the first time in years. He took up Tai Chi, quit smoking and came off the medication that controlled his alcoholism. He became a health counsellor and Tommy was one of his first patients.

Both men had to overcome several lifetimes of conditioning to sit in the room together. Hardened, macho, working-class men were not expected to ask for help or to offer it. Danny and Tommy had broken the toughest rules of the lot – their own. Emboldened, they decided to branch out.

In the early '90s, 60 per cent of Drumchapel men were unemployed – countless more were also depressed, medicated and agoraphobic. So Tommy and Danny set up a men's issues group for mutual support.

A handful of men joined and together tried to break the emotional logjam. It was hard going. A woman had to be drafted in at first to probe beyond the gruff, defensive replies. Men outside the group dismissed them as 'poofters'. It took a group outing to climb Ben Nevis before the first cracks in their behavioural armour appeared. At the misty summit, cold, disorientated and far from home, the strain finally showed. Some were frightened, others were angry. On the way back – a year after meeting – they finally opened up, talked, and realised no-one could tackle the plight of the sickest men in Europe but themselves.

Soon there were 30 regulars taking cookery classes, Tai Chi lessons and hill walks.

Men once revered as skilled craftsmen – the Kings of Labour – were overcoming all sorts of misgivings to sign up for glorified night school. Slightly older than the rest, Danny rallied spirits and laid down the law.

'According to Danny, we had a duty to the younger guys, who looked up tae us. We weren't to throw our weight around, get pished, pick fights or try to look hard. Danny said the old macho stuff was our worst enemy. He told us to take care of ourselves, one anither and oor families.'

For once, when the men were ready, so was officialdom. In January

1993, the Government's chief medical officer Robert Kendall said: 'It's time someone started to think seriously about the health needs of men, particularly in deprived areas. It'll be much harder to persuade men to attend clinics... imagination and ingenuity are needed. But the challenge is waiting for someone to rise to it.'

Unfortunately, that someone wasn't Danny Morrison.

Danny died in June 1993 after trying to ignore pain which he believed to be the return of his untreatable lung cancer. In fact, Danny died from highly treatable pneumonia.

Just as Danny had encouraged the Men's Group during life, so the manner of his death became a further spur. Tommy contacted the Health Board and proposed a Men's Health Centre in Danny's memory, staffed by local volunteers. He found a chink in the wall. The proposal was approved – for one year only and with just £86,000 in funding. Doors opened in October 1995.

Amazingly, it was Tommy, not a clipboard-wielding graduate, who got the co-ordinator's job. A photo of Danny was turned into an oil painting and placed in the window as an encouragement to come in. Sure, there were forms to fill in; administrators from a different, leafy, suburban planet; evaluation processes, annual targets, performance indicators and occasional panic-inducing visits from the suits. But the dream was a reality. Tommy Riley and the boys were no longer on their knees. They had a reason to get up every morning, a chance to help themselves and become role models for a new generation of Drumchapel youngsters – Danny Morrison had not died in vain.

I came along to visit, halfway through that trial year, to record and print a discussion about men's health in *The Scotsman*. I was Assistant Editor at the time, and gender issues were my bag after proposing and editing *The Scotswoman*, an edition of the paper produced by female staff on International Women's Day 1995, when the masthead changed for the first time in 178 years. The men went home and an eminently readable paper with new perspectives made a small piece of social and newspaper history.

Although many senior editorial staff dismissed the exercise as pointless tokenism, *The Scotswoman*'s main legacy, ironically, was a weekly Men's Page. It only lasted a year, but during that time managed to showcase the Drumchapel Men's Health Project.

Tommy Riley and six volunteers turned up for the interview. I was so busy asking questions, making sure the tape recorder was working and checking the spelling of names that I didn't really hear what was being said. The project was already running into the sand.

Men were indeed turning up, services were being used and the Centre was busy enough. Smoking cessation classes were popular, discussion groups for unemployed men were full and aromatherapy to counter stress was first mocked and then quietly attended. Within nine months there was a waiting list of 72 weeks for acupuncture and 18 weeks for aromatherapy.

Two of the men's stories were particularly moving.

Terry (22 years old in 1996) walked through the doors of the Danny Morrison Health project in its first week. He had just been discharged from Gartnavel Royal Hospital after treatment for severe depression. Terry had tried to commit suicide when his relationship failed after his girlfriend had a miscarriage.

'It was caused by amphetamines we were both taking. I had been on them since the age of 11.'

After discharge from Gartnavel, his doctor put him on tranquilisers and anti-depressants.

'I was walking through Drumchapel like a zombie. My so-called friends didn't want to know me cos I was in the psychiatric hospital and they thought I was some sort of headcase.'

After attending the men's health centre, Terry's life improved dramatically.

'It helped immensely to talk to other guys. Slowly but surely the acupuncture helped take the drug cravings away and the aromatherapy calmed me down. I've been drug-free for two months now, I'm going to the gym four days a week and I've put on two and a half stones.'

The transformation of John (49 in 1996) was no less amazing. A painfully thin, 70-a-day smoker of unfiltered roll-ups who was stressed by the failure of his cartoon business, John turned to shiatsu and massage.

'I was dedicated to being totally unhealthy, living badly, over-smoking and generally being over the top. I had dying Scotsman syndrome.'

John started acupuncture to quit smoking.

'After one session on the needles I chucked the fags and have never looked back.' A course of Tai Chi led to further improvements in general health, posture, fitness and peace of mind.

'I've been told my attitude has improved. I'm not so obnoxious now. My language has gone to almost Christian proportions because I'm not under the stress I was. I've been repackaged into a sellable product for work again.'

But uncertainty over future funding of the project was a constant worry. Policy changes higher up the public health food chain meant 'self-help' and 'gender specific' projects had apparently fallen from favour. Measurable improvements in the health of Drumchapel men were taking too long to materialise and the stress of a daily job after years of unemployment was taking its toll on Tommy. Quietly, the authorities were tiptoeing away from Drumchapel's brave experiment and Tommy knew it. He had always been a teetotaller. Now he was taking a few swift shots every night – after making a well-cooked family meal – because over and above the job there was always that extra burden: expectations. Tommy had to prove the naysayers wrong about him and his friends. He had to demonstrate the capacity of 'schemies' to help themselves. And, the heaviest burden of all, he had to be the big, brave, unstoppable force that father figure Danny Morrison would have wanted him to be.

But that day in 1996, he didn't let on. And I didn't notice.

The basic health statistics of the men gathered for interview were daunting enough.

Only one of the seven didn't smoke. Only one – a recovering alcoholic – didn't drink heavily. And only one – the man whose drinking and smoking levels had shot through the roof – had a job.

For men who knew they were likely to become the next set of Scotland's grim health statistics, the group was disarmingly frank about the self-destructive habits that shaped and limited their lives.

'Aye, we're the Magnificent Seven alright.'

Sense of humour intact at least.

First smoking. All disagreed with the received wisdom that friends and family are a big support in the drive to quit. According to Tommy, they were actually the main reason he'd started again:

'I'd been off smoking two weeks and my wife complained because I was so grumpy. Folk at work were another factor. Before, I'd maybe only have two or three draws at a fag as I talked on the phone or typed. But now I only go out to smoke and I smoke each fag all the way. I also have a few ciggies at one time cos I don't know how long it'll be before I can come out again. I'm definitely smoking more now. The smoke-free zone is better for non-smokers but worse for me.'

Richard Booth also questioned the prevailing belief that smoking is antisocial: 'I'd estimate 80–90 per cent of men here smoke. It's the social norm – it's about giving and taking. It means you've got something to offer – a bit like being in the trenches. You need mates. If you have a packet of fags to hand round, you can be one of the crowd.'

So if family and friends are not triggers to quit, what is?

Davie said, 'I can't sing properly.'

The men nodded sagely as if everyone had that problem.

'I'm in a band and I cannae hit the top notes. So I came aff for six months.'

What went wrong?

'Women trouble. Isn't it always?'

The Greek chorus nodded gravely again.

'I found myself on the way to the pub to get smashed, so I got myself into a shop to buy 20 fags instead – for a recovering alcoholic it's the lesser of two evils.'

Martin chipped in.

'But drinking makes misery manageable. None of us has a paid job, but we still have the drinking patterns of a worker. My dad would come home from work and have a drink. It was a reward...'

'... and it was about space, too,' said Tommy.

'Women had the kitchen and, in a way, the whole hoose as their ain space. I suppose a man's place has been out working or at the pub or slumped in front of the telly. And what have we now? I suppose two out of three's not bad, eh?'

The observation was a bit too close to the bone for laughter. Had any of the group asked a doctor for help? Alan was the youngest:

'It's only since I started here at the men's centre that I've had the confidence to use the doctor properly. In the past I wouldn't go, or I'd go but not open my mouth. I'd just do what I was tellt. I wouldn't talk to them.'

Why not?

Tommy tried to explain:

'GPs have got real power over you. In the old days they were the ones who decided if you got a sick line – that's the only reason I ever went to see them. If it wasn't for that most guys would just go to the chemist instead, because they're more normal, less judgemental – chemists aren't authority figures. The doctor hands you a bottle and says take it. The chemist explains what's in it – they don't talk to you like you're stupid.'

If fat is a feminist issue, health is a class issue. There's no way these working-class men will expose themselves to the ego-crushing experience of judgement and disapproval by a superior-sounding man from another class and another universe. And statistically they're right to expect a man from a different socio-economic background inside the white coat. Relatively few youngsters from the big estates make it to university – you'd need an even bigger sense of mission to make it out and voluntarily return.

There are relatively few surgeries in the most deprived Scottish communities – even if the big peripheral estates and east end schemes have the biggest health problems.

Martin didn't think any GP could make much of a difference.

'The thing is that unemployed men – the bulk of us here – are like lost souls. Six of us are volunteers – that gives us a focus to each day and above all a place to meet that isn't the pub. I'd say the biggest thing the health board could do for men in schemes is give them a working reason to get out of the house. That'd make men more receptive to other health messages.'

A good idea, but was anyone in authority listening?

'Of course not. They just put mair cash into 'health messages' that dinnae work here.'

It's a Catch 22 that would drive me crazy. But the Drumchapel Seven were calm, or perhaps just resigned to their fate. Davie had a theory about that:

'The thing is that for men, if you start to worry, you have to act. And we don't know how to act, wit tae dae about oor situation... so we don't worry.'

I had rarely heard so many important chunks of reality laid bare in one interview. So many expert views challenged. So many hidden barriers described and revealed. So many useful insights. Their words stayed with me. The *Scotsman* article was duly written. As a result I (not the Men's Health Group) was asked to give a talk about Scotland's enduring 'Sick Man of Europe' status a few months later to members of the British Medical Association in the very grand Royal College of Surgeons in Edinburgh's Georgian Queen Street. I sat at the front of the steeply-ranked auditorium where far smarter folk than me have held forth and watched 100 GPs take their seats. Sensible, confident, well-heeled and well-informed men and women. How could such catastrophic health outcomes be happening on their watch? There was no point in reciting statistics. All I could do was try to demonstrate the vast chasm lying between all of them and the men I'd just met in Drumchapel.

I asked how many drank red wine. Almost every hand went up. Then I asked how many had even sampled El D (Eldorado – one of the fortified wines popular amongst the poor). No-one.

I explained that the men in Drumchapel had reacted in precisely the opposite way. When I'd asked them about consumption of wine, none of the Danny Morrison men had immediately understood what I was asking about:

'You mean Lanny (Lanliq) or El D (Eldorado)? You mean fortified wine?'

'Naw, she means table wine. Red wine. Naw we dinnae drink that – tastes like vinegar. You'd need to mix it with something – lager maybe. Even then, wine is for wimps.'

The Drumchapel men wouldn't touch red table wine with a bargepole – the Royal College men had never heard of Eldorado.

It is 54.5 miles from Drumchapel to the Royal College in Edinburgh. It might as well be a million miles. How can one set of Scots heal another whose lives, lifestyles, attitudes and habits they hardly know and cannot possibly understand?

In the 16 years since that visit to Drumchapel, the social gap between underclass and professional class has only widened. And yet advice for people facing depression, suicide, violence, addiction and poverty is still devised by people for whom illness and stress have quite different meanings and impacts. I say this not to judge or be hostile. Relatively speaking, my life is stress-free too.

Back in 1996, Tommy told me: 'I was looking at a DSS leaflet listing all the health risks associated with manufacturing jobs. They were all jobs we'd done. Almost everything we've done in our working lives here in Drumchapel has been dangerous. It's very hard to look at a fag and think it can do more harm than what's happened already.'

Davie's rejoinder to that has stayed with me ever since:

'Our masculinity is based on the ability to withstand damage. We have tae prove our worth by struggling against something. Now the work's gone, where does the damage come fae? How can we prove we're fit tae be called men? The damage we withstand has to be self-inflicted noo. It comes fae fags, booze and drugs.'

Those sentences stopped me in my tracks. Davie had put his finger on a profound truth. But because it came from a non-professional, his insight went nowhere – like the men's group, and the Healthy Cities project that funded it.

It's not that these guys have been accidentally missing the health messages of polite society. They come from a hard, unforgiving world that despises them. 'Proper' men in workless housing estates don't relate to the underlying feminisation associated with caring about anyone's physical health. Life in Drumchapel is not a L'Oreal ad. Scottish society has told these guys time and time again, *you're not worth it*. Staying hard, staying tough, remaining impassive in the face of an uncaring world, passing the pain to smaller, weaker, more vulnerable people down the line – that's the way most men survive a hopeless, disempowered existence. The decision to unravel this macho stance on the vast housing scheme of Drumchapel in the hard years after Thatcher took real courage.

Courage that wasn't matched by Greater Glasgow Health Board, or the Scottish Executive.

Would it have been too risky to come up with the £86,000 needed annually to keep the Danny Morrison project going? Was that paltry sum of cash spent on projects with demonstrably better outcomes for working-class men? Was it even spent in Drumchapel?

And what happened to Tommy? I finally tracked down Martin, who's now leading a community health project in nearby Scotstoun. Choosing his words carefully, I could hear that things with Tommy weren't good.

'He took the end of the project hard. I'll tell him you were asking for him. If I see him, like.'

I said that's fine. What's to be gained for Tommy having old hopes and disappointments raised again?

'There was a bloke connected with the project who said success in a place like Drumchapel can be measured like this – still nae suicides. Let's just say that.'

Martin made a point of going to see Tommy, as I imagined he might. And Tommy called today – as I knew he would. There is no happy ending. There is just a man whose lifelong habit of honesty requires him to tell me the rest of his story... exactly as it is.

> I'm an alcoholic, I have COPD and asthma. The doctor says I've nae chance. Some nights I can hardly breathe, my legs are wasted and I cannae walk. I sit here in the flat watching oot the windae. The wife comes tae visit every day. My kids come along every week. But there's nothing tae be done. It could have been different, aye it could. When the money ran oot, in August '96, we had 40 volunteers. Forty guys trained tae deal with aw the difficulties of men fae Drumchapel. The Danny Morrison Centre ran oot o cash and there was a wee donation from Billy Connolly's company TicketyBoo. I kept working without pay for seven months, but I was drinking heavily. I couldn't get the stories of the guys oot o ma heid. The Health Board never gied us a trained psychiatrist on the project. So we took the burdens of these guys onto oorsels. We weren't trained for that. The educated and qualified professionals didn't have the answer. We had it. The answer was us. Ordinary people ready to fix oorsels. But we needed their support. We needed time, belief and professionals ready to fit into oor lives. We never got it.

* * *

If only the men of Drumchapel had found a professional champion like Dr Mary Hepburn.

'If I lived in awful circumstances, I would use drugs,' she told *The Herald* in 2007. 'If I had been brought up in a broken home, within a dysfunctional family, where there was a lot of violence and mental, physical or sexual abuse... in those circumstances, anything that made life more pleasant would be welcome.'

In one sentence you can see why the authorities feared her, 'hard to reach' patients loved her and fellow health professionals were... divided.

As my Caithness-born mother might say, Mary is thrawn and entirely unconcerned about the controversy caused when she calls a spade a spade. And she often does.

The winner of the 2012 *Scotswoman of the Year Award* is a 60-something, softly-spoken, London-born, Shetland-bred consultant obstetrician who's spent her professional life trying to understand why health matters so little to Scotland's poorest mothers. As a result, she's managed to connect with damaged women whose behaviour usually prompts public rejection and official indifference. That hard-won connection means Mary is gradually improving life chances in Scotland's poorest communities. Each newborn baby whose mother manages to breastfeed has a slightly better chance of not developing asthma, diabetes or bronchial problems, not growing up with dependencies and therefore not resorting to drugs or prostitution – a slightly better chance of holding down a job and producing healthier children of their own. In a world that looks for quick fixes and instant solutions, that's too slight a set of improvements and it all takes too long. But without massive social and political change, nothing quicker works. If the poorest mums can be supported, coaxed and persuaded, they can quit the self-damaging habits of a lifetime for a few crucial months around birth and make all the difference to the health of their babies.

Such is the glacial pace of change in the large, hopeless housing estates where Scotland's poorest people struggle daily with forces powerful enough to immobilise even the strongest individual. Dealers on every street, loan sharks on every corner, jobs nowhere – and 'clean' society judging it all from the safe vantage point of a few physical miles and a different social universe.

It would take an unusual, determined and unassailably optimistic person to make this environment and these people their life's work.

Step forward Mary Hepburn.

Mary's own upbringing was happy and unconventional. Her mother, Jess, was a bright linguist who worked in Bletchley Park during the war. Her GP father, Tom, was the product of an Edwardian manse. Indeed, Mary was born in a Salvation Army hospital in Hackney (a genuine Cockney) while her father was working in London. The family moved to Shetland a couple of months later, and the three-month-old Mary regularly accompanied her father on his rounds (including some trips by boat to other islands) attending humans, sick cows and injured sheepdogs. Not your average childhood.

The family moved to Perthshire when Mary was 13. It was a massive culture shock.

'I came from this wonderful, classless society in Shetland – a feral upbringing where you did what you wanted, everyone mattered and no-one was considered different. We arrived in this snobby place where at school they picked on you for having a strange accent and not being good at hockey.'

So Mary played truant. Eventually she and a friend stayed off school for a fortnight. Her teacher decided not to tell Mary's father because he was a doctor. Her friend's dad was told immediately. Furious, Mary went home and confessed. Her father pointed out she had more to lose than the school authorities and advised her to pass the exams and make sure she didn't get caught again.

So Mary's school years weren't wasted. She excelled academically but also gained insight into a health-related condition unknown to most of life's achievers: exclusion.

'Up against authority you have no control and no way to fight back except simply not to turn up. I wasn't punished for it – others were. They still are. I use dad's advice with the women I treat. Don't get caught and protect yourself.'

When Mary studied medicine at Edinburgh University in the '70s, entrance standards for women were still higher than men to ensure the 'proper commitment' and deter 'time wasters' who might go off and have babies. It was only after she graduated and took a succession of jobs in different specialties that she realised an unconventional career path was considered time wasting too.

So Mary's first training in obstetrics was part of a GP training pro-gramme which meant a move to Dublin in 1978, where mothers with more than 15 children were still commonplace, abortion was illegal and there was limited access to contraception.

'On my first day in Dublin there was a woman whose fetus had an undeveloped brain, a condition incompatible with life, so the baby would die at birth. It had been diagnosed at 20 weeks but termination was illegal and to deliver early would be murder. So the mother went to 52 weeks gestation. I was horrified by this but even more horrified to discover she agreed with this approach. Another woman with severe medical problems miscarried in her 20th pregnancy because she was so ill. I told her she might not survive another pregnancy and advised her she needed reliable contraception but she declined and said "so be it – this is the will of God".

I had never encountered anything like it. As doctors we were trained to give out advice and expected patients to want to follow it. I'd never heard anyone in such an apparently clear-cut situation say "I can't follow your medical advice" or "I don't want to". These women made me realise I had no right to make assumptions. My job was to say "I'm here to help you work out what health care is acceptable and then ensure you get it".'

Back home in Glasgow that Irish experience proved invaluable.

'The women I treat now often can't stop smoking, can't stop drinking or using drugs. They can't control their environment, often can't leave their abusive partner, can't get better housing. There's no point being moralistic. They can't get new lives. So we accept that and say, "Let's explore what you can do and how we can help".'

In many ways, it would probably help the cause if I just left the story there. You probably get the general picture, feel relieved that life for most Irish women improved after the '70s (despite the recent tragic death of Savita Halappanavar) understand drugs have compounded the hopelessness of exclusion and wish all struggling with multiple deprivation the best of luck.[1]

What follows may simply demolish that sympathy. When men 'lose the plot', they generally lash out at female partners – adults who can theoretically seek help. When women lose the plot they often implode, harming themselves and the one group society views as sacrosanct – their new-born babies. The fact that some mothers allow drug habits to jeopardise babies lives is infinitely more shocking than the knowledge some fathers do the same. We're not ready for that knowledge. Nor do we realise that the failure to protect and care for their babies frequently costs mothers their own lives.

In 1985 Mary Hepburn, together with a midwife, opened an antenatal clinic in the unemployment blackspot of Possilpark. Local

---

1 Savita Halappanavar died from sepsis (chronic infection) after being denied an emergency abortion at an Irish hospital in 2012. Her death sparked an international outcry over Ireland's strict anti-abortion laws.

women weren't using the hospital-based clinic and she figured a local base would be easier to access.

'In those days the medical profession recognised the link between poverty and ill-health, but failure to attend for care was viewed as the responsibility of the poor people themselves.'

Mary realised it wasn't that simple and turned the clinic into a one-stop-shop that could help patients with all their medical and social problems. It sounds simple and obvious now. At the time, though, it was revolutionary.

Fellow health professionals thought Mary was mad, senior staff warned she would be passed over for promotion, advised her to give up the clinic and concentrate on the more routine parts of her job. Without support from Professor Malcolm Macnaughton, Mary's project might have stopped right there. He authorised a second clinic in the Glasgow Royal Maternity Hospital (Rottenrow), created a new consultant post and the Glasgow Women's Reproductive Health Service was established with six community-based clinics across Glasgow and the hospital ward.[2]

'People didn't think poverty-related bad health was something you could improve like you could improve the management of diabetes. Maybe that was my advantage, coming from outside Glasgow. The first thing that hit you about the city was its poverty. It was so evidently the biggest factor everyone was dealing with – patients and medical staff alike.'

Even so, there wasn't a stampede to attend Mary's new clinic in Possil, so she asked mums-to-be why they didn't come. Social workers were part of the answer. The women believed their babies would be removed automatically at birth without any chance of appeal. They believed doctors, nurses and social workers were in cahoots, so they didn't come. Strange that. If Possil women really couldn't care less about their babies, what difference would removal make? And yet Mary knew it was the one eventuality they all dreaded.

'We explained the right social work support would give the best chance of a mother keeping her baby, and that we would all work together as a team. We introduced social workers as people who could

---

2   Possil, Easterhouse, Castlemilk, Pollok and Drumchapel and 'Mary's hospital clinic' at Rottenrow, and later at the Princess Royal Maternity hospital.

help solve benefit or housing problems. But we didn't lie. The thing that made people come was that we treated them with respect. We didn't condemn them for their problems, but we didn't collude with them either.'

Mary's first patient at the Possil park clinic was Carol, 'an abused, traumatised woman' who stuck with Mary's clinic during three pregnancies and managed to more or less abstain from drugs during pregnancy and around the time of birth. That may sound like a very minor achievement, but it gave Carol's children a better start than trying and failing to achieve total abstinence.

Mary Hepburn is not a sentimental woman. And yet clearly Carol has a special place in her memory – perhaps because she so visibly struggled to trust anyone in a white coat.

'She took a friend along to that first clinic and sat facing the other way, answering my questions via the friend who then passed the answer on. It was pretty strange.'

Carol couldn't make eye contact. She couldn't bear to see disappointment and frosty disapproval on yet another closed, professional face. Accepting the strange circumstances of this first consultation was a test. Mary passed.

'Carol had three children and each time she said "this one's going to be okay because I love it to bits". She took her first baby home then lost custody of him because of her chaotic lifestyle. She worked so hard to try and get him home again, getting stable on prescribed substitute drugs and managing a routine. She would be so close when she would do something so chaotic they couldn't give her custody. It was as if she was scared she simply wouldn't be strong enough to stay away from the damaging behaviour all around her.'

When Carol got pregnant a second time, she was sent to Mary to arrange a termination. Instead she asked for another chance at motherhood, determined to turn her life around.

'I said alright, have another baby – but let me take care of you.'

Despite their best efforts, Carol's second child was also taken into care. Devastated by this failure, she still turned up to meet judges when Mary's clinic was nominated for (and later won) the Community Health Service of the Year Award. The head judge asked why women attended the WRHS clinic when they failed to appear anywhere else.

Mary said, 'We offer non-judgemental care.'

Then he paused to ask the scowling figure, scuffing her foot and avoiding eye contact.

Carol said, 'Cos they dinnae treat you like shite.'

'I rather think that's the same sentiment,' was the head judge's unexpectedly game reply. But the hard truth is that being treated with respect wasn't enough to save Carol.

'When she lost her third baby she said, "That's it. I won't be trying again. I'm a useless mother." Her sister, who was an alcoholic, got her baby home about the same time, and I remember saying I don't think Carol will be able to cope with that. A few weeks later she was dead after an "accidental overdose". She had a terrible life. She lost her mum when she was ten and her dad was an alcoholic. She was tragic and totally destroyed by her life experience – destroyed in so many ways and just 30 when she died.'

If there's a better working definition of hopelessness, I've yet to hear it. In many ways – just like Danny Morrison in Drumchapel – Carol's lonely death provided a reality check and a spur to keep going.

The clinics soldiered on and Mary started to get some results where other health care teams failed to get even attendance. In the first year, 12 patients turned up at the Possilpark clinic. In the second year there were 64, and 130 in the third. The secret was (almost) unconditional acceptance of patients' lives and a willingness to bend pointless and counter-productive rules. No-one in Mary's team expected women to completely succeed in doing what was medically correct or even in their own best interests. But that didn't mean caving in to self-destructive habits either. Every day, the staff at Mary's clinics had to use their own judgement to devise reachable standards of care.

'If you held a clinic in the afternoon – which was what the women asked us to do – you were letting the women be chaotic. So we held them in the morning; by the afternoon patients were spread to the four winds. We told mothers this is a practice period – you can prove you can be a good mum. If you can get out of bed, come to the clinic and get organised, you are demonstrating you can take care of your baby. Even if they didn't come, they knew why we had morning clinics – we weren't just being bloody-minded. We would knock on doors as we came into work to make sure they were awake. Sometimes we would visit women at home, but we didn't do all the antenatal checks there – we insisted they come to the clinic to demonstrate responsibility. It helped if we offered a reason; we need an official stamp for this form, there's medicine we can't take out of the clinic etc. We didn't allow the women to take prescribed methadone home in case they were tempted to sell it or someone else took it – with supervised daily dispensing we knew exactly how much each patient had taken.'

The clinics blended respect with realism. In the late 1990s, Project Prevention advocated a different approach – paying drug-using women to be sterilised. The American born-again Christians grabbed headlines then disappeared back to the States. Mary persevered with the less newsworthy business of change by negotiation.

'I would say: I can understand why you want a child, but if you have one now you'll have a great deal of stress because you've no house and your drug use is out of control. So your health is compromised and there's a higher risk your baby might have health problems at birth and social work might think you can't cope. What about taking contraception while we sort out those problems and you can get pregnant at a better time?'

There might never be a better time. And the women weren't daft – they knew that. But reasoning produced a less damaging outcome. And that's all Mary's clinics were aiming for.

'When we got the ward at Rottenrow Hospital, socially disadvantaged women using drugs made up half of our patients. So the ward was specifically designed to have all beds visible from the nursing station. I asked one woman if she liked it. "Effing hell," she said, "youse can see what we're doing." And I said, "Spot on. You are so right! But there's a benefit for you. We can see when you need help and we know you're not using drugs in the ward."'

It would have been easy and tempting to slacken this regime of constant monitoring. But though 'hands off' environments might appear more respectful of a patients' right to privacy, respect without involvement can simply cause more trouble.

'In one Canadian city they built a wonderful state of the art maternity block for drug-using pregnant women. I advised them on setting up the service and went back later to see how they were getting on – they reported terrible problems with women using drugs in their rooms. They said, 'You can't go in if they've put up 'do not disturb signs'. I said, "The hell you can. You don't politely leave folk to commit suicide.'"

Just as the Danny Morrison Men's Health project in Drumchapel was finding on the other side of Glasgow, avoiding suicide was the first realistic measure of success. For Mary's clinics, raising the abysmally low rate of breastfeeding was the next.

In the 1990s, about 50 per cent of her patients were drug users – many were injecting drugs and a few were HIV positive. American experts were resolutely opposed to breastfeeding by drug using mothers, European experts tended to agree and – the biggest problem by far – Mary's own patients were absolutely revolted at the very thought.

'If I had even mentioned breastfeeding in the early days the women would have walked out. One young woman saw a mother breastfeeding and asked "can you really feed them that way?" As a student in Edinburgh I would ask a woman how she planned to feed the baby and she would often say breastfeeding. Asking the same question in Aberdeen, I would get a surprised response – "what other way was there to feed a baby?" In the disadvantaged areas of Glasgow, however, women just didn't recognise breastfeeding as an option. One woman in Govan said, "Oh you mean SMA or Oyster Milk (Ostermilk)?"'

Why the big regional difference? Glasgow mums have historically lived near their own mums, thanks to the predominance of council housing where points are acquired by having local family. One theory goes that a generation of mothers encouraged to use artificial milk after the war as more liberating, clean and modern than breast milk have had a disproportionate influence on their daughters and granddaughters. The useful proximity of free childcare also encouraged the younger generation to bottle feed so child-minding duties could be shared. Of course the explanation could be far simpler. The higher levels of deprivation in Glasgow could just have created more damaged women and more unhealthy lifestyles.

There's an emotional argument too. Some women in deprived parts of Glasgow have been sexually abused as children, others work in prostitution and regard breasts as part of the sex trade – almost all are completely distanced from their own body and their own physical needs.

Writers have successfully lionised Glasgow's Hard Man. The

'hard woman' is harder to glamorise. The 'hard mother' is nigh on impossible. But the blunt truth is that pregnancy means new, inject-able breast veins. That's a horrible thought. Breasts are intimate, soft, sensitive – no matter what an over-sexualised world has done to their public portrayal. But habitual drug use creates a world beyond the outsider's ability to comprehend, where pain is pleasure and the chance to self-anaesthetise is a 'luxury'.

This is the enduring *Trainspotting*.

It's not glamorous or chic. Drug-using mums are generally regarded as the lowest of the low. Beyond help – and beyond any ability to change.

Except the WRHS clinics have proved they are not. The proportion of women breastfeeding there rose over a decade from zero to 24 per cent – without leaflets, expensive pilot projects or TV campaigns.

'We hadn't been trying to sell breastfeeding to these mums. We didn't know how. When I was Registrar we handed out leaflets that effectively said one glass of wine at conception meant your baby was knackered for life. Handing that to women who'd conceived on a sea of alcohol was pointless. A bit like the iceberg image in HIV ads – none of the women knew what an iceberg was. The images were meaningless to them. So I started to think – what's in it for these mums to breastfeed? They hate it so much there has to be something in it for them. Promis-ing they'd get their figure back quicker didn't work – most women were in size zero jeans a week before they delivered. I asked one woman, "If I said breastfeeding made your wean brainier would you breastfeed?" "No-one wants a brainy wean," she said. "I was bottle-fed and I'm fine." "But are you really fine," I'd ask? "Your granny died when she was quite young, your dad is already dead and your mum has heart problems. How about giving your baby a better start?"'

That sort of persuasion helped a little bit, but after extensive market research, Mary found two arguments were most effective – breastfeeding reduces the risk of cot death and breastfed babies are less likely to need treatment for withdrawal symptoms. Slowly but surely, the persuasion worked.

'If you come from Possil Park and you grow up in a family with smoking, damp housing and a rotten diet, if you are chronically stressed, drinking, using drugs and expecting to give birth six weeks prematurely to a low birth-weight baby – breastfeeding will have a relatively greater impact on your child's health. You will protect it against cardiovascular disease, extend its life expectancy and turn the baby into a healthier adult who will in turn have a healthier child. If a pregnant woman in a leafy suburb is the right weight, not smoking, not stressed, having a healthy pregnancy and expecting a 10lb baby, breastfeeding will make a smaller contribution to its health and life expectancy. The most important people to get breastfeeding are socially deprived women.'

There's another reason breastfeeding is so important for babies of drug-using mothers. Normally it's best for babies to remain in the womb till full term. But poor women are often so damaged that their placentas don't work well and after a while the baby isn't growing on the scan. So Mary's team intervene and induce birth. The result is often a very low birth-weight baby (these constitute five per cent of all Scottish babies, but 20 per cent in Mary's service). Premature and underweight, these babies need all the help they can get. And yet until recently they didn't get breast milk.

'In America a breastfeeding woman was convicted of manslaughter for using amphetamines a fortnight before her baby died in a cot death. It's incredible – by breastfeeding she was doing the right thing. The baby of a mother who uses drugs has already been exposed to drugs for many months in the womb. Breastfeeding gives the baby continued small amounts of the drug taken by the mother and this reduces the risk of withdrawal symptoms or treatment with morphine and gives all the other considerable benefits of breastfeeding.'

Wouldn't cold turkey and total abstinence by the mother be better all round?

'The first drug-using mother who asked me for help in 1985 said, "Admit me into hospital, don't let me have drugs, don't let anyone see me and don't let me out." That seemed easy enough. I spent every evening and weekend at the hospital talking her through it. She lasted 12 weeks drug free and had a beautifully healthy baby. But shortly after getting home she was using again and ended up losing custody of her baby. It's often safer to maintain women on a prescribed substitute drug. We were popular with critics of drug-using women when we tried for abstinence – and less popular when we moved to prescribing methadone. But though motivation for abstinence is high during pregnancy, the cost of failure (to the mother and baby) can be even higher, so overall it's a risky time for women to try. On the other hand, with drugs where there is no safe substitute for pregnant women, abstinence is the only option. Overall we're aiming for stable lifestyles to give mothers the best chance of keeping their babies.'

Smoking was another unhealthy habit Mary's clinic had to partly tackle, and partly accommodate.

'We had a smoking room beside our ward. So when we admitted women for stabilisation they could use the room. We didn't let them go out for a smoke because dealers were waiting outside. So they sat in this little brown room all day and chain-smoked. One of the anaesthetists noticed our patients had a lower rate of epidurals than the rest of the hospital. If they came to our ward they could chain smoke but the minute they went to the labour ward they couldn't. So they stayed in the ward. You could go into the smoking room and see a woman gripping the sofa arm with pain and terrible contractions, dragging on a cigarette. You'd ask, "Are you ok?" and she'd say, "I'm alright." And then finally she'd be off for 20 minutes giving birth and back having a cigarette half an hour later.'

So the smoking ban caused mayhem in Mary's ward and, helped end the stabilisation process for drug-using mums – because almost all of them smoked too.

'Should we let the women go out for five minutes to smoke? I spoke to some drug users and addiction staff and they all agreed with me and said absolutely not. It's not fair. They'll go out for a cigarette, they'll be offered drugs and won't be able to refuse so we'd be setting them up to fail.'

Of course Mary's staff could have been judgemental, lost all engagement with the mothers, prompted more stress and perhaps more smoking. Instead – as usual – the team found a least worst solution, working with public health and smoking cessation teams to devise a high dose regime of nicotine replacement therapy that included 24 hour patches, chewing gum and mock cigarettes to help the women stay in hospital long enough to complete their detox without potentially destructive trips outside. While they were in detox, smokers also received intensive support from a smoking cessation midwife. It worked.

Detox restarted and 80 per cent of the first 20 women completed the week long programme – the same completion rate with the old smoking ward.

Tough love is that tough. And it comes with sadness and relatively few rewards.

Of the 12 women Mary saw in that first year in 1985, only one is known to be alive and the whereabouts of another are not known. All the rest died ten to 20 years ago as young women. There's a price to pay for failing to be a good mother. It is the ultimate price.

Put bluntly, Mary believes some mothers kill themselves when it becomes apparent they will never be adequate mothers.

'Women would often come along years after their first pregnancy to express gratitude for the care and respect they had received. Sometimes though, just after those visits, I'd hear the women who lost their children were dead. I realised they were actually coming to say goodbye. Their deaths were usually classified as accidental. Sometimes they clearly were not. One woman who'd recently lost custody of her child worked as a prostitute to get the money to hire a nice hotel room and inject herself with a massive overdose – these were women who cared very little whether they lived or died.'

The Confidential Enquiry into Maternal and Child Health (CEMACH) is a five yearly, UK-wide review of maternal mortality which has traditionally focused on medical factors (bleeding, infection etc). But deaths due to use of alcohol or drugs were included in the psychiatric chapter and Mary was asked to comment on this section. Reading through the UK records of alcohol or drug deaths amongst new mothers, she was struck by the similarity with her own experience in Glasgow. Most deaths were classified as accidental, and yet the details suggested that wasn't quite right. One woman was told at her pre-birth case conference she wouldn't be allowed to take her baby home... a couple of days later she died from an overdose. Another woman who had lost her own child looked after her sister's children over Christmas and was found dead shortly after her sister took the children home. Without their children, these women had nothing to live for – and they knew it. Yet society judged them harshly even in the manner of their death. See, they couldn't even manage a safe fix.

It's heartbreaking to think how lonely these women must have been at the end. Terrible to realise that even their perfectly executed deaths would be dismissed by an uncaring world as yet another botched job by a junkie.

Deprivation increases maternal mortality 20-fold. If a medical condition had the same effect it would prompt outrage.

Twenty years ago, Mary's clinic managed to get more than 90 per cent of babies home with their mums. Fifteen years ago it was 80 per cent. Now the rate is lower.

'In the mid-80s, opiate use took off amongst 17–24 year olds, but they didn't generally drink. Women using alcohol were older, drug users were younger, and they didn't get on. In 1989 I went to the USA and they had women of all ages who did both. I said we don't have that combination, and they said you will. They were right. Now on average mothers who use drugs are aged 25–35, they are using drink and drugs together and they've been using drugs for longer, so they have more secondary health problems. Outcomes of pregnancy are just horrendous now – dramatically awful – amongst all the socially disadvantaged women we look after.'

Perhaps those 'dramatically awful' outcomes contributed to Greater Glasgow Health Board's decision to blame the messenger and close Mary's ward in 2007 on the grounds that the women cared for in the ward must find it stigmatising to be treated separately. This was completely contrary to the evidence. In the mid-'90s a study found pregnant women who used drugs valued the attitudes, knowledge and understanding of WRHS staff. A second study showed women looked after in Mary's clinics and specialist ward had the most positive view of their care in hospital. Sadly, once the ward was closed, breastfeeding rates halved (though they are slowly starting to climb again).

Now there are three clinics and most women attend hospital-based services. Just as well perhaps, since their high risk pregnancies mean hospital attendance is almost inevitable to monitor their babies.

As things stand, a happy ending is unlikely. In Glasgow the health gap between rich and poor is wider than ever.

'Sadly, I'm now looking after women that I delivered as babies, which is a bit scary, because generations are getting shorter. Over the years, pregnancy outcomes have got worse, which is disappointing and paradoxical. We're seeing sicker women with sicker babies. Over time those babies grow up to become sicker young women without prospects and they too cope, like their mothers, by drinking, smoking and taking drugs. This is an effect of poverty – our women now present as early as the rest and attend more often but still have pregnancy outcomes that are comparable to East, not Western Europe and are getting worse. The heaviest babies born to disadvantaged women under my care in deprived Glasgow are now born to asylum seekers.'

Is this the Scotland we want?

Scots spend billions suppressing our own pain instead of tackling unhealthy habits, so it's not surprising we choose to deny the existence, judge the behaviour and suppress the painful reality of life for Scotland's sickest men and women instead of looking deeper. The life experiences of Tommy Riley, Danny Morrison, and Mary Hepburn's deprived and drug-dependent mothers taken together represent a catalogue of social failure. Their addictions, illnesses and early mortality would be warning signs in a healthy society. Instead we suppress the disturbing evidence in the same way we suppress our own symptoms of ill-health in a sea of tranquilisers and painkillers. Scotland is a medicated society where the definition of health is 'getting by' or the absence of pain, not the presence of what James C Thomson called 'rude health.' The Edinburgh naturopath was diagnosed with an acute lung condition in the 1900s and told he had less than three months to live. Searching through bookshops he devised a simple regime based on wholefood and vegetables, fresh air, light, water, physical activity and no drug intervention. He stuck to his 'Nature Cure' and 'gradually but painfully' built himself up to a reasonable state of health, opened a clinic and wrote booklets on naturopathy, one of which, updated by his son Leslie in 1987, observes the following:

> It is impossible for any doctor, surgeon or physician to do our healing
> for us. What is called 'modern scientific medicine' is, in practice, an
> attack upon symptoms with no regard for basic causes.[3]

Are Scotland's armies of professionals trying to do society's healing? Does social policy constitute an 'attack upon symptoms with no regard for basic causes'? Is Scotland intent on removing the reasons for fundamental disease or just the visibility of adverse symptoms?

---

3   Thomson, LC & J Living with Nature Cure Thomson Kingston Edinburgh (1987)

We've tried ignoring and demonising 'bad mothers', offering solutions they can't realistically access and closing the services that do work because progress is too slow. Real progress in a chronically unequal society will always be slow. And yet we won't really tackle the inequality and hopelessness which drive the 'Scottish Effect'.

It's easier to blame individual women for 'choosing' to neglect their children. Easier to call for children to be taken from such mothers at birth. Easier, unfair – and utterly impractical. According to the Association of Directors of Social Work in 2010, there were roughly 5,000 places in residential and foster care in Scotland and an estimated 50,000 children living with parents addicted to hard drugs. Society can't remove all these children at birth because there is simply nowhere for them to go.

Children are best cared for by their own parents or family – as long as they can provide good enough parenting. So Mary's preferred solution is simple and characteristically carefully phrased.

'I want women whose parenting skills may be compromised by use of alcohol or other drugs, mental illness, learning disability or a background in care to spend time in residential accommodation around the birth of a child with intensive support and training. That kind of intervention would give mothers the chance to become the best parent they are capable of being – but the baby would be protected while proof's obtained, and if it all goes wrong services can work with mothers to remove the child in a planned and less traumatic way, maintaining her involvement. It'll be very expensive in the short term, but it's likely to mean fewer Baby Ps in the long term.'

At a time like this, when popular public services are being cut, this rational argument for the poorest, drug-using mothers stands next to no chance of success. And yet the more unequal Glasgow's life chances become, the more young mothers will join the ranks of 'bad mothers' and 'accidental deaths'.

What Mary Hepburn has achieved is little short of miraculous in a world where professionalism often excuses distant, badly-configured care by people who don't want to investigate further. Mary herself is in demand across the world, where the health of poor women is in collapse – but less so here. Visiting Eastern Europe, Mary meets enthusiastic politicians and service providers still confident they can turn lives around. Yet Mary and fellow travellers in Scotland have faced an uphill struggle trying to change professional and public attitudes. The pioneering methods of the WRHS are not widely known, not analysed and still not standard here. Just like the pioneering men's health centre in Drumchapel.

The poorest, sickest, most disempowered Scots are blamed for their own ill-health and for pulling down averages to saddle Scotland with the unenvied status of sick man and woman of Europe.

What's needed is for Scots to accept that passive, hopeless done-to communities and profoundly unequal life chances are Public Enemy Numbers One and Two.

Correcting the inbuilt tendency towards bad health and self-harming needs compassion, understanding, long-term funding, a slow transfer of control and considerable vision. The hopeful sign is that Scotland's top medical professionals have begun to speak this language too.

Glasgow Centre for Population Health has found deprivation profiles in Glasgow, Liverpool and Manchester are almost identical, but premature deaths in Glasgow are more than 30 per cent higher across almost all ages and both sexes. The project found deaths from cancer and heart disease were fairly similar in all three cities (see Figure 6, Mortality compared.) But 'non-medical' causes of death – drug and

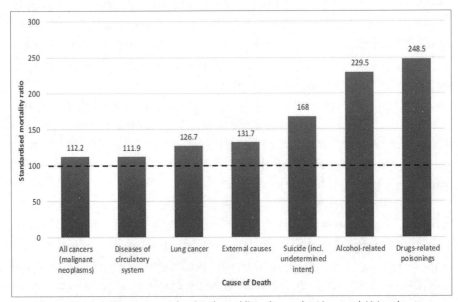

Figure 6: Mortality compared – the dotted line shows the Liverpool / Manchester average in each category.

alcohol misuse, suicide and violence – were far higher in Glasgow. Which begs the next question: why are Glaswegians so prone to these life-shortening behaviours?

There's no easy answer, and absolutely none that sits conveniently within the confines of medical science alone. Chief Medical Officer Harry Burns cites the work of Israeli medical sociologist Aaron Antonovsky, who talked about the sense of coherence (soc) necessary for adult health.

Antonovsky defined it as:

> The extent to which one has a feeling of confidence that the stimuli deriving from one's internal and external environments in the course of living are structured, predictable and explicable, that one has the internal resources to meet the demands posed by these stimuli and, finally, that these demands are seen as challenges, worthy of invest-ment and engagement.[4]

In other words, it's a mixture of optimism and control with three com-ponents – comprehensibility, manageability, and meaningfulness.

That may sound like advanced management-speak, but bear with me.

Comprehensibility is defined as the extent to which events are perceived as ordered, consistent and structured. Manageability is the extent to which a person feels they can cope. Meaningfulness is how much one feels that life makes sense, and challenges are worthy of commitment. Antonovsky suggested people with strong socs feel less stress and tension and believe they can meet demands – and strong socs arise from the person's natural coping style, their upbringing, financial assets and social support.

This is backed by other research which shows a child's home envi-ronment has a greater impact on literacy than birth weight, gender, dep-rivation and mother's education. Other studies – including Thomson's Nature Cure – have demonstrated the enduring physiological impact of stress arising from the home environment and local circumstances.[5] Research shows neglected or abandoned children have abnormally high levels of the stress hormone cortisol, as well as lower growth hormone

4   A. Antonovsky, *Health, stress and coping: new perspectives on mental and physical well-being* (San Francisco: Jossey-Bass, 1987).

5   'The Effective Provision of Pre-School Education [EPPE] Project: A longitudinal Study' funded by the DfES (1997–2003 University of London, 1999).

levels. These imbalances inhibit the development of nerve tissue in the brain, suppress growth and depress the immune system.

According to Dr Bruce Perry, chronic stress over-stimulates an infant's brain stem so the child may display increased aggression, impulsivity, and violence later in life as the brainstem floods the body with adrenaline and cortisol every time a stressful, hard to handle situation crops up.

The regular release of stress hormones in a child's brain arrests growth in portions responsible for attachment and emotional control – and unused functions are 'pruned' during the first year of life. So the result of neglect is often a violent, impulsive, emotionally unattached child.[6] And a badly adjusted youngster and young adult incapable of seeking out or sticking to the common-sense, drug-free regime of simple food and physical activity outlined by James Thomson.

Daily life in areas of multiple deprivation often produces a world devoid of comprehensibility, manageability or meaningfulness, where adults rely on medication to cope because underlying problems cannot be tackled and thus become 'avoidant' parents with negative health impacts on their own children. It's the ultimate vicious circle. But rather than pick our way through this long causal chain, Scottish society tends to blame, judge, punish, imprison and isolate. It doesn't help. But it reassures 'decent citizens' they are not to blame. And they are not. The system is to blame. But we are all part of the system.

Glasgow's higher mortality rate isn't longstanding. Before 1950, the Glasgow average wasn't so different from the Scottish average, and neither was so different from European mortality rates. Just as Mary Hepburn observes, something happened in the 1980s. What could that be except the advent of Margaret Thatcher and the sudden end of a comprehensible, manageable or meaningful way of life for tens of thousands of Glaswegians?

It's a theory, no more. But the health-destroying impact of stress through hopelessness and grief and across generations is now recognised.

A legion of engaged professionals like Mary, long-term backing for community volunteers like Tommy Riley, and new government priorities to reduce inequality, empower communities, and pile resources

---

6   B. Perry, 'Incubated in Terror: Neurodevelopmental Factors in the Cycle of Violence,' *Children in a Violent Society* (New York: Guilford Press, 1997). See also M.H. Teicher et al, 'The Neurobiological Consequences of Early Stress and Childhood Maltreatment', *Neuroscience Biobehavior Review* (2003, Jan-Mar; 27) pp 33–44. pp 1–2.

into Early Years Care could yet transform this situation – slowly. If we're serious about health, we must be serious about the belief that Scots, with the right resources, can heal themselves. Everything else has been tried – and in our poorest communities, everything else has failed. The proof is in the data.[7]

Look at the consistent pattern. Every important aspect of living is correlated with background. Life chances, performance and outcomes are high in rich neighbourhoods, low in poor ones. Not loosely or randomly or occasionally, but absolutely, always and rigidly. Not last century but last year. There is simply no doubt. Scotland cannot blossom while so many people are disempowered and stuck in hopeless lives. If we don't think a new approach is needed, we are defying logic – nothing has shifted this pattern to date. And if we don't think that's possible – despite all the positive examples from communities, volunteers and committed professionals – we can all go home.

The snag is that in Scotland, home is often where the trouble began.

---

7 Figures 7–10 were compiled by the Improvement Service using health, education and crime data for the most and least deprived communities in Scotland in 2011. Each cohort represents the ten per cent of neighbourhoods which contain the most and least income-deprived people. These two groups (of the least and most income deprived) each represent over 700 neighbourhoods (there are 6,505 'neighbourhoods' and 500 to 1,000 people per neighbourhood. So each of the two ten per cent groups represents over 350,000 people living in Scotland). Each table shows health, education and crime outcomes for the two 'poorest' and 'richest' ten per cents of neighbourhoods in Scotland. Figure 7 shows Emergency Hospital Admissions per 100,000 people. Figure 8 shows crime rates are recorded by the Scottish Index of Multiple Deprivation (SIMD), 2012 and only include crimes recorded by the police. Figure 10 shows Pupil Performance measured by 'average tariff' scores from pupils SQA exam results from 2010–11. UCAS use these scores to establish entry into higher education. Figure 9 is calculated from the total number of live births 2009–11. The 'richest' and 'poorest' neighbourhoods have been selected by the percentage of their population who are income deprived. All data is publicly available from the Scottish Neighbourhood Statistics website: http://www.sns.gov.uk/.

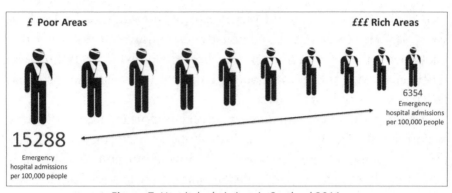

Figure 7: Hospital admissions in Scotland 2011

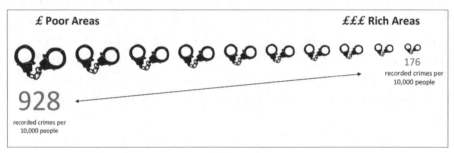

Figure 8: Recorded crime in Scotland 2011

Figure 9: Underweight babies in Scotland 2011

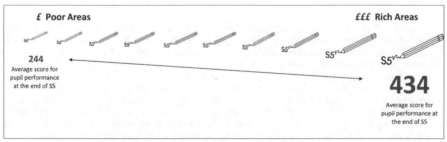

Figure 10: Academic attainment S5 in Scotland 2011

CHAPTER THREE

Our Homes are not our Castles

KINGS, QUEENS, CURRENCIES, wars, inventors, languages, geography and latitude all command attention in the conventional story of Scotland. Yet a nation is distinguished – above all – by the way its people live. And Scots have lived in quite distinctive ways for the last century and beyond.

First of all, there are flats. North of the border families in cities have tended to live in flats, not houses, sharing space in a predesigned (not converted) way. Almost a million Scots still live in stone tenements – a housing type not even included in official registers elsewhere in Britain.

Secondly, Scots have tended to rent, not own, for most of the last century with tenants outnumbering owner-occupiers until as recently as 1991, in contrast to trends in the rest of the UK.

Thirdly, Scots tended to live in council-owned, not private, property. In the 1970s Scotland built proportionately more public sector homes than Eastern Europe.

Fourthly, Scottish housing conditions within living memory were more squalid, life-shortening and overcrowded than anywhere else in these islands, including Ireland.

These profound differences are not generally considered very important in the formation of Scottish identity and political loyalties.

Why not?

Housing has carved the shape of Scotland, the limits of hope and the pace of social endeavour. It has reinforced class identity and voting loyalty, installed solidarity as a national characteristic to be ignored at a politician's peril and helped produce a conundrum.

Better understanding of our housing legacy might help us unravel a major conundrum.

Today Glasgow is both the community-led housing capital of the UK and home to Europe's largest, bleakest housing estates.

How can one place contain such extremes? Welcome to one

manifestation of the contradiction which prompted the poet Hugh MacDiarmid to reflect on the 'duelling polarities' within Scottish society and declare 'I'd aye be whaur extremes meet'.[1]

The tenants of West Whitlawburn in South Lanarkshire already live there.

In the last 30 years they've blossomed from being powerless tenants on a run-down peripheral council scheme into members of a dynamic housing co-operative – one of only nine in Scotland.

Their story of home-grown transformation demonstrates the underlying capacity of Scots: 'The first cheque I ever signed in my life was for £2.2 million. Weird, cos I only had ten pence in my pocket at the time'.

Phil Welsh was neither joking, nor an MBE back in 1988 when West Whitlawburn's big moment came. After a working life at the steelworks of Clydebridge in North Lanarkshire (now defunct) Phil, then in his mid-40s, was at home feeling ill and slightly sorry for himself while his wife Sadie attended yet another tenants' meeting about repairs to the high rise block where they lived on the fifth floor. So far, so normal. Except that April evening after a long day's work, textile machinist Sadie Welsh took a unilateral decision that changed the lives of everyone she knew. It could have become a turning point for Scotland. She 'volunteered' Phil for a new steering committee which took West Whitlawburn out of council control and into local ownership. The rest became history – albeit one few Scots have heard. 'One day we were tenants, the next we were Landlord,' recalled Phil. 'We really had no choice – either we kept living in unacceptable conditions or we took control from the council, took a risk and bid for housing grants to run West Whitlawburn as a co-operative – we chose the second option.' So – almost a year after that first meeting – on 20 March 1989 tenants in one of the most run-down estates on Glasgow's southern periphery ended decades of council under-investment by voting to own and run the estate themselves. Phil was one of the driving forces in Glasgow's most successful housing co-operative. Muriel Alcorn has been another.

---

1   The 'idea of duelling polarities within one entity' was thought typical of the Scottish psyche and literature and the phrase 'Caledonian Antisyzygy' was first coined by G. Gregory Smith and elaborated upon by MacDiarmid in *The Modern Scot*.

From my flat up on the tenth floor I can see Ben Lomond from the kitchen window and Coatbridge to Rutherglen from the living room. I wouldn't change it for the world.

Muriel came to Glasgow from Dunblane in the '70s to start nursing. She was scared of heights but in 1979 happily accepted the tenth floor council flat where she still lives today:

There were so many children and old folk – they needed to be closer to the ground than me.

Muriel's new life in council-run West Whitlawburn was great for a while, but soon the '60s-built high-rise blocks started showing defects no amount of well-meaning DIY could hope to fix:

Water penetration, dampness, the heating didn't work, the windows didn't fit, there was no security and the verandas leaked. When there was an east wind in the winter you froze. When you went to make complaints at the Housing Department you never met the same person twice and you could go ten or twelve times about the same repair. Of course if you were working that was impossible.

Muriel Alcorn and Phil Welsh in West Whitlawburn.

Frustrated but convinced the flats could be fixed, Muriel, Phil and five others formed the first steering Committee of West Whitlawburn Housing Cooperative in 1989. It wasn't easy. For lifelong socialists and believers in state provision, 'going private' – even though it was actually 'going co-operative' – instinctively felt wrong. But in the 1980s not much felt right about the housing estate marooned on Glasgow's most remote southern edge.

One winter's day in 2010 I turned up for a guided tour to get a better idea of the transformation with Phil Welsh.

'It was flat roofs to blame – they were OK for Spain but not the west of Scotland.'

'Phil, isn't it weird how everyone still tries to find a charitable explanation for near-criminally sub-standard design and construction?'

'Aye, you've got a point. The windows weren't properly aligned, the panel joints were exposed, the flat roofs leaked – it was a recipe for dampness.'

'So the flats were basically thrown up in a hurry to meet post-war government housing targets?'

So far, so sadly familiar.

'Aye, but then came the final straw.'

It must have been weighty. The first council housing was generally high quality, but as money ran out, most was not. Sterile, faceless, badly constructed and marooned council estates were thrown up all around the towns and cities of the Central Belt – many high rise in the modernist style of Le Corbusier, whose radical idea of a vertical garden city included schools, community centres and shops halfway up tall, slender housing blocks built on stilts above parkland. Yip, if you half-close your eyes, look at the tower block disasters all over Britain, I suppose you could get the drift. In the '50s and '60s though, high rise was the only game in town. Indeed, in 1965 Housing Minister Richard Crossman was so convinced prefabricated tower blocks were the answer, councils had to complete lengthy 'why not' sections in grant application forms if they opted for a different system.[2] Few did until 1968, when a gas explosion demolished a load-bearing wall in a tower block at Ronan Point in East London. Four people were killed,

---

2   H. Sherlock, *Cities Are Good For Us* (London: Paladin, 1991).

17 were injured and society woke up to the fact that tower-block living wasn't working – in all sorts of ways.

Nor were many of the sprawling, 'low rise' council estates much better. Many Glasgow council tenants had to thole conditions councillors, MSPs, poverty workers and indeed passing journalists wouldn't tolerate for a minute – bronchitis-inducing dampness, chronic overcrowding, repair delays, sofas left in communal closes, malfunctioning waste disposal systems in high rise flats, no right to paint doors, no right to say boo to a goose, and no chance whatsoever of seeing a goose in the wastelands surrounding each stalag-like block. Added to all this, there were often next to no local amenities save a pub and a shop.

It didn't have to be like that. Scotland's Norwegian neighbours responded very differently to the same post-war housing crisis with the same urban tenement housing type.

The Norwegian Housing Bank, set up in 1947, gave grants to people to build their own homes in rural areas with help from friends and neighbours (community self-help called *dugnad*) and city dwellers were offered flats in co-operatively owned blocks (with allotments nearby to grow vegetables). Denmark also adopted a co-operative housing model. As a direct result, many of today's stone-built Copenhagen tenements have solar panels on the roof and small lifts retro-fitted on the outside (all paid for by owner contributions) which can stop at each landing because communal stair windows have been replaced with glass lift doors. It means the elderly can live on any floor, house price inflation is controlled because there's an upper ceiling on sale prices, housing is relatively affordable and rents are calculated to create a pool of cash for repairs.

Such a rational co-operative housing system was not given house room in the construction of Britain's post-war welfare state. Here the underlying philosophy was always benign paternalism or, as Phil described it, 'stand there till we fix you' socialism.

Scots were given next to no control or involvement in decisions so council housing produced units – but not necessarily active inhabitants or muscular communities. For decades, units sufficed. Many families were extremely grateful for housing with indoor toilets, baths and kitchens and a municipal landlord who wouldn't suddenly evict or

External two person lift in Danish tenement Housing Co-op.

double rents – eloquent testimony to the terrible conditions Scots had endured on the land and in the Glasgow pre-war, private sector slums where diseases like TB and cholera first prompted Scottish councils to intervene.

West Whitlawburn tenants – like tens of thousands of other Scots – expected little from their housing and were not disappointed. So the last straw that prompted radical action in 1988 must have been a whopper.

It was.

Glasgow Council had been given £6.6 million by the government to refurbish the estate. West Whitlawburn had hard-to-fix high-rise flats. So the council decided to spend all the repair money on easier-to-fix low-rise blocks in East Whitlawburn instead of dividing the spend evenly. Better value for money.

The tenants association in West Whitlawburn was outraged, and decided not to take the loss of improvement cash lying down. Their timing was perfect.

Six pilot housing schemes had already been transferred from council to housing association control. Breaking up large council estates suited every important interest at the time – principally the Con-

servative Scottish Office and the Labour-run city council. So the West
Whitlawburn buyout got a speedy green light from the authorities. At
the start, the only hesitation came from the residents themselves. Sixty
per cent voted to transfer away from council control – but for Phil
Welsh, that wasn't enough.

> We were terrified. We'd never done anything like this in our lives. We
> knew we needed to take control of our ain hooses but we needed mair
> people to back it wholeheartedly. So we went around and harangued
> them for a month. Thirteen per cent more folk voted yes the second
> time. That was good enough.

In fact, Muriel, Phil, two shop assistants, Susan Stevely and Isabel
Dunsmuir, along with two retired men, Bobby Inglis and Frank
Gallagher, amongst others, put their local reputations on the line to
create change. Without this team of well-connected, street credible,
community leaders, West Whitlawburn would still be a failing estate
like its council-controlled Eastern neighbour.

'Did any of you have experience of running something this big?'

'Naw. We were naïve – didn't quite know what we were taking on.
Naebody had management experience.'

'Well Phil was a shop steward...'

'Och well hardly...'

'How long, Phil?'

'Well, since I was 18 in the Boilermakers Union.'

'And he ran amateur football teams...'

'Teams plural – as in more than one?'

'Well aye – Clyde United, Eastfield United and the Belvoir Bombers.'

'Phil, you'd been a shop steward and organised grown men in three
football teams, lived to tell the tale and you don't think that's management experience?'

'Aye, ye can see how we made him Chair after just three months.
Dinnae be modest, Phil.'

'Aye, it disnae suit you.' There's an outbreak of wheezing laughter
amongst the volunteers round the table.

'But you set up a housing co-operative not a housing association –
why was that?'

Phil sits forward, 'People fae miles away can sit on a Housing

Association Board. Only folk fae the neighbourhood can sit on the housing co-operative. It was an opportunity to get things done for oorselves. And that's how folk like Frank and Bobby were so important – they were retired so they had time to talk to people, head off problems, meet all the council folk we couldnae cos we had jobs. The women were the business-like ones – maybe because they worked in shoaps, maybe that's just how they always were. We didnae always agree but we had diversity. That made a good team.'

Phil and the first co-operative leaders grabbed their opportunity with both hands. The new Scottish Homes gave WWHC £2.2 million to pay Glasgow Council for 540 homes. Since then, £50 million has been spent bringing the flats up to standard and building new homes for sons and daughters who want to stay locally. With no debts to service, all subsequent rental income funded the co-operative. From the day West Whitlawburn opted out of council control, the two halves of the old estate developed very differently.

Dampness, security and renovation were immediately voted top spending priorities by co-op members in the West. But according to WWHC Director Paul Farrell, the big difference wasn't better kitchens, snazzy external cladding, new roofs or even new heating systems.

'The seismic shift in the West came from feelings of ownership, pride, confidence and social esteem.'

That may sound like the stuff of hopeful mission statements. In West Whitlawburn, it is tangible. In the West, the streets and pavements are gritted, litter- and graffiti-free. Common closes and glasswork are cleaned several times a week. Empty flats are quickly filled with new tenants. In the East they're not. In the West, 500 people are waiting to fill the 50 vacancies which arise every year. In the East, vacant flats have their windows smashed and remain boarded up until new tenants arrive. Much of that is down to security. In the West there's loads of it and most residents – even younger tenants – support it wholeheartedly. Concierges are on duty 24 hours a day watching the 28 external and 185 internal cameras of the extensive CCTV system and responding fast when needed. 'At the start there was mistrust. People asked if the cameras were there to report folk to the DSS or to detect 'frequent visitors'. We said they weren't. It just took time to prove'.

Drug dealers moved out of the West fairly quickly – clients weren't happy having every move recorded so trade suffered and trouble moved on.

In 1993 the committee voted to become a fully mutual co-operative – cleverly opting out of the government's damaging Right to Buy scheme: 'Aye, we had to dae that before we built those new semis round the corner for young families. There'd have been nae point ploughing the cash in if it just ended up as big profits for some individual tenants ten years doon the line. Folk all agreed. So we just did it'.

It took another two decades and a new Scottish Parliament before democracy formally ended the haemorrhage of council housing stock WWHC had effortlessly avoided. What a difference a decade makes.

'It was wild here in the old days. People could disappear for weeks in the multis. If you lasted a year as a caretaker in a multi-storey environment without CCTV, you were doing well.' Graham Pearson was a concierge until back pain meant early retirement. He still lives in 'the East' and volunteered to take me 'across' for comparative purposes. There was much discussion about this – Phil and Paul decided their presence might be 'provocative' while Graham was entitled to walk round because he lived there. Territorial limits around the Whitlawburns are still so graphically drawn.

'It feels like we're planning a trip across the Peace Wall in Belfast or something...'

'... or like the Berlin Wall in the old days. I've no been but that's what some folk say.'

'Do you go over to the East?'

'I've no real cause to go there – so no. I huvnae been over for years.'

The 'East' begins 100 yards beyond the last multi-storey block in West Whitlawburn. So Graham and I saunter across. There's a central square with tufty patches of grass strewn with litter outside the council housing office. A road runs through the middle and a parking space has the words 'Furniture pick-up' painted in yellow on the ground. 'Aye that's the latest 'advance' over here. Kids were setting fire to sofas cos they were bored. The sofas were lying aboot and naebody came to pick them up. Some auld folk were nearly killed when the fire spread to their flat. So this is the solution. If everyone takes their auld sofas oot here in the middle of the park, then when the kids set them alight, they cannae hurt anyone. Result, eh?'

Unwanted furniture collection in East Whitlawburn.

In the West we offer tae come and tak oot auld furniture – we dae it oorsels and tak it doon tae a storage area where it gets locked up till the cooncil comes tae collect it. Nae litter, nae temptation, nae fires, nae problem. But here...

Graham walks on, casually pointing out crumbling brickwork, single-glazed windows and – on that winter's day – icy paths like skating rinks.

'Nae old folk will risk coming oot wi paths like that. And naebody will go in tae ask after them either.'

In the West it's very different.

We drop into the bungalow that serves as nerve control for all the security cameras and meet Raymond, who's just started his shift.

'The paths are cleared every morning and 70 homes with elderly, disabled or vulnerable tenants are fitted with alarms. They can buzz doon to the concierge if they're lonely, frightened or ill – in the middle of the night even – and we pop up to check on them, have a natter or a cup of tea.'

Knowing how keen most men are on 2am cups of tea – especially when they have to make them – I find such selflessness amazing.

'It's not what security staff would expect to do as part of a routine night shift, is it?'

'Why not – we're here all night and that's what we're paid for. It's nae bother.'

Raymond looks up over the low bank of CCTV screens and nods at an old man with a stick shuffling past.

'That's John. In the bad weather we went up with his shopping. He likes a can of cider. That's his life.'

Eleven deaths have been averted thanks to the monitoring system and quick detection of heart attacks, epileptic fits and choking attacks. Personal contact in the wee, small hours and 24 hour support has also prevented the precautionary admission of frail, elderly people to accident and emergency facilities – a measure which cost the NHS in Scotland almost 1.5 billion pounds in 2009-10. The co-op resolutely refuses to turn these life-saving interventions into 'cost effective' statistics but they are canny enough to know higher than average management costs have to be defended – especially in difficult times. So they've produced social accounts which list the ways in which an empowered, well-managed, self-regulating community protects dignity and saves cash. The improvement in West Whitlawburn life was confirmed by an independent survey in 2000 which showed 83 per cent of residents thought services were good or very good; 76 per cent saw their homes as good value for money; 71 per cent thought the neighbourhood was good or very good and 92 per cent of respondents found reporting a repair easy. Since there's been no comparable satisfaction survey in 'the East' it's hard to demonstrate what an astonishing transformation that represents.

West Whitlawburn was also the sole Scottish focus of a UK-wide academic study on housing co-operatives in 2001 in which residents spelled out the way things had changed.[3]

'The Council used to make decisions, but didn't have to live with the consequences.'

'Before with the Council, we had caretakers. They finished at 6pm and that was that. They were no help, none at all. They were like little generals.'

3   Tenant Control & Social Exclusion report by Professor David Clapham, Philippa O'Neill & Nic Bliss for the Confederation of Co-operative Housing 2001.

'With the co-op you are a person, with Glasgow City Council you were just a number.'

'The co-operative housing team has a genuine interest in their job. There hasn't been anything that I couldn't come down and discuss with the staff.'

'With the co-op, what they said they were going to do, they've done and they keep you up to date. You're not left in the dark.'

Praise indeed.

wwhc has also branched out from simply supplying houses. The outlook is simple – 'If local people have a plan to do something and its legal, we'll support it.' The busy Bonus Ball Resource Centre runs a healthy eating café a newsletter, a senior citizens exercise club, a fitness centre, a mother and toddler club, a fruit-selling operation and a junior gardening club. The centre also houses a youth committee with its own budget, 'if you target 14 to 17 year olds now, they'll take over running the estate in their 20s'. The co-op supports the local credit union and local football teams, pays for a welfare rights adviser, sponsors folk to reach and stay in higher education, and gives donations to bereaved residents. In short, the co-op has expanded its caring role to make up for the shortcomings of other public agencies. wwhc is fast becoming a mini version of the *folkhemmet* – the People's Home, as Nordic nations christened their all-embracing welfare states. All it needs is more control, more levers (sound familiar?) and the rest of Scotland to catch up.

In all these long decades, however, West Whitlawburn has somehow failed to make the headlines – in Scotland anyway.

That's even more amazing when you realise Phil and the gang were not the first kids on the housing co-operative block. Glasgow's community-controlled housing movement really started in 1971 with Central Govan Housing Association. Soon after, a new Housing Act kick-started regeneration and gave Glasgow Council the chance to build on the Govan model to encourage the creation of housing associations all over the city and in Paisley and Clydebank. As the Director of Glasgow 1999 (City of Architecture) Deyan Sudjic observed:

> It was the involvement of Glasgow people in rescuing their homes
> from generations of neglect that triggered one of the most successful
> episodes in the history of social housing in Britain.

Between 1974 and 1995, Glasgow City Council approved 20,000 housing improvement grants and 58,000 repair grants – most carried out by tenant-led housing associations. In the boom years, Glasgow's public spending on renovation amounted to 10 per cent of the total UK renovation budget. Thanks to this rush of grassroots activity, encouraged by the Council, Scotland went from no community-led housing to a substantial international presence within a decade.

By the late '80s and early '90s, Glasgow's massive council estates had fallen behind the housing associations and a second wave of community takeovers began (including West Whitlawburn.) The final chapter should have opened in 2003 when housing stock transfer in Glasgow became the flagship policy of the (then) Scottish Executive's Community Ownership Programme under Wendy Alexander. That ambitious project aimed to transfer housing from cash-strapped councils across Scotland to community-led Housing Associations. The idea was that Glasgow's council stock would be shifted first to the Glasgow Housing Association (GHA) and then from that temporary staging post via 'second stage transfer' (SST) to Local Housing Organisations (LHOs) owned and run by residents. Such a bold move could have produced dozens of people's republics like West Whitlawburn – but it didn't.

The GHA turned out to be rather possessive. True – it did spend £1.2 billion over a decade to repair or modernise 70 per cent of council homes and cut average heating bills by a third. But then 'devolving power' ground to a halt. It took a seven-year campaign by Glasgow tenants to wrestle 18,950 homes from GHA control and transfer them to 24 existing community-controlled housing associations (CCHAs), leaving the GHA as Scotland's largest social landlord with around 45,000 homes and 25,000 homeowners for whom it provides factoring services. Amazingly, though, the Community Controlled Housing movement in Glasgow is even bigger.

Fifty associations own 58,000 homes and house the majority of Glaswegians who rent. That's big. But community leaders feel they've had to fight for cash every inch of the way and constantly prove and re-prove their credibility with each new set of councillors and government funders. The starry-eyed idealism of the 1970s is long gone. Despite generations of warm words, community-owned housing is still not in with the bricks of mainstream provision. Nor have they these grassroots powerhouses been given health, job creation or education cash to continue the regeneration job like the de-facto micro-councils they have effectively become. Instead they must win short-term, one-off grants or qualify as pilot schemes.

It's crazy. A collection of houses is not a community. And yet housing associations have been expected to provide both despite having funding and jurisdiction over bricks and mortar alone. For too long now, successive governments have willed the empowerment of tenants without willing the means. Even though the latest statistics suggest small, local community-controlled housing associations (with no aspiration to grow beyond their locality) make far more efficient use of staff than the big, professionally led, growth-orientated ones apparently favoured by the Scottish Government.[4]

Beyond Glasgow, tenant control has been slow to catch on. The rest of Scotland has just 10 per cent of the community-controlled total. Sometimes tenants outside Glasgow voted against stock transfer – sometimes the process just stalled. The net result is that councils are still large players in providing affordable, rented housing while some tenant-controlled associations have even been quietly dumped, merged or taken over by more conventional neighbours in the name of best value, compliance, efficiencies of scale and other 'professional' priorities.

What of it? Well given participation and election turnouts in Scotland's most deprived neighbourhoods are ultra-low, tenant control can kick-start democracy – and that's not to be sniffed at.

Phil and Muriel remember vividly how they handled the stress of management responsibility... and a bank account containing £2.2 million.

'You divorced yourself from it. It didnae worry me.'

'Once you started, you had to see it through. There was a lot of dogged determination.'

'You saw other like-minded folk around you – that helped. When I had fears, the others allayed them. Some folk pass on bad habits.

---

4   Scottish Housing Regulator stats 31 March 2012 show CCHAS have one office-based member of staff for every 59 houses, 13 biggest national/regional RSLS have one per 45 houses & GHA's have one per 43 houses.

People on the steering committee influenced each other to stay positive.'

'We said to each other, 'We can't live in this pigsty anymore. We need to pull ourselves up.'

'Aye – we were not going to be beaten. At the start when they got all cash the East Whitlawburn folk were cockahoop. Hardly any of those folk are even there now. One way or another they've left or passed on. We achieved something we can see every day and pass on to oor weans. When we go to conferences we get respect fae folk. Over in the East, it's still faceless control.'

'Aye, we're tenants and managers – so we're always in the firing line here.'

Perhaps not every community is ready to combine control and involvement in the full-blooded, co-operative way West Whitlawburn has done. But maybe that's because there's been less and less whole-hearted government backing for community-controlled housing since the heady days of the 1970s. For the last half century, the Tories skewed the market in favour of individual home ownership, whilst Labour staked everything on the economies of scale delivered by massive council estates and then embarked on a partly realised stock-transfer to housing associations. The SNP reintroduced council housing and ended the Right to Buy.

Nowadays 'community involvement' often means giving tenants a choice of kitchen worktops – not transferring power, assets and control. Scotland is doing 'empowerment lite' when the benefits of 'full fat' tenant control are staring Ministers straight in the face – or should be. In truth, segmented Scotland doesn't really look across such epic class divides. So the sterling example of West Whitlawburn doesn't confront anyone except the long suffering tenants of the east and the mildly irritated housing officials of South Lanarkshire Council.

Like all local heroes, the founders of WWHC are too busy working in their own community to spend time broadcasting achievements, hob-nobbing with distant MSPs or creating a powerful lobby for further change.

In the current grim economic circumstances created by 'too large to fail' institutions, you'd think small, successful, co-operative ways of working would be sought out. You'd think West Whitlawburn would be flavour of the month. Instead, their story, their fight and their capacity remain relatively unknown – in Scotland at least.

After that visit in 2010, I wrote about West Whitlawburn in a *Scotsman* column, part of which was then reproduced in a *Spectator* column by Alex Massie, who concluded:

> Of all the criticisms of David Cameron's Big Society the one that makes least sense is the notion that... it's of no use in poorer communities. Nothing could be further from the truth. If it's anything the Big Society is about untapped 'social capital' and there's more of that, in more communities, than the scoffers and titterers on the *News Quiz* would have you believe.

Unsurprisingly – after such a prominent connection with the Big Society idea – the Cabinet Office in London called Paul Farrell a week after the *Spectator* piece was published, suggesting WWHC should apply for a Big Society Award. They did – and in December 2012 were declared winners, to the amusement (and horror) of lifelong socialists like Phil.

At least David Cameron reacted. The PM's people spotted a bunch of winners and seized an opportunity to make political capital – or try. There was no such reaction in Scotland.

Why not?

WWHC has paid for itself many times over since 1988, with reduced emergency hospital admissions and care provision. Along with lives saved, violence and anti-social behaviour have been reduced (along with associated costs of rehousing) and the co-op is tackling drink, dietary and skills problems.

Oxfam's recently published Humankind Index shows ordinary Scots can see the potential of such local empowerment. The joint top priorities of that 2012 survey were affordable, safe and decent homes and physical and mental health, closely followed by living in a neighbourhood where you can enjoy going outdoors and a clean and healthy environment. It seems punters intuitively understand that health, housing, locality and community are all connected. People are welded to place. And just as better health cannot be 'done to' people without their active involvement, better housing in the sense of providing a vibrant community setting for homes cannot be 'done to' people either.

Even when it's tough – especially when it's tough – people in every community are able and willing to cope with the pressure. As long as they can rely on one another and have had the chance to try.

Tenants do have a say in the 13 largest social landlords where around a third of board members are tenants – but that's nowhere near the 100 per cent of grassroots involvement in tenant-run West Whitlawburn or the 86 per cent of community controlled housing providers. And when you look at the number of shareholders – the people with the right to 'sack the board' – the 'democratic deficit' outside the tenant-controlled sector is even greater. Shareholders in Scotland's 13 largest landlords constitute three per cent of the houses owned while in Scotland's 81 community-controlled providers[5] shareholders constitute 26 per cent of houses owned.[6]

Put simply, the bulk of tenants across Scotland still don't have an active hand in running their neighbourhoods. And even in Glasgow – Scotland's Co-operative Capital – professionals have failed to keep devolving control and cash to communities which proved their capacity decades back. A big opportunity for local empowerment has been missed.

Today there are nine fully fledged housing co-ops in Scotland like West Whitlawburn, representing about one per cent of total housing stock.[7] That's not enough.

Much energy is expended by professional people trying to fix people evidently capable of fixing themselves. What the most active folk in each community generally need is backing, budget and belief. But they don't get it. Instead the vast majority of politicians, academics and journalists ignore practical, community-led success stories like West Whitlawburn in their restless quest for magic bullets, cures, solutions, examples to pilot and heroic individuals to present with

---

5   106,484 houses are controlled by 3,111 shareholders amongst the largest landlords – 82,967 houses and 21,500 shareholders in the community controlled sector. Figures derived from Scottish Housing Regulator Register 2012. Total excludes rural housing associations which are hard to fit into the urban CCHA model.

6   A few of Scotland's biggest landlords do actively promote widespread involvement. Dumfries and Galloway Housing Partnership have around 600 shareholders and 10,000 odd houses (equivalent to 17 per cent of all the houses they own). But in the GHA (Scotland's biggest single landlord) the only shareholders are board members themselves.

7   There are just nine fully fledged housing co-ops in Scotland like West Whitlawburn out of 180 social landlords and 32 councils with 5,123 housing units out of 288,053 RSL units and 318,260 council units – that means the beefiest form of community-controlled housing like West Whitlawburn provides just 1.7 per cent of all social housing and constitutes five per cent of all social landlords. It's not a lot.

awards. As a result, the general public quietly despairs of ever 'fixing' Scotland's most disadvantaged communities and discounts the crazy notion they could fix themselves.

An often patronised friend of mine who worked in one of Belfast's dodgiest areas during the Troubles regularly brought meetings to a (hilarious) standstill with this observation:

> A consultant is someone who sees a thing working in practice and wonders if it might just work in theory.

By that definition, Scotland has had a set of consultants with their collective hand on the tiller for too long – the net result is that the top-down, passive housing options of the last century are still the only properly funded options of this one.

For many, it's a poor choice. Individual home ownership in a run-down unemployment blackspot is like individual car ownership in a traffic jam – it brings only the illusion of control.

But renting a flat in a vast, unresponsive housing estate is just as disempowering – it brings only the illusion of involvement. The only thing that hasn't been tried properly across the whole of Scotland is full-blooded, well-planned, properly funded community-run housing in Scottish cities, acting as a future base for asset-owning development trusts or even small, new, community-sized municipal councils. If genuine, meaty land reform or a new system of land tax pulled down the cost of land, community-run housing associations could transform the poorest neighbourhoods.

But that probably won't happen.

Billy Connolly once summed up Scotland's hopeless peripheral schemes as 'deserts wi windaes'. The West Whitlawburn folk proved it doesn't have to be that way. A hundred co-operatively owned West Whitlawburn Housing Co-ops could cut vandalism, tackle gang culture and reduce hospital admissions in areas of multiple deprivation faster than any advertising campaign. A hundred properly-funded, miniature West Whitlawburn-sized councils could change Scotland. And yet, although the Scottish Government used the estate to launch its white paper 'Towards a Healthier Scotland', politicians have been slow to back the housing control revolution that make health improvements possible. Why is it so hard for successive governments to have faith? Why was it so hard for Scottish councils to let go? And why have so few other communities followed WWHC's example and seized the moment?

Scots still can't decide if this level of self-management and local ownership is a good thing. Community buyouts in rural areas to deal with the neglect of feckless, absentee owners are one thing – voting to opt out of democratic local control in cities is somehow regarded as 'privatisation' instead. Even if councils have presided over decades of neglect, even if folk have been shunted about like furniture and even if councils have been perfectly good but distant landlords, there's a slight feeling of defensiveness, maybe guilt, amongst folk like Muriel and Phil, who've spent 20 years helping to fix their own communities.

Why is there such strong attachment in Scotland to the council, the council house ideal and such wariness of more empowering alternatives?

The answer lies in the past and the appalling conditions of life before council housing.

1951 was a heck of a year

All About Eve won best picture at the Oscars starring Bette Davis as an aging Broadway legend and Marilyn Monroe, her young rival. The Soviet spies Guy Burgess and Donald Maclean fled to Moscow. Marlon Brando starred in *A Streetcar Named Desire*. Colour TV was invented and the first zebra crossing appeared on British streets. Footballers Kenny Dalglish and Kevin Keegan were born. And yet in that same year, half the families of Glasgow lived in just two rooms.

Think about that.

When Celtic and Liverpool legend Kenny Dalglish struck his first leather caser, most Glasgow lads spent every waking moment in the same room as two or three siblings and both parents – and probably slept beside them as well – indeed half of all Glaswegians were just this 'overcrowded.'

By contrast the proportion living in such cramped conditions in London in 1951 was just 5.5 per cent.[8]

Fifty per cent overcrowding in Glasgow – five per cent in London.

---

8 T.C Smout, *A History of the Scottish People* (London: Fontana, 1987).

The disparity is utterly astonishing – the fact it's not common know-ledge even more so. And though the problem of chronic overcrowd-ing was worst in Glasgow it wasn't confined there. The 1951 census shows 15 per cent of all Scots lived more than two to a room com-pared to 2.6 per cent of the population in England and Wales.

It takes a minute for the enormity of that difference to sink in. 1951 was just nine years before I was born. I can still cycle uphill to get the paper and recognise judges on *The X Factor* – so we're not talking ancient history here. Within living memory, home life for many Scots was chaotic, privacy-depriving, dignity-denying and even life-shorten-ing beyond anything experienced in such numbers south of the border.

Amazing really. Scotland's experience of overcrowding was probably responsible for epic levels of 'home avoidance' amongst generations of working men who sought escape in public houses and even the army, while women tolerated massive, Soviet-style housing schemes and hard-to-heat high rise blocks – all because they offered that supreme luxury: personal space.

Happily, most of the current generation have no first-hand expe-rience of chronic overcrowding and appalling housing conditions. Unhappily that means this generation cannot guess what shaped the outlook and expectations of our grandparents and their grandparents.

The 1861 census was the first in Scotland to ask questions about housing conditions and the results were shocking. A third of 'houses' consisted of one room (the 'single end') roughly 14 by 11 feet and inhabited by five people. A survey the following year in Edinburgh showed 1,530 single ends had 6–15 inhabitants in each. At such densi-ties, people slept like sardines in rooms without furniture or sanitation and rose every day to work for ten to twelve hours without time off. Not all the inhabitants of the room were even family members – one Edinburgh family in ten lived in a single end with a lodger.[9]

Hygiene suffered and disease was endemic. In 1861 Dundee had 91,664 inhabitants and just five WCs – three of which were in hotels. The city's main water supply, the Lady Well, was polluted by offal from the slaughterhouse. One contemporary writer observed that the 'absence of conveniences... is a great preventative of thorough cleanli-

---

9   Thomas Ferguson, *Scottish Social Welfare 1864–1914* (Edinburgh: E&S Livingstone Ltd, 1958)

ness and purity... As a consequence, the atmosphere is foully tainted, and rendered almost unendurable by its loathsomeness at those periods when offal and nuisance require to be deposited on the streets.'[10]

In 1861, the *Builder* journal observed of Edinburgh:

> We devoutly believe there are no smells in Europe or Asia which can equal in depth and intensity, the concentration and power, the diabolical combination of sulphurated hydrogen we came upon one evening in a place called Toddrick's Wynd.

And yet, that was an improvement.

In 1839, J.C. Symons, Government Commissioner for the investigation of the condition of the hand-weavers, said of Glasgow:

> I have seen human degradation in some of its worst phases, both in England and abroad, but I did not believe until I visited the wynds of Glasgow, that so large an amount of filth, crime, misery, and disease existed in any civilised country. In the lower lodging-houses ten, twelve, and sometimes twenty persons of both sexes and all ages sleep promiscuously on the floor in different degrees of nakedness. These places are, generally, as regards dirt, damp and decay, such as no person would stable his horse in. In this part of Glasgow most of the houses have been condemned by the Court of Guild – but it is just these dwellings which are filled to overflowing, because, by law no rent can be charged on them.[11]

In 1861 an Edinburgh city centre tenement suddenly collapsed, killing 35 people. A young boy, Joseph McIvor, was the only survivor. His rescuers heard him shout from the rubble: 'heave awa lads I'm no deid yet'. In honour of his miraculous escape, the new building that replaced it was called 'The Heave Awa Hoose', and an ornate lintel bearing an image of the sole survivor is still visible on the High Street – a permanent reminder of the danger of geriatric tenements. But this tragedy was less about the design weakness of the tenement. It was really a judgement on appalling levels of overcrowding. By the 1800s, Edinburgh's oldest 8–10 storey stone buildings were already 300 years old and occupied by 5–10 times more people than originally intended. The Improvement Act of 1867 brought in after the 'Heave Awa'

10   J. Symington, *1866 The Working Man's Home* quoted in T.C. Smout, *A History of the Scottish People.*
11   J.C. Symons, *Arts and Artisans at Home and Abroad* (Edinburgh: 1839).

disaster let the council tear down the most dangerous buildings. But overcrowding survived, even though a system of ticketing was introduced in Glasgow and extended to all Scottish burghs in 1903.

Dr James B. Russell – Glasgow's pioneering Medical Officer – said in 1888 of children who died young:

> Their little bodies are laid out on a table or a dresser so as to be somewhat out of the way of their brothers and sisters who play, sleep and eat in their ghastly company. One in five of all who are born there [in Glasgow's overcrowded slums] never see the end of their first year.[12]

The fact that overcrowding continued despite government control speaks for itself. A report on Paisley in 1906 showed that 46.9 per cent of ticketed houses inspected were still overcrowded.

The problem endured.

In 1911, single ends still made up 10 per cent of the Scottish total (and though houses with no windows had mercifully disappeared in 1881, my mother still recorded people living in caves around Wick during the 1951 census.) A 1913 survey showed that 94 per cent of Edinburgh's single ends shared one toilet and 43 per cent shared a sink. Living in one or two rooms measurably damaged health – infant mortality was 277 per 1,000 in the single ends of the Cowgate, compared to just 46 per 1,000 deaths in the 3–4 roomed homes of Merchiston.[13] Babies born to the overcrowded poor were five times more likely to die – and if they survived, probably five times more likely to be malnourished, short, thin and bronchial. What a health legacy.

Still, the problem endured.

The Royal Commission on Housing in 1917 found 'an almost unbelievable density' in Scotland compared to England – one witness to the Royal Commission said living in one room meant 'a constant succession of lifting, folding, and hanging up and if this regime is relaxed for even a short time the confusion is overwhelming.'[14]

The difference in living conditions on either side of the border was truly epic. Social historian Christopher Smout says that:

---

12 J.B. Russell, 'Life in One Room, 1888': A Lecture delivered to the Park Parish Literary Institute, Glasgow, 27 February (Glasgow, 1888).

13 W.W. Knox, Urban Housing in Scotland 1840–1940, SCRAN online.

14 S.G. Checkland, The Uppas Tree (Glasgow, 1976) The Royal Commission in 1917 found more than four people per room in 10.9 per cent of Glasgow houses (0.8 per cent in English cities), more than three people per room in 27.9 per cent (1.5 per cent in English cities) and more than two people in 55.7 per cent (9.4 per in England).

there was no privacy, no play space, no work space, no place to get out of the tensions of family life, to think, relax or sulk. There was not even space to die. To say the Scottish Housing problem was of a different order of magnitude from the English is only the literal truth.[15]

Pause a moment and take that all in.

1917 may feel like ancient history, but it isn't. Overcrowding in Scotland was lethal when my grandparents were teenagers. In 1917 they were acquiring (or failing to acquire) the positive outlook, physical attributes and general health they would pass on to my mother and later she to me. The housing conditions and health experienced by our grannies shapes us still – it can take that long to lose the physical inheritance of poverty and deprivation. Especially when chronic dampness became a big problem in cheaply built 70s and 80s housing.

Why were those conditions so bad? The massive, rapid urbanisation of the Victorian era was a big factor. Thanks to early industrialisation, Scotland's urban population was rocketing and Glasgow's population trebled in the half century up to 1911. Someone had to house the workers, didn't they? But squalid conditions weren't just a hangover from old times. Clydebank was effectively a brand new town in 1901 with a population of 30,000 – compared to just 816 in 1871. But in 1911 four fifths of Clydebank's brand new houses contained just one or two rooms as well.

There were other reasons for the persistence of chronic overcrowding in Scotland compared to England and they were all still present until this century when feudal land tenure was finally abolished – high land prices, feudal land ownership and relatively high rents for new council homes.

Of the houses built in Scotland in the period 1919–39, 67 per cent were in the public sector, compared to just 26 per cent in England. But those first council houses had high rents (between 46–52 per cent of a Dundee textile worker's wage).[16] That was partly because every aspect of housing (and everyday living) had traditionally been more expensive in Scotland than south of the border – the feudal system here meant

15 T.C. Smout, *A History of the Scottish People* (London: Fontana, 1987).
16 Ibid.

developers had to pay an annual fee to original landowners, which pushed up land prices. Building standards were higher in Scotland, but crucially, wages were also lower. Richard Rodger suggests real wages in Scottish burghs were 11–12 per cent below that of big English industrial cities.[17] And those figures are average wages. As Sean Damer points out, many Scottish workers were casually employed on piece-work rates, from day-to-day or from contract-to-contract. So Scots were unable and/or unwilling to risk spending the same proportion of their lower income on housing as their southern cousins.[18] Ultimately, housing accounted for 8 per cent of the average Scots income in 1951, compared with 10 per cent south of the border. Finally, and perhaps most importantly, the Scots (unlike the English) had no poor law to help workers during spells of unemployment.

All of this was a recipe for high rents, low and irregular income and, therefore, chronic overcrowding. So, during the last century, the living standards of ordinary Scots were significantly worse than folk in the rest of the UK. Such a profound experience of deprivation doesn't easily leave folk memory – nor does the equally profound experience of solidarity that made such a life bearable. All of it shaped our parents and grandparents – and they shaped us.

And whether it was ever said openly and explicitly, an unpalatable truth was passed on which inhibits trust to this day.

Wealthy land-owning Scots exploited fellow Scots in sub-standard housing for as long as they could get away with it. Class, not national-ity, was the main predictor of life chances. Affluent Scots did not come to the rescue of fellow Scots – far from it.

In the 19th century, dreadful conditions in private-sector housing had been tolerated by councils led by educated Scotsmen who were also slum landlords. According to Brian Elliott and David McCrone 95 per cent of the men sitting on the Lord Provost's Committee, 87 per cent of the Treasurer's Committee and 86 per cent of the Plans and Works Committee in 1875 Edinburgh were also landlords and proba-bly all Scots.

Regulation was half-hearted – but with deeper, structural reasons

17 R. Rodger, ed. *Scottish Housing in the Twentieth Century* (Continuum, 1989).
18 S. Damer, *Glasgow Going for a Song* (London: Lawrence & Wishart, 1990).

for overcrowding, how could regulation alone tackle the basic problems of undersupply and unaffordability?

Given the enduring health and social problems generated by overcrowding and poor living conditions, you'd think modern political debate would recognise the importance of Scotland's housing inheritance. It doesn't.

Historians have documented the horrors of how Scots once lived. And for those with curiosity, a strong stomach or any doubt, flick through the work of Richard Rodger, Ian Adams, Robert Baird, Christopher Smout, Tom Devine, Catriona MacDonald, Richard Finlay, Sean Damer, Chris Whatley and many more. It's all there. And yet somehow the research, arguments and statistics have failed to find their way into the consciousness of everyday Scots political debate.

Perhaps that's the job of non-historians. In his recent book *And the Land Lay Still*, James Robertson's main character Don observes:

> When he'd gone off to war he could hardly believe the amount of space there was; in barracks, in tents and the backs of lorries and out in the open air. It was almost worth having a war for – the men used to joke – having a bit of elbow room.

In his classic *Docherty*, William McIlvanney also paints a vivid picture of the squalor and brutality that bred generations of Glaswegians:

> High Street was the capital of Conn's childhood and boyhood. Everyone whom circumstances had herded into its hundred-or-so yards had failed in the same way. It was a penal colony for those who had committed poverty, a vice which was usually hereditary.

And yet despite all of this, our appalling housing heritage rarely rears its head in discussions of Scottish identity. The misery described so eloquently in *Angela's Ashes* was not just an Irish phenomenon. Overcrowding, illness and premature death were an unremarkable part of the average Scottish experience until the 1950s – and for some luckless Scots, well beyond. The home is the basic building block of health, outlook and national wellbeing. And yet until relatively recently the Scottish home contained one of the worst domestic environments in Europe. Even when overcrowding finally began to ease and physical conditions improved, a new housing problem awaited Scots. The problem so manifest in West Whitlawburn in 1989. The powerless-ness and passivity of the council tenant.

The Scots rent, the English own

During the last century, Scots were not just more overcrowded than the rest of the UK. They had a different housing experience in two other important respects as well. From the start of the council housing boom, Scots tended to rent, while the English tended to own.[19] And Scots tended to rent from councils whilst the English tended to be private sector tenants.

Those important differences have determined how Scottish lives, loyalties and locations developed during the 20th century.

In 1971, 70 per cent of Scottish households rented compared to just 49 per cent of households in England.[20]

In 1981, 35 per cent of Scottish householders were owners compared to 57 per cent in England.

In 1981, 56 per cent of Scottish householders were public sector tenants compared to 31 per cent in England.[21]

Bigger tenure differences existed within the United Kingdom than between neighbouring states like Denmark, the Netherlands and Germany.[22] But who – other than Margaret Thatcher – even noticed?

Until very recently Scots did not live in a 'property owning demo-cracy' and even though the Scot Noel Skelton may have coined the phrase, his fellow countrymen took a long time to share the outlook, behaviour or voting patterns that went along with it.[23]

Take the familiar saying, that an Englishman's home is his castle. In shared, rented, tenemented, flatted and publicly owned Scotland,

---

19 Tom Begg's *Housing Policy in Scotland and Communities and Local Government* (2010). Housing Statistics Live Table 801: Tenure Trend .

20 In the public and private sectors combined.

21 1981 Scottish Census shows household split: 35 per cent owners, 56.2 per cent social renters, 8.9 per cent private renters. English census 1981, 57.2 per cent owners, 31.7 per cent social renters, 11.per cent private renters

22 Home ownership levels 2011: Denmark 51 per cent, the Netherlands 49 per cent and Germany 42 per cent. Eurostat Housing 2012.

23 Skelton first used 'property owning democracy' in two *Spectator* articles in 1923. His *Oxford Dictionary of National Biography* entry notes 'he himself had meant a reinforcement of individualism through indus-trial profit sharing, agricultural smallholdings and co-operative schemes. But after Eden revived the phrase as a party slogan it became associated... with state promotion of house ownership.' Interestingly, Skelton's 'package' combined with widespread land ownership fairly well describes the Norwegian system.

the saying holds less meaning. In England the inviolable nature of the domestic domain has been embedded in Common Law since the 17th century.

In 1628, lawyer and politician Sir Edward Coke wrote:

'A man's house is his castle and each man's home is his safest refuge.'[24]

In 1763, William Pitt wrote that the:

poorest man may in his cottage bid defiance to all the forces of the crown. It may be frail – its roof may shake – the wind may blow through it – the storm may enter – the rain may enter – but the King of England cannot enter.

In 1800, the idea crossed the Big Pond when the biographer of Henry W. Grady (writer on the US Constitution) included this line:

'Exalt the citizen. Teach him that his home is his castle, and his sovereignty rests beneath his hat.'

In Scotland, the sanctity of home-owning has been a far fuzzier concept. A citizen's sovereignty cannot 'rest beneath his hat' when three floors of tenement-dwellers also rest there and the 'home' is owned by all-powerful municipal authorities or private landlords who could remove you at a week's notice.

Living for the most part in rented council flats until the 1990s, the average Scot did not regard his or her home as a castle, and was part of a different housing model to Britain's property owning norm. That different model could have taken us in a positive direction – towards efficient and lower cost district heating, an earlier appreciation of tenements and the need to maintain density in European-style cities. Taking Scotland's different housing model seriously could have helped improve it – half the population could be living in well-managed, warm and affordable housing co-operatives by now. But that could only have happened if Scotland's unique housing situation was thought to matter in terms of policy-making, law-framing, town planning and journalistic accuracy. In practice, it didn't. Scotland has long been just a variation on the theme. More's the pity.

Some check on the growth of unadulterated house worship in England could have released hot air from the housing bubble. Some

---

24 *The Institutes of the Laws of England*, 1628.

check on the rise of monolithic council estates in Scotland could have encouraged a more co-operative third way, harnessing the energy of passive, warehoused communities. In the event neither side of Britain's stale housing equation has really checked the other. Instead, British post-war housing history has seen a pendulum swing fully one way – then the other. On both sides of the border, most people lived in private rented accommodation until the First World War – an estimate for England in 1918 showed 23 per cent owners, 1 per cent social renters and 76 per cent private renters.[25] After the Housing Acts of 1919 the pendulum started moving.

In England it swung away from private renting to home ownership and towards dependence on an unregulated property sector which unbalanced the entire economy of Britain, soaked up savings which could have started small businesses, and eventually fuelled the current recession.

In Scotland it was a different story – the pendulum here swung fully towards council housing.

It took two decades of Right to Buy policy before Scottish home ownership even reached the 50 per cent mark for the very first time.[26] Scots didn't reach the UK property owning average until 2003. And yet these watershed moments passed without much of a mention (see Figures 1–3).

Before 1991, Scotland had been a nation of council tenants.

That means for half of a formative century, Scots were dependent on the municipal state for shelter. Although Scots had a close connection with council flats, and children often took over council house tenancies, the perception of the home as an appreciating, saleable asset was largely absent from Scottish thinking until 1991.

Proper plumbing, piped water, separate bedrooms, heating systems and inside toilets immediately improved life expectancy, child mortality and general health. Relatively high quality housing created a wave of gratitude towards the political party credited with building these homes. Generations of unwavering support for Labour was hence-

25 Estimates by Alan Holmans of Cambridge University Department of Land Economy 1918. Census questions on housing tenure in Scotland only began in 1961.

26 1991 Scottish Census shows household split: 52 per cent owners, 40.2 per cent social renters, 4.9 per cent private renters.

27 Figures 1–3 Sources: 1961 to 2001 Scotland Census, National Records of Scotland. 1999–2010 Scottish Household Survey. England; 1939–71: 'Housing Policy in Britain,' Alan Holmans, Table VI. 1981–91: DOE Labour Force Survey Housing. 1992–2008: ONS Labour Force Survey.

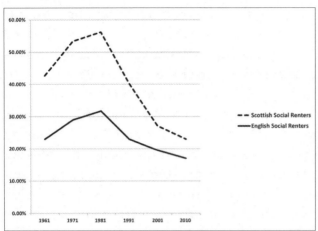

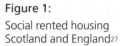

Figure 1:
Social rented housing
Scotland and England[27]

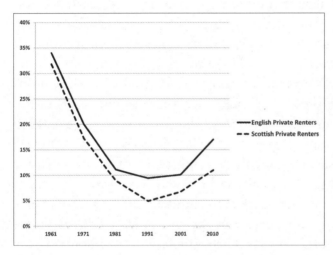

Figure 2:
Private renting
Scotland and England

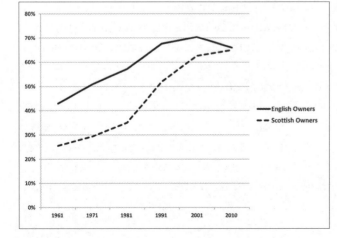

Figure 3:
Housing ownership
Scotland and England

forth matched only by generations of unwavering hostility towards the private sector from whose 'Rachman-like' clutches Scots believed they had been saved... by solidarity, trade union organisation, collective action, British municipalism and the British Labour Party.

In the early 20th century a massive 60 per cent of Scots lived in the urbanised stretch from Greenock in the West through the shipyards of Glasgow and mining towns of Lanarkshire and West Lothian to the capital of Edinburgh. London embraced the council house more wholeheartedly than any other city in England – but only 17 per cent of English people lived in London. So the council housing revolution and associated improvements in health were directly witnessed by the majority of Scots.

Is it any wonder then, that in the early 20th century, Scottish councils were hailed as municipal saviours and private landlords were regarded as implacable foes? Many Scots believed the institution of the council house effectively saved their lives.

The act of delivering council homes across the whole populous Scottish Central Belt allowed Labour to seal the deal with a generation of Scots and their grateful descendants. The Soviet-style, grim looking barracks that often appeared on streets without trees, shops, churches, town halls or bus shelters nonetheless offered contemporary luxury inside. They offered the one thing overcrowded Scots craved – space.

Though some council houses were built in the 1920s, Britain's council house boom really began in the 1950s as a Liberal policy enacted by the Tory premier Harold Macmillan. But the homes fit for heroes were actually delivered on the ground by local Labour councils. For decades, the electoral spoils went to the victors.

Scotland's experience of council housing nurtured and sustained a Labour-supporting, unionist default in urban Scotland for half a century. It also had social impacts.

There was no point in Scots contemplating extensive DIY, kitchen extensions or conservatories. Most council house tenants famously couldn't change their door knockers without council permission. Perhaps that's why Scots have always slightly mocked the 'sit-ooterie'. The idea of enlarging living space has long seemed impossibly difficult and therefore pretentiously ambitious to the average council house dwelling Scot.

Likewise, how could you get territorial or sniffy about intrusion or even have ten minutes to yourself if you shared a main door, back green, bins, close (and until 1951 possibly also the toilet and sink) with several other families, lodgers and friends? How could you be sucked into a consumer revolution with its focus on individual taste and personalisation when the layout of your flat was the same as every other flat for miles in all directions, with the same council-provided fittings and possibly the same inherited utility furniture and co-op dividend-stamp purchased cups and saucers?

I used to think it was remarkable that all my mother's family across several generations and many hundreds of miles all had the same rose-patterned tea-sets for 'best.' Perhaps this was no coincidence in a world where diversity, ownership, choice and involvement were still seen as luxury extras within the reach of English-accented, management-members of the ownership class. Scots settled instead for security and space.

Of course, on the face of it, this all changed in 2003, when Scots finally joined the rest of the UK aboard the property owning gravy train – just in time to see it come right off the tracks. Life – like comedy – is all about timing.

Now this is not to say renting is inherently bad or ownership inherently good.

Not at all.

But compared to other renting nations like the Germans, for example, renting Scottish-style had some downsides. A council flat for life meant having (probably) little say in its décor, location or maintenance. A private flat could mean a six month lease with equally little control. In the country the choice was often Hobson's Choice – a tied house (often on a peppercorn rent with eviction likely at the end of the job) or a tenant farmhouse with equally little say or security.

In Germany renting was more secure, long-term and higher quality. Today around 90 per cent of Berliners are tenants (by choice) and labour force mobility is high. The big difference between the Scottish and German experience of private renting has always been security.

Private German renters generally have unlimited leases and can demand continuation if their landlord tries to evict them. Private renting in Scotland, by contrast, was a low-quality, insecure option –

that's why the municipal state was forced to come to the rescue with council housing in the first place.

German housing associations and councils own 12 per cent of rental accommodation and 75 per cent is owned by small, local landlords. The proportions in Scotland are almost exactly the other way round.[28]

Council house allocations in Scotland used points to determine housing need. Points were also allocated for being local. That helped generations of Scottish families stay in the same neighbourhood, but it did tend to deter moves to new areas in search of work. The same was not true for more mobile renting Germans. A newspaper description of the modern German tenancy is instructive:

> Once you've signed your contract, you pretty much own the place, you can change almost everything, from the colour of the walls to sanding the floors and it's very hard for landlords to just kick you out whenever they want. If anything doesn't work properly (water, electricity, heating, even when the pipes tick too loudly in winter), you have the right to cut the rent, sometimes by 50 per cent, if the landlord doesn't fix it fast enough. I've lived in rented accommodation in London for two years, and you get treated like shit here by the landlords – and it's all legal. Hell, just a few years ago, if the landlord somehow lost your deposit, he didn't even have to pay it back! But politically, I don't think any party in the UK would dare to change the law, because even the poorest sod in Britain somehow sees himself as a potential homeowner and wouldn't want the law to change.

If Britain had German style, long, affordable leases our social and political history might have been very different. But we didn't.

Ironically, one of the few politicians to notice or care about the impact of housing type on voting and political outlook was Margaret Thatcher, who believed Scots would remain immune to the blandishments of conservatism until they too had a stake in the property owning democracy. She believed council housing produced dependency (not to mention a new generation of grateful Labour voters every few decades) and she determined to break the power of councils providing homes just as she would break the power of unions in the workplace. Rate capping, public sector borrowing limits, the abolition of

---

28 http://www.guardian.co.uk/money/2011/mar/19/brits-buy-germans-rent.

direct labour organisations (responsible for repairs) and the creation of semi-public, semi-private 'off-balance-sheet' housing associations to take over new builds – all these innovations combined to knock the stuffing out of council housing.

Like Moses, Maggie didn't live long enough (politically speaking) to see the Promised Land. In 1981 – when her Right to Buy legislation was formally introduced – 53 per cent of Scots were public sector tenants, compared with 31 per cent in England. But even though public sector housing was moribund and out of favour, it was still 22 years before Scots started nibbling at the carrot. That year the proportion of tenants fell to 29 per cent and new council housing was virtually non-existent.

And yet the Conservatives got no thanks at the polls. Some Scots did make money buying their council houses at a discount and moving up the property ladder— but many were saddled with homes they couldn't maintain or resell. Councils lost housing stock and had to place the homeless in expensive Bed and Breakfast accommodation. Thirty years after Maggie's great housing reform, when the SNP cancelled the Right to Buy in 2012, not a tear was shed – and hardly a single Tory vote had been won.

Mind you, whether thanked or castigated, Maggie's property revolution did reshape Scots housing preferences and spending patterns until the 2008 property crash.

Even if Scots were loath to admit it.

Altered government priorities, personal desires to own homes and the realisation that the optimism of the housing boom had failed to address the desires of more affluent Scots, all made Scotland more receptive than some care to admit to the prospect of a 'property owning democracy'.[29]

But Maggie's home-buying Scots weren't just embracing ownership – they were also rejecting the way council housing had panned out.

Dampness became a huge campaigning issue. The Clean Air Act in 1956 meant Glasgow District Council stopped installing coal fires in new housing stock to end the street pollution that caused so much respiratory illness. But according to housing campaigners like Cathy McCormack in Easterhouse, air pollution simply came indoors instead:

29   C.M.M. MacDonald, *Whaur Extremes Meet* (Edinburgh: Birlinn, 2009).

The result was condensation and damp and carpets that turned green. Taking away coal fires started the real dampness epidemic... and sky-high fuel bills.[30]

In the late 1970s Cathy had a young daughter with asthma and a baby son with constant runny eyes, chesty colds and thrush. Yet council officers famously blamed dampness on residents 'boiling too many kettles' and 'not heating the house' enough.

For Cathy the real explanation was far simpler:

> We lived in what was basically a concrete bunker. It had a gas fire in the living room and an electric fire on the wall of one bedroom, but no heating in the other rooms or in the hall. There was nothing to keep the heat in or the cold out and there was no adequate ventilation. The wooden window frames had slits at the top but we had to cover them up because they let in gale force winds.

With structural defects like these, council tenants spent years pleading, arguing, reminding, cajoling, remonstrating and despairing before homes were brought up to a basic standard. Smaller jobs often required the same level of tenacity and perseverance. Perfectly capable men and women had to queue at local housing offices to arrange for council workmen to fix leaking taps, broken showers, fallen tiles or dodgy wiring – jobs many tenants could have done in half an hour themselves. But they weren't allowed.

Decades of campaigning effort by Cathy and other Easthall tenants did pay off. Academic work by hypothermia expert Dr Evan Lloyd of Edinburgh University on the internal effects on the body of ever changing temperatures means the link between cold, damp and heart disease in the West of Scotland is now understood.[31] Central heating is mandatory in all Glasgow council homes and energy audits tell would-be tenants how much heating will cost. Cathy's flat is now run and managed by a housing co-operative – not the council. But it's still cold. And damp conditions are still not recognised as one of the main factors that might explain the 'Scottish Effect'.

If building standards had been higher, tenants might not have cared

---

30   C. McCormack with M. Pallister, *The Wee Yellow Butterfly* (Glendaruel: Argyll Publishing, 2009).

31   E.L. Lloyd, C. McCormack, M. McKeever & M. Syme, 'The effect of improving the thermal quality of cold housing on blood pressure and general health: a research note', (*Journal of Epidemiology & Community Health*, 62, 2008). pp 793–797.

that they lived without control over their home environment. But once problems did emerge, the council's reaction often revealed that resourcefulness, self-help, autonomy and community development had never really been part of the council housing deal – and yet it could have been otherwise.

The Labour Party had actually proposed a tenants' Right to Buy in its 1959 manifesto. Individual ownership of poor quality homes on low incomes would probably have been as unhelpful in the 1950s as it was later in the 1990s. But it could have started Labour on a path towards more tenant involvement and a housing co-operative model like the kind being rolled out by social democratic parties elsewhere in Europe.

It didn't happen. And why should it? Scots were very familiar with top-down control.

The first post-war generation of Scottish council tenants was initially delighted with affordable and secure housing... but soon frustrated.

According to the writer and critic Ian Jack:

> in the decades between Attlee and Thatcher, Scotland could fairly be described as a nation of council tenants... They [could] be wearisome places, these council estates. Long looping crescents of grey pebble-dashed houses, a few shops selling processed food and fags, a bus shelter with the glass removed. Here the most regular visitor from the outside world is a chiming ice-cream van.[32]

Protection from the maelstrom of the market too often meant learning to bite your lip and wait your turn for council help. And wait. And wait. Until that fateful day in 1988 when the tenants of West Whitlawburn decided to wait no longer.

Of course councils were also civic saviours.

Municipal intervention to provide clean water from Loch Katrine probably saved tens of thousands of lives. Visionary Glasgow council leaders had to overcome considerable opposition in 1859 when one Professor of Chemistry said the action of loch water on lead pipes would be hazardous and the Admiralty insisted loss of water would interfere with navigation of the Forth.[33] But the Corporation forged ahead.

---

32 I. Jack, *London Review of Books* (Vol 11, 1989).
33 A. Aird, *Glimpses of old Glasgow* (Glasgow, 1894).

Scots can also be grateful that councils enthusiastically grasped the nettle to build homes even before the Housing Acts of 1919. If they hadn't intervened, who would have come to the rescue of Scotland's overcrowded poor?

The business of being a council tenant was far, far better than being a private tenant in an overcrowded slum – but not empowering enough (or affordable enough) to transform society. The tenant movement in Glasgow and Scotland was far stronger than in England – but not strong enough to achieve a wholesale move to community-owned housing.

Of course, not all co-ops are perfect. Decentralised, co-operatively owned housing organisations in the Nordics and Low Countries also have problems of maintaining involvement and engaging the poorest people. But they know that task is an essential one, and spend time and money to make co-operative structures work. They know the trust and capacity which result from local grassroots control are worth their weight in gold. Somehow in the high level battles between our Leviathans – labour and capital, Labour and Conservative, landowner and tenant – the need to nurture mutual trust and human capacity have all but been forgotten.

So of course council housing saved Scots from squalor and exploitation in the early 20th century. But compared to the experience of other countries, it also tended to encourage dependency, stifle local initiative and prevent the establishment of mixed neighbourhoods. But few among the first grateful generation of council tenants would ever complain.

The memory of chronic insecurity on Scotland's land was far too recent.

Scotland's rural housing legacy

The bad housing deal each new generation of Scots has accepted speaks volumes about the worse deals our parents and grandparents endured. The seeds of Scotland's private and public sector slums were sown centuries earlier – on the land. Few of the Scots pushed and pulled into cities during the 18th and 19th centuries had ever known security in housing – one reason for the speed of Scottish urbanisation. Without ownership or long term leases, families were easily moved. In

The Poor Had No Lawyers, Andy Wightman comments on the earliest Scottish Land Register compiled in 1874 which showed 18,031,066 acres (92.3 per cent of the total land mass) was owned by just 1,809 landowners.[34] Put another way, out of a total population of 3,559,847 Scots, only 132,230 (3.7 per cent) owned any land at all. 96.1 per cent of the population were tenants.[35]

This was a far more insecure situation for rural Scots than prevailed in Norway, where an ownership survey in 1661 showed that 19 per cent of farmers owned their own land, 21 per cent of farmers or businessmen leased land, a mere 8 per cent was owned by nobles and 52 per cent belonged to the Crown or Church.[36] In areas like Agder, 57 per cent of all land was already owned by farmers.[37]

Once Church land was sold off in the 18th century, more Norwegian farmers became very small landowners or *bonder*. Norwegian tenants outnumbered freeholders by three to one before 1661, but freeholders were twice as numerous as tenants a century later.[38] Needless to say all Norwegians who owned a small bit of land built a house on it – as did *husmenn*, who technically didn't own land, and even urban Norwegians who built wooden cabins in rented city centre allotment gardens and decanted there with their families to live every summer. So strong is the connection between families and homes in Norway that under Odal law (*Odelsrett*) – which also operated for centuries in Orkney and Shetland – a family member can still redeem a family farm within three years of sale.[39] That's how much security ordinary Norwegians have enjoyed over their land and their homes for hundreds of years.

Such a dramatically different landowning and housing reality created a dramatically different democracy. One reason Norway had one of the widest franchises in Northern Europe was the Constitution of 1814, which extended the vote to all male landowners over the

---

34 Return of Owners of Lands and Heritages Scotland 1872–1873 produced by Angus Fletcher, Comptroller-General of the Inland Revenue.

35 Thomas Johnston, *The History of the Working Classes in Scotland* (Forward Publishing, 1929).

36 J. Follesdal, *Norwegian Farms* (Norway: Rootsweb, 1998).

37 Knut Mykland, ed. *Norges Historie*, Bind 7, Gjennom Nødsår og krig, p. 221 (Oslo: J.W. Cappelens Forlag, A/S, 1979).

38 O. Østerud Agrarian, *Structure and Peasant Politics in Scandinavia* (Oxford: Oxford University Press, 1978).

39 Since 1687 the farm must have been owned and worked by the family for two decades to qualify.

age of 25 with the result that 45 per cent of men became eligible to vote overnight.[40] This compared with 0.173 per cent of Scots enfranchised by the British Reform Bill of 1832. Enfranchising landowners gave the vote to almost half of Norwegian men but fewer than half of one per cent of Scotsmen in the early 19th century – and the result wouldn't be very different in either country today.[41] The breadth of the Norwegian electorate meant that a cross-section of society had 'skin in the game' and had to be politically accommodated. At first educated officials in Oslo looked down on these peasants as 'the estate of the most foolish', but soon the liberal intelligentsia joined forces with them to make Government more responsive to Parliament, and forced through new, elected, representative municipal councils in 1837 to permanently restrict the local power of central 'Danophile' elites and state officials.[42] This paved the way for the subsequent development of democracy through proportional representation, a political culture of compromise and the embrace of equality as the nation's guiding social and economic policy objective.[43]

When the Norwegian National Housing Bank was set up in 1947 it gave rural Norwegians small grants to build their own houses. With widespread land ownership and widely retained house building skills, self-build was quicker, cheaper, more practical and more empowering than building council houses for people.

In Scotland the story was different.

For most of Scotland's history farmers have not owned the land. They have been tenants of a landlord. With the security of property the lord could borrow and invest whilst the peasant could not. The lord could plan for the future and bequeath his land. The peasant had an insecure lease and no right to bequeath.[44]

In 1814, the average Norwegian man had the vote and owned his farm. The average Scotsman had neither. The big difference was feudalism.

40 K. Heidar, *Norway: Elites on Trial* (Oxford: Westview Press, 2001).

41 Norwegian women didn't get the vote until 1913. J.R. Christianson, 'Norway: A History from the Vikings to Our Own Times', *Scandinavian Studies* (69.1, 1997).

42 D. Arter, *Scandinavian Politics Today* (Manchester: Manchester University Press, 1999).

43 M Hilson, *The Nordic Model – Scandinavia since 1945* (London: Reaktion Books, 2010).

44 Andy Wightman, *The Poor Had No Lawyers* (Edinburgh: Birlinn, 2012).

David I (1124–1153) first imposed the system of feudal tenure on Scots, creating in the process a hierarchy of ownership, with the Crown as the ultimate feudal superior granting title to land in return for military or other services from selected nobles. Landowning nobles would in turn make sub-grants for other services, and so a hierarchical structure was created with each property having a number of owners, co-existing simultaneously – and generally they all had to be paid by tenants. Even landowners were also vassals with obligations to their feudal superiors. Sometimes that meant military service – far more often it meant payment of feu duty (with no service offered in return.)[45] It was often money for old rope. Until feudal tenure was abolished in 2000, the Church of Scotland, for example, was getting £30,000 a year from feudal fees.

By contrast, a Norwegian law passed in 1674 limited the amount a landowner could charge a new tenant farmer to take over a farm and capped the fee for renewing leases every three years, encouraging longer leases and more security.[46] There is no better way to understand the full grip of feudalism than to read Andy Wightman's comprehensive study in *The Poor Had No Lawyers*, Tom Devine's detailed accounts of landowner fortunes across the centuries in *The Scottish Nation* and James Hunter's account of Highland society in *The Making of the Scottish Crofting Community*. But in brief, the laws of primogeniture and entail – passed by the old Scottish Parliament – worked to prevent the natural forces of family subdivision, bankruptcy, absence and even lunacy from breaking up large estates.

Scotland's large, feudal landowners generally handed their massive landholdings down from father to son since primogeniture meant younger sons and daughters in Scotland had no legal claim on land until 1964. Estates rarely came on the market and were always sold intact – in transactions far too large and expensive to be contested by Scottish tenants. This overarching certainty – that most ordinary Scots would never own land – lies behind almost all the disempower-

---

45 At its most constructive, 'feuing' allowed developers in Edinburgh and Glasgow to impose 'perpetual conditions' dictating how buildings should be constructed and maintained (one reason Edinburgh's New Town has remained just as it was in the 18th century).

46 J. Follesdal, *Norwegian Farms* (Norway: Rootsweb, 1998).

ing arrangements of Scottish life that were to follow. One key feature always endured. The total control of those at the top – even when those men were eventually democratically elected.

In feudal Scotland powerful supporters of central authority also became Earls and Barons with the power of 'pit and gallows' over local people. These 'heritable jurisdictions' gave feudal lords total power to exercise local justice. So Scotland's largest landlords were also judges empowered to pronounce the death sentence on their tenants. Misuse of feudal power was one reason many prominent Scots actually supported Union with England in 1707 after lairds blocked any attempt to abolish feudal practice in the old Scottish Parliament.

In 1697, the commentator and Edinburgh printer James Donaldson observed that 'when a tenant makes any improvement of his ground the landlord obligeth him either to augment his rent or remove – it's become a proverb: 'bouch and sit – improve and flit.'[47]

In 1706, Dr John Arbuthnot – a Scottish doctor, satirist and the inspiration for Swift's *Gulliver's Travels* – wrote a spoof Sermon on the Mercat Cross where he suggested Scotland's celebrated history of freedom was false consciousness promoted by vested interests, nobles and clerics. English prosperity, he argued, was intimately linked to the real freedoms of the common people on the land enjoying long leases and security of tenure. Union with England would be:

> A liberating experience for the Scottish people promising independence from the petty tyranny of lairds and freedom of conscience.[48]

Lord Belhaven proposed a scheme whereby tenants might use the surplus of a good year's harvest to pay landlords a lump sum for a long, low-rent lease heritable by their family – making Scottish tenants more like England's free-holders. William Seton, MP of Pitmedden, argued that union might help 'neuter' the feudal Scottish nobility, removing their institutional playground (the unicameral Scottish Parliament), and 'substituting an arena where the English Commons had consolidated their interests in a separate chamber'. He hoped union would

---

47 J. Donaldson, *Husbandry Anatomised* (Edinburgh, 1697).

48 This work was clearly intended to encourage Scots to support the Act of Union. Once passed, Arbuthnot was made a fellow of the Royal College of Physicians of Edinburgh, and Physician in Ordinary to the Queen, which made him part of the royal household.

lead to the liberation of tenants from the burdens of lairds and usher in an era of improvement and the end of rack rents and short leases.

However, despite all these great promises of radical change upon Union with England, nothing changed for the ordinary Scottish tenant in 1707. Article 20 of the Union with England Act guaranteed all inherited positions in Scotland would continue as before. After all, the parcel of rogues in the Scottish Parliament had to be won over. It took the Jacobite Rising of 1745 to convince the British Parliament of the threat posed by the standing armies of feudal Scottish nobles in times of peace. Heritable Jurisdictions in Scotland were finally outlawed in 1747, transferring legal powers to sheriffs appointed by the King, stripping Scotland's nobles of the power to demand military service and stipulating that new titles created after 1747 would grant no rights beyond landlordship (collecting rents). So Scotland's vanquished landowning nobles threw themselves – or rather their factors – whole-heartedly into this new limited realm of supreme control.

Of course, there were honourable landowning exceptions. Sir William Forbes, for example, laid out the village of New Pitsligo in 1783 and effectively handed control to his tenants:

> … before his death he had the satisfaction of seeing assembled on a spot which at his acquisition of the estate was a barren waste, a thriving population of 300 souls, and several thousand acres smiling with cultivation which were formerly the abode only of the moor-fowl or the curlew.

With such astonishing improvements, one can only imagine what kind of new progressive Scotland might have emerged if outright ownership or secure tenancy had been the norm.

But without security, tenants were easily cleared.

Government sources described conditions on Barra, owned in 1849 by Lieutenant Colonel John Gordon of Cluny:

> The scene of wretchedness which we witnessed as we entered the estate of Colonel Gordon was deplorable, nay, heart-rending. On the beach the whole population of the country seemed to be met, gathering the precious cockles. I never witnessed such countenances – starvation on many faces – the children with their melancholy looks,

big looking knees, shrivelled legs, hollow eyes, swollen like bellies –
god help them, I never did witness such wretchedness.[49]

Between 1849 and 1851, about 2,000 people were forcibly shipped
from South Uist and Barra to Quebec – Colonel Gordon's answer to
the problem. Some embarked voluntarily, with a promise they would
be taken free of expense to Canada, where government agents would
give them work and grant them land. It didn't happen. They were
turned adrift at Quebec and had to beg their way to Upper Canada.
The Canadian newspapers published accounts of the miseries endured
by the immigrants, who could speak only Gaelic.

> Those unwilling to accept the Colonel's promises found themselves
> hunted – men were attacked and rendered senseless before they were
> thrown with arms bound onto the waiting ships. Members of families
> were torn apart and put on to ships with different destinations in the
> Americas. In February of 1851, a group of [remaining] 61 destitutes
> made their way from Barra to Inverness and sat down, helpless, in
> front of the townhouse. (F. Thompson, 1988)

Events like this across the Highlands and Islands led to the Crofting Act of 1886, which did at last give security to Highlanders over
small heritable plots of land. But this had little immediate impact on
rural overcrowding because crofts were generally packed with landless members of the crofter's extended family, were too small to allow
self-sufficiency and were located on the poorest land. Aberdonian
landowners (including Sir William Forbes' descendants), combined
to block application of crofting tenure beyond the crofting countries
where the evidence-gathering Napier Commission actually visited.

In 1906 men from overpopulated Barra and Mingulay seized land
on neighbouring Vatersay, which had been cleared by the owner,
Lady Gordon Cathcart, to make way for a sheep farm. The Vatersay
Raiders were arrested and jailed in Edinburgh, but were later released
as the result of public outcry. The island was bought by the state and
58 crofts were created for its new inhabitants – carefully excluding the
original raiders, it's said locally, who died landless. A cautionary tale

---

49   F. Thompson, *The Western Isles* (Batsford, 1988).
50   L. Riddoch, *Riddoch on the Outer Hebrides* (Edinburgh: Luath Press, 2007).

about the dangers of being first to stick your head over the parapet, but a great triumph for direct action by islanders.[50]

Land raids like Vatersay erupted across the Scottish Highlands – in Barra, Tiree, Uist and Sutherland – prompting the (re)establishment of the Highland Land League as a political party in Glasgow in 1909. Like the 19th century movement of the same name, it sought the restoration of deer forests to public ownership and the nationalisation of land. Members pledged to defend tenants facing eviction and supported home rule for Scotland.

During the First World War, politicians made lavish promises about land reform, and soldiers returning from war were in no mood to accept government inaction. Land raids began again against the backdrop of revolution in Ireland and Russia.

But by 1922 the cold winds of depression had reached the furthest corners of the Highlands and Islands:

> ... thousands of men began to withdraw their applications for land and applied instead for a passage on the emigrant ships. Almost all the 300 people from Lewis who boarded the *Metagama* [in 1923] were young men with an average age of 22. They were off to Ontario in Canada where they had each been offered 40 hectares of land. Another country had held out the opportunity that Scotland had promised but failed to provide.[51]

The message of their anger and betrayal was transmitted across miles and generations. In August 1918, the Highland Land League affiliated with the Labour Party and later members also helped form the Scottish National Party.

The memories of dispossession and the fight for dignity and a livelihood passed from rural to urban, from the powerless tenant to the empowered activist and eventually into the thinking and the hands of politicians who could reshape Scotland. Men like Tom Johnston, the Labour Secretary of State for Scotland, who used the urgency created by war to finally overcome landowner intransigence and install hydro-electric dams to bring electricity to the Highlands in the 1940s.

---

51 A. McIntosh Gray & W. Moffat, *A History of Scotland: Modern Times* (Oxford: Oxford University Press, 1999).

A portrait of Johnston takes pride of place today in the drawing room of Bute House – the official residence of Scotland's First Minister – by request of Alex Salmond himself.

Meanwhile, beyond the crofting counties in the Scottish Lowlands, tenants had to fight their own battles against a law of hypothec which gave landlords security over tenants' moveable property as a guarantee of paying rent – a situation which may have driven up rents since the landlord could be confident of getting paid either way. Tenant farmers were also hit by the growth of Lowland sporting estates and the destruction of their crops by protected game. The plight of rural tenants led to the creation of the Scottish Farmers' Alliance, which pressed for land reform and a defeat for landlord candidates in the 1865 and 1868 elections. Concessions and the 1883 Agricultural Holdings Act (Scotland) finally gave tenants the right to compensation for improving land.[52] Tom Devine has examined the complex system of tenancy, sub-tenancy, hinds, cotters, crofters and farm servants in Farm Servants and Labour in Lowland Scotland:

> Most permanent farm workers in Scotland were farm *servants* (rather than labourers) who were hired over a period of one year, if married, and for six months if single. Married servants were paid almost entirely in kind, receiving such allowances as oats, barley, pease, the keep of a cow and ground for planting potatoes. The rental of the cottage was paid for by the labour of the wife or daughter (or a woman brought in) during harvest.[53]

A six month hire sounds short, but it was longer than the weekly and monthly hires of southern England. Getting food instead of cash also sounds rough, but it did cushion Scottish workers against inflation. The long hire farm servant system also let farmers compete for labour against the burgeoning textile and manufacturing industries of central Scotland. But it created two damaging legacies:

> Accommodation and employment were linked. To be unemployed in the country meant not simply to be without work but without a home. Cottages surplus to requirements were pulled down. The unemployed farm worker had often therefore no alternative but to

---

52   T. M. Devine, *The Scottish Nation* (Allen Lane, 1999).
53   T. M. Devine, *Farm Servants and Labour in Lowland Scotland* (Edinburgh, 1984).

move to seek work. They could not, like the rural unemployed of southern England, depend as easily on the Poor Law... because the able-bodied unemployed in Scotland had no legal right to the dole. Finally, for single male servants (many bunked together in basic bothies) migration was likely at the age of marriage... because of the scarcity of family cottages.[54]

It was 'the impulse to marry', as Aberdeen University's Malcolm Gray put it, which brought the most severe housing problems. Unmarried men slept rough around the farm, boarded in the farmhouse. or lived in bothies where many slept two to a bed for warmth. Some married ploughmen (called hinds in the Lothians) lived in cottages attached to the farm. But these were like gold dust. So marriage and children usually meant dislocation, upheaval and even the end of life on the land for many country people. Some married farm workers left for towns, others became day labourers living in villages, but many opted to stay in the bothies of unmarried men, living apart from their own families who stayed in nearby towns and villages. A survey in Aberdeenshire showed 92 out of 212 married men were living like this in 1893, only seeing their families once a fortnight.[55] Women fared worse.

Since so much of the new industry in Scotland recruited men for heavy labour and since lack of housing meant a constant haemorrhage of country families unable to live together, single women filled the labour gap on the land. Sue Glover's tremendous play *Bondagers*, first performed in 1991, described the women's plight. Borders farmers in the 19th century required all male agricultural workers (hinds) to provide female farm labourers (bondagers) to work in the fields (on half male pay) as part of their bonds of employment. One reviewer of the play wrote:

> The women fantasise about a life with no leaking roofs, only kind men around them and summers that last all year long. They cling to the idea of emigrating to Canada, though none of them know any-thing about the place. The reality is one of brutal hardship, the dread of winter and unwanted sexual advances from men. The women sleep with the children to protect themselves.

---

54   ibid.
55   Royal Commission on Labour 1893, (Clackmannan).

The bondager was normally hired by the hind for a year, a cost he had to bear all year round so she was available for farm work (paid directly by the farmer) during busy times like harvest. This system of bondage in Borders Scotland continued until the Second World War.[56]

So tied housing, dependency, dislocation and an inability to complain were all built into the Scottish rural experience. Such separation of families in the homelands of apartheid South Africa prompted international outcry. But in Victorian Scotland, housing insecurity was widespread and unremarkable. Without the chance to own land and buy security, no better deal was available.

By way of contrast, the ratio of owners to tenants in Norway in 1939 was a whopping eleven to one (almost the reverse of Scotland). It was also common for Norwegians to combine farming with work in industry or shops – in 1939 almost as many people were part-time farmers as full-time. Such flexibility, useful for Norwegians coping with harsh living conditions and fluctuating markets, was only possible because they had security on the land they continued to own, even if they went off for a time to work in cities. In 1984, after a century of urbanisation, one in fifteen Norwegians still owned some land.[57] Indeed, today, one in ten Norwegians owns a second home – usually a fairly basic wooden cabin without running water, indoor toilet or electricity (though more luxurious cabins are now popular) as a way of reconnecting with the modest, outdoor, hardy and independent-minded way of life which had become a model during the nation-building period that preceded Norwegian independence in 1905.[58]

Access to land in Scotland did improve in the early 20th century when land prices collapsed between the wars, and by 1951 'bondage' was rare. But even today tenant farmers still face difficulties exacerbated, ironically, by the Land Reform (Scotland) Act of 2003. The act gave secure tenants the right to make a pre-emptive bid to buy the land they farmed and this 'undoubtedly seriously affected landowner willingness to let land and led to a preference for other mechanisms such as contract farming, annual crop licenses or in-hand farming.'[59]

56   Elisabeth Mahoney, *The Guardian*, Wednesday 19 September 2001.
57   Statistics Norway, NOS Census of Agriculture and Forestry 1989.
58   Ibid.
59   'Barriers to New Entrants to Scottish Farming', Scottish Government, 2008.

In short, once the new Scottish Parliament moved to give tenant farmers more security, landowners simply removed land from tenant farmers' reach. Now areas like Islay have a big problem of young would-be farmers who simply can't get started because there's no access to land.[60]

Our countryside is still relatively empty. Tenant farmers find it hard to get a start. In cities, most tenants still live in large estates with no real say in their management, whilst those in community-controlled housing need new resources to turn their communities around. Certainly many homeowners are happy bunnies. But others are stuck with negative equity and mortgage payments they can't afford, let alone the cash needed for repairs and home maintenance. New build lags well behind demand – not just because of the recession but because of the way an enduring land scarcity – arising from the concentrated patterns of land ownership, drives up the cost of housing in cities and the countryside. To this day, the National Trust insists anyone who lives on 'their' island of Canna can occupy only tied housing.

Yip, feudalism was formally abolished in 2003, but its imprint is still all over Scotland. And lest you've forgotten, 1,000 people own 60 per cent of Scottish land today. A bit better than in 1874, when 659 individuals owned 80 per cent – but still an eye-wateringly concentrated pattern.

Circumstances have indeed changed since the bad old days when country folk first moved into overcrowded city housing beside beautiful buildings like Glasgow's City Chambers or the churches of Alexander 'Greek' Thomson.

Housing standards are generally much improved, but the gap between rich and poor in modern Scotland is still Dickensian and control over land is still an issue. A recent Scottish Government report showed the people in the most deprived areas are five times more likely to live beside derelict land. It's a modern version of the galling plight faced by the Vatersay raiders a century back. Now though, there are no land raids.

The poorest Scots still cope through solidarity, endurance and the capacity to maintain low expectations – except where tenants have taken joint action to improve their lives.

---

60   Highlighted by Ian Hamilton during 2012 local election coverage: http://www.bbc.co.uk/news/17907704.

In many ways things are better for the poorest Scots than they were in the 1970s. But in some very important ways they are worse.

Back then, half the population lived in council housing and there was little stigma because social housing was the norm. Today, home ownership is the norm and perceptions of those left behind in social housing have changed radically. It's become all too easy for right-wing newspapers and cost-cutting Whitehall Ministers to character-ise tenants in the social sector as scroungers and cheats – the modern 'undeserving poor'.

In the past, many Scots lived cheek by jowl with the poorest folk and the sheer scale of council housing meant many estates were effec-tively mixed communities where most worked, some had children who went to college and others had good manual jobs.

Now the profile has changed, and social housing has a concentra-tion of the unemployed, disabled, unskilled and chronically ill. Con-venient, some say. Deliberate, say others.

It's easier to scapegoat people you never meet.

In 1863, Glasgow's first medical Officer of Health, W.T. Gairdner observed that:

> Gross sanitary neglect inevitably leads to the production and multipli-cation of a class which is not only helpless and progressively in a state of degradation... but has in itself no power of redemption so that it becomes a truly parasitic class, living on the classes above it and abso-lutely precluded from every kind of spontaneous improvement.[61]

The big problem facing Scotland then was to know what to do with this 'dirty, criminal and improvident class', this 'sunken tenth', this 'residuum of the disreputable', as poor people were variously labelled throughout the Victorian era – even though the reasons for squalor were beyond their control. Long hours (5am starts were common in the 1900s) were combined with very low rates of pay and the constant fear of losing all income through injury or (more commonly) lay-offs. Tens of thousands of city workers were casually employed, so whilst the average wage would finance life on the breadline, few workers in practice received the average wage. This had tangible health impacts:

Out of these conditions came the classic Glaswegian 'wee bauchle'

---

61   W.T. Gairdner, 'Clinical Observations in the Royal Infirmary of Glasgow', *The Lancet* (1863).

and 'wee wummin.' They were wee. Their diet was totally inadequate
and not a few had rickets due to vitamin deficiencies and lack of sun
in tenement streets. To accuse these workers of being slum-makers
because they didn't want anything better is intolerable cant.[62]

A hundred and fifty years later, what's really changed? Rickets are
back, so is TB and health outcomes in the poorest neighbourhoods
are worse than anywhere else in Western Europe.[63] And those poorest
neighbourhoods are almost all located in social housing.

Just as distinctions were once drawn between the respectable and
unrespectable poor, the decent and hopeless working class – so the distinctions are drawn today.

Is it possible that those who got out and moved on simply want no
reminder of the terrible living conditions they left behind? If the past
now seems like another world, what can modern Scots make of those
who still depend on social housing – are they another people?

Is it possible that now – as then – the real watershed in Scottish life
is between those who have managed to escape bad housing and those
judged harshly for apparently choosing to stay?

The social housing that once saved the majority of Scots now stig-
matises a minority. It's wildly unfair. And it drives a wedge of deep
mutual mistrust into the heart of Scotland.

Series like BBC Scotland's *The Scheme* filmed in Onthank near Kilmarnock have allowed characters like 'have a go' emaciated heroin
user Marvin – more loyal to his dog than his pregnant girlfriend – to
become counter-cultural heroes, applauded by some for not giving a
toss about appearances and egged on by others eager to watch a man
survive against the odds, using only his stubborn instincts. The series
has been called poverty porn – and it is.

Parts of comfortable Scotland have watched fascinated as a man
inhabits his own chaotic, empty, beer-can-strewn flat, reassured his
fate isn't their fate, astonished at the conditions he will accept and
repelled at the same time.

Does the average viewer inhabit the same society as Marvin? Tell
me that has no impact on the independence referendum.

---

62 Damer. Glasgow Going For a Song (London: Lawrence Wishart 1990.

63 Glasgow children once again have symptoms of rickets: http://www.scotsman.com/the-scotsman/opinion/
comment/lesley-riddoch-sunshine-vitamin-in-short-supply-1-237380.1.

We are still judging individuals instead of understanding the problems created by centuries-old patterns of inequality in Scotland. Still expecting the poor to adopt the values of 'comfortable Scotland' without the comfort.

In short, the poor scare the living daylights out of moderately affluent Scots because despite every effort, we can't fix them. That's the point. No-one can ultimately fix other people.

We can stop judging, stop ghettoising, stop underfunding community initiatives, stop micro-managing and start changing the ground rules of society so communities have the tools, cash, support, skills and expertise to fix themselves. Not as one-off, tentative, pilots and rule-bound handouts – but as of right.

Now that's a lot to say. I know.

But our housing past poses constraints, bad memories, unsatisfactory models for living and some tough questions.

The poor of other nations expected better and were treated better – in part because they had already experienced better. Twentieth century urban Norwegians became homeowners in part because they had already been homeowners on the land. Centuries of smallholding created expectations which Norwegians took with them into cities and beyond into their newly independent state.

The Scots – by contrast – were accustomed to bad treatment, tenancy and insecurity on the land and brought those low expectations with them into Scotland's industrial cities, mills, factories and towns.

More than that – the housing insecurity that arose from feudal landownership helped create the large landless class that was crucial for the industrialisation of Scotland after 1750. The accumulated wealth of the feudal aristocracy and intermarriage with a wealthy trading class led to the establishment of Scottish banks and created an industrial feudalism able to exploit landless labour.[64]

Scottish employers in general invested less in plant and equipment... and competed not through the level of investment... but through

---

64   'The intermarriage of the Younger and Balfour families centred around brewing and banking and the Tennant and Ogilvy families fused landed interests with new wealth extracted from chemicals. The Marquess of Linlithgow was a Director of the Bank of Scotland and Standard Life; the Duke of Buccleuch of the Royal Bank, Standard Life and Scottish Equitable; the Earl of Mansfield of the National Bank and Scottish Equitable and the Marquess of Tweeddale of the Commercial Banks, Edinburgh Life and Scottish Widows'. A. Dickson & J.H. Treble, *People and Society in Scotland* (Edinburgh: John Donald, 1992).

control over the workforce. Wages were lower. Managerial direction was tighter. Scottish Labour had to be cheap. It also had to be
plentiful. This was not just because Scottish industry itself was more
labour intensive, but because methods of labour control required the
maintenance of a significant unemployed reserve. Authoritarian, hire
and fire management depended on it (Dickson and Treble, 1992).

Scotland's history of insecure housing made much of this possible.
And yet, in political debate, housing and housing tenure are considered
relatively unimportant in Scotland's story and the home is viewed as a
mere housing unit – a private, feminised domain where non-economic
activity like childcare takes place, beyond the sphere of production
and therefore of little interest to economists aside from its property
value. Doubtless many serious thinkers believe there are more important fish to fry. And yet our parents shaped us. Their parents shaped
them. So their experiences still matter – for better and for worse.

And that shines a solitary happy light on one peculiarity of Scottish
housing, which is the building block and salvation of Scotland's
modern urban renaissance.

The humble tenement.

Even if didn't look that way to a young Irish immigrant in 1973.

CHAPTER FOUR

Tenements and the Miracle of Sharing Space

MY FAMILY 'crossed the water' from Belfast to Glasgow one squally morning in October 1973. My brother had been sick several times on the Larne-Stranraer ferry. More importantly, my two pet goldfish had died aboard the *Antrim Princess* in a bleach-cleaned sink. A decade later, when the benighted vessel was turned into a floating casino and berthed on the Clyde, I boycotted it on principle.

In 1973, despite my piscine sacrifice, the Gods were not appeased.

We arrived in angry weather to rain swept city streets flanked by high, scowling cliff-faces of blackened stone. Each building was massive, daylight-stopping and overbearing, with a single shared entrance like the tiny door into a vast human ant hill. I was 13, this was my first encounter with Scottish tenements and they were terrifying. There were no trees on the streets. There was no exception. Glasgow was high, daunting, stone-built and sooty-black – nothing like Belfast with its front and back door terraced homes (whose design unintentionally encouraged concealed arrivals and fast getaways).

Back then, my Irish school pals were wide-eyed with horror at the notion I might have to live in that terrible, wild and dangerous place called Glasgow. In Belfast, we were dodging the bullets – or at least arranging for gruff-sounding boyfriends to phone in bomb threats to postpone exams. We were accustomed to sitting one desk space away from windows criss-crossed with wide strips of heavy-duty sellotape to ensure glass came out in large injury-minimising chunks during explosions. We were forbidden to wear Bay City Roller tartan-trimmed trousers lest we provoke roaming paramilitary tartan gangs. We were locked in at night with padlocks. But in 1973, Glasgow's reputation was far worse than Belfast.

The Rangers Supporters Club in Sandy Row was the biggest social club in Protestant East Belfast. Indeed back then, Ireland, north and south, was united only by its inability to produce a football rivalry to match the sectarian force of Glasgow Celtic and Rangers. Massive, distant Glasgow was the place to go and visit – if you were hard enough. It was the place of long-lost cousins, separated parents and drug deals. A place of strong accents and small, aggressive people who'd fight over nothing at the drop of a hat. Unlike civilised Belfast, you understand, where only informers were knee-capped and crimes against the person unrelated to terrorism were practically non-existent. Or 'dealt with' locally. Or unreported.

As young well-heeled Prods, we were the conduits of our parents' opinions and the views of their coffee morning and golf course-frequenting peers. So we believed – like them – there were rules to violence in Belfast. If – like us – you lived in Presbyterian suburban East Belfast, surrounded by soft-accented east-coast Scots, gardens, affluence and tranquillity, and if your dad wasn't in the police, judiciary or Millionaire Row, then your family was not a legitimate target. Probably.

And it seems crazy now. But in Belfast we felt safe, in the way that kids always feel safe amongst familiar surroundings, whatever they happen to be. And a large part of that familiarity was the ubiquitous terraced house – reassuring low-rise, red-brick rows of individual homes with bunting, and kerb stones painted red, white and blue in the summer marching season. Indeed, this reflected a surprising truth. Falls or Shankhill, West or East, Republican or Unionist – all parts of Belfast's divided society occupied the same terraced housing type as distant England.

Glasgow was very different. In the 1970s there was hardly a terrace or indeed a brick-built building in sight. Even Edinburgh's famous colonies contained flats, not English style two-storey terraced homes. Offices and shops, homes and bedsits, highbrow and lowbrow, all were accommodated as flats in tenements – stone buildings with shared entrances containing between six and ten flats (evenly split on either side of the central stone staircase or sometimes gathered three to a floor behind an epic, monumental facade). As a grieving, disoriented 13-year-old, I immediately spotted the difference between my old home and my new one. That sense of dislocation was rapidly replaced with astonishment that so few Scots noticed it too. Ponder for a moment.

Thanks to tenements, 529,000 families (almost a third of urban Scots) do not have front and back doors, do not have a roof over (just) their own heads, do not have a (private) garden or (personal) garden gate or possess a home they regard as their castle. Space is shared, life is shared and though traditions like stair-washing rotas and 'windae hinging' have largely gone, pride in tenement-living remains. Glaswegians always encourage visitors to look up and examine the plinths, facings and general ornamentation.

And it is indeed all there... if you look up.

But of course, back in 1973, you didn't. You didn't look round either. Glasgow had a higher murder rate than New York and spray-painted slogans indicated the ubiquitous presence of gangs and contested territory.

It's worth recording just how bad Glasgow's reputation was before gentrification, café culture, the Garden Festival, Miles Better and the 1990 City of Culture. In the '70s, some Glasgow suburban estates like Easterhouse were the size of small towns, built without shops or pubs and so full of threat that even cool, lip-curling Frankie Vaughan hadn't coaxed knives, machetes and guns from gangs during a 1950s amnesty. Unlike well-kept, war-torn Belfast, peaceful Glasgow was strewn with litter, cigarette butts and dogs' dirt. Mum cautioned me against wearing a favourite Chelsea Girl white jacket into town – every surface was dirty, she said. Perhaps she hadn't updated her thinking since first venturing down from Wick in the 1950s to bag a trophy outfit in the chic and elegant boutiques of Sauchiehall Street. Even then Glasgow (where her brother George contracted TB) was shopping heaven – like any real metropolis, a place full of contradictions.

Anyway, at the age of 18 I got itchy feet and went to Oxford University, then a Cardiff postgraduate course in 1984 and a two-year London BBC training course the year after that. I worked for three months back in Belfast, three more on the Radio Bulletins Desk in Broadcasting House and another three in the television newsroom at White City alongside the next generation of Britain's self-important young decision makers.

Life was fast-paced, demanding, unpredictable, fun... and a bit unnerving. I remember two comments from the final reports of my BBC Trainee years. 'If we had known you lacked ambition you would not have been selected for this highly competitive course', after I revealed my intention to head back to Scotland once training was complete. Surpassed only by 'Lesley will make a great addition to a BBC news-room – not this one', after a TV Newsroom attachment marred by my stubborn insistence that BBC guidelines were being 'stretched' during reporting of the Miners' Strike. Ah, the bolshiness of youth.

Not surprisingly then, my 'Caledonia' moment came early.

I came home, got a job with Radio Scotland in my mid-20s and bought a flat in a Partick tenement five doors down from Billy Connolly's uncle (they said). Finally, after seven years on a whistle-stop tour of Britain's most iconic cities and a motley selection of their cheap-est bedsits and shared flats, I knew first-hand what I'd only suspected at one remove during teenage years spent in a detached house in the eerily sterile suburb of Bearsden. Tenemental Glasgow, Edinburgh, Perth, Inverness, Stirling, Dundee and Aberdeen were profoundly different to other British cities.

I tried to get insurance for my 'minority housing type' and was asked to choose from five options. Did I live in the cheapest home to insure – terraced, or was my house semi-detached, detached, a cottage or – the daddy of them all price-wise – a 'town flat'?

Well, none of the above, really. It was a second-floor tenement flat.

The woman in the Bradford and Bingley office on Byres Road looked at me with exasperation. I felt the queue willing me to back down.

'Isn't the Scottish tenement flat really the equivalent of the English terraced house?'

The woman looked at me with silent fury.

'It's a flat. In a town. So it's a town flat. Do you want the insurance or not?'

It was hopeless. The 'f' word put my humble abode into the same category as a wealthy London financier splitting time between a small mansion in the country and an opulent apartment round the corner from Harrods. The premium for a 'town flat' was more than twice that of a terraced house – the average British working class home. But that's what I had to pay. Despite the weary collusion of locals (well it was a queue) it was clear no Scot would have concocted such a tene-ment-denying set of housing options.

The average British insurer, like the average British law-maker, was interested only in the average British resident. Since the population of Scotland is ten times smaller than England and since the UK has been a London-dominated, centrally-run, difference-denying entity for many centuries, tenement flats were never going to be a 'mainstream' housing option. And yet in the 1980s, between a third and a half of all Scots lived in flats – the bulk of them urban tenements.

It's hard to make direct comparisons between Scottish and English Housing Statistics. National Housing Surveys in the early '70s covered only England and Wales and today there is still no category for 'tenements' in England and a lack of clarity about what their 'purpose-built flat (low rise)' category actually includes. Housing stock surveys were also conducted in different years.

But from the statistics for 2010/11, it is clear that Scots householders are still almost twice as likely to live in flats as English householders. Given the large-scale demolition of tenements over recent decades and the growth of hitherto alien building types like maisonettes in Scotland, there would have been a much higher proportion

Housing Types	England	Scotland
Terraced	28.4%	23.2%
Semi-detached	26.2%	20.3%
Detached	17%	21.4%
Bungalow	8.9	–
Tenement	–	22.3
Flat (Low Rise)	13.6%	–
Converted Flat	4.2%	–
Flat (High Rise)	1.7%	–
Other Flats	–	12.5%
All Flats	**19.5%**	**34.8%**

English and Scottish Housing Condition Surveys 2010/11
(NB: *some housing types not directly comparable*)

Figure 4: Scots almost twice as likely to live in flats today

of tenement-dwellers when I tried to insure my flat back in the 1980s. And yet, until devolution took most aspects of housing policy away from Westminster, Scotland's million plus tenement dwellers inhabited a world of housing policy which all but ignored their very existence.

The confusion over tenements didn't immediately end with the arrival of the new Scottish Parliament. The following year, in 2000, Strathclyde Region had fewer registered child-minders than anywhere else in Britain. Was that due to the ubiquitous presence of obliging local grannies – or the legacy of UK-wide fire regulations requiring front and back door access to private child-minding facilities? That rule, at a stroke, removed the vast majority of Scotland's tenement dwellers from the available pool of approved child-minders. Important? No-one seemed to think so. Benefit payments were similarly affected. In 2009, 60-somethings were entitled to a lump sum of £250 to help with winter energy bills and £400 was available for the over-80s. But payments were made at a reduced rate for pensioners sharing a home, so many Scottish pensioners got less than their entitlement because each tenement flat shared the same street number. A national scandal? Hardly. How many homes in Scotland had adequate roof insulation in 2002? It wasn't clear, because each household was thought to have a separate roof even if eight tenement households actually shared one long roof. Holyrood's new bean counters (London-trained civil servants) were temporarily in a mess – caught between Scottish tenemental reality and their English terraced housing default. Despite being officially ignored for almost a century, though, tenements have remained massively popular north of the border. The latest Scottish House Conditions survey lists 529,000 tenements in Scotland in 2011. That's 22.3 per cent of the total housing stock, making the tenement the second biggest housing type in Scotland (until 2009 it was the biggest). All of which means tenements are still pivotal in maintaining a distinctively Scottish urban way of life.

Tenement living reaffirms the communal tendencies of Scots, requiring owners and tenants to share space, stairs, closes, back courts, cleaning and maintenance responsibilities and north of the border the term 'tenement' still lacks any of the pejorative connotations carried south of it. Wikipedia tells us:

Age of dwelling	Detached	Semi-detached	Terraced	Tenement	Other flats	Total
	ooos	ooos	ooos	ooos	ooos	ooos
Pre 1919	100	61	63	178	56	459
1919–1944	47	91	35	29	100	303
1945–1964	29	142	182	100	70	523
1965–1982	115	103	204	94	48	565
Post–1982	217	84	67	128	23	519
Total	509	482	551	529	297	2,368
Percentage per type	21.4%	20.3%	23.2%	22.3%	12.5%	100%

Figure 5: Scottish House Condition Survey: Key Findings 2011[1]

A tenement is, in most English-speaking areas, a substandard multi-family dwelling in the urban core, usually old and occupied by the poor. In Scotland it still has its original meaning of a multi-occupancy building of any sort, and in parts of England, especially Devon and Cornwall, it refers to an outshot, or additional projecting part at the back of a terraced house, normally with its own roof.

In the Scottish Housing Conditions Survey a tenement simply refers to 'any block of flats sharing a common central staircase without a lift, particularly constructed around 1919'.

The tenement as a key part of Scottish urban life is part of a European success story providing medium-density city living. The terraced, low-rise English model of urban living – creating sprawling hard-to-service suburbs – is not (no offence chaps). And yet modern Scots are moving out of cities, councils are constructing English-style semis, terraces, and maisonettes and Scottish cities are losing density and working-age families.

Why are modern Scots losing confidence in the sturdy tenement – why don't we value what we've got?

---

1   http://www.scotland.gov.uk/Publications/2012/12/4995/downloads.

How could the fact of tenement living be overlooked for so long by policy-makers north and south of the border? Certainly Scots have always been heavily outnumbered within UK averages. But there's more. Terrible housing conditions have long been Scotland's secret shame. And the humble tenement has become the convenient scapegoat – in part because of its shady, feudal origins.

The origins of tenements

The tenement has a long history.

In ancient Rome, 'insulae' were large apartment buildings housing the plebs. Literally. The ground floor level was used for tabernae, shops and businesses with living space above which reached ten or more storeys – some had 200 stairs. Actually, the fabulous 18th century building that houses Edinburgh City Chambers is even higher: just three storeys above the Royal Mile but soaring 12 storeys above Prince Street Gardens at the 'back' to cope with the steep hill. In the 11th century, apartment buildings in the Egyptian capital rose to 14 storeys and had roof gardens complete with ox-drawn water wheels to irrigate them. I don't think any Edinburgh tenement managed to outdo that.

But visitors raved about the unique feel and appearance of this 'Athens of the North' – even if that name (invented in 1823 as part of a fundraising campaign to complete the Acropolis on Calton Hill) annoyed the heck out of Londoners with its conception of London as Rome (the centre of the world's greatest empire) and Edinburgh as Athens (the centre of learning).

Still, beauty was beauty.

'The antique grandeur of [Edinburgh's] Old Town and the subdued cold, classical beauty of the New Town of Edinburgh constitute an aspect so striking and picturesque that we have nothing to compare it with,' trilled *London Builder* magazine in 1861. Claude Levi Strauss observed that the man-made Old Town was a fabulous foil for the breathtaking natural centrepiece of Arthur's Seat. 'The city is both natural object and a thing to be cultivated; individual and group; something lived and something dreamed; it is the human invention *par excellence*.'

Perhaps without knowing it, the father of modern anthropology was describing the effect of the tenement – the building block of all that is distinctive about the look and feel of central Edinburgh.

And yet the design of the more generally feted New Town seemed to abandon the tenement for a mix of townhouses, Georgian terraced houses and terrace-style colony homes.

The late Charles McKean, Professor of Scottish Architectural History at Dundee University, had a theory about that. To explain the pervasive influence of the tenement on all subsequent Scottish design, Charles once hauled me up to Edinburgh's famous Royal Mile on a bitterly cold February day to survey the towering tenements before us.[2]

> In centuries past, each floor housed a different strand of Scottish society with shops/merchant booths on the ground floor, the nobility or wealthiest in the largest apartments on the first floor or *piano nobile,* then the gentry, and then craftsmen up into the attic rafters. And even though they had little social connection with the tradesmen, the better off were forced to rub shoulders with the worse off every day on those narrow stairs.

'So in Old Town tenements the classes might be separated and stratified – but there was basically no getting away from one another?'

'Exactly. Now conceive the New Town as a tenement on its back, with each class occupying a different (parallel) street rather than a different floor.'

Suddenly, I could see it.

'So Princes Street with its shops would be the 'ground floor', the 'attic' would be those wee colony flats beside the Water of Leith – and the gentry had all the streets in between.'

'Precisely.'

Out trip was suddenly well worth the icy blast. OK – that is just a theory, albeit an intuitively persuasive one. But the local and international popularity of Scotland's cities is a cast-iron fact. Edinburgh and Glasgow regularly pop up in Top City lists compiled by the public, *Time Life* and *Conde Naste*. Why? Because modern cities need density to function.

---

2   The interview was part of a *Guardian* podcast in which I asked why Scotland isn't fulfilling the potential of its natural resources or people: http://www.guardian.co.uk/commentisfree/audio/2008/dec/29/scotland-energy-lesley-riddoch.

These days the idea of Glasgow without tenements is unthinkable. Tenement flats in the wealthy West End boast Charles Rennie MacIntosh Art Deco tiles in 'wally closes', elegant sash windows and beautiful wooden shutters. Tenement flats in Edinburgh have original wooden floors, generous proportions and views across the Forth estuary or up to the Castle. Many ordinary flats in working-class areas have decorated tiled inserts around old open fireplaces. Today, tenement-style cities are the European norm – and Scots are a part of that larger, sustainable, rational and space-sharing tradition, living in flats like the French, Germans, Dutch, Norwegians and Danes – in fact, like just about everyone excepted the terraced-house cities of England. In many ways it's not the high-rise Scottish tenements that need explanation but the low-rise English housing style.

So why did Scotland take a different direction in housing its people? Explanations vary. Feudal law meant landowners could demand an annual payment in perpetuity for the right to occupy land. So the higher the building, the more feu payments for the same piece of ground and the healthier the profit for the landowner. Some suggest Scottish geology provided sandstone, granite and other building stone and solid, weight-bearing ground for construction – England's clay soils favoured timber, brick and lower loadings. Yet European tenements are also built on every type of geology. Others think the Scots built high behind defensive city walls and this created a template copied during later centuries, though Charles McKean dismisses this as: 'Typical post-Enlightenment nonsense. Not a single Scottish town had been laid out for defence in the European manner, and by the mid-17th century none were walled. English medieval cities were much more heavily fortified than Scottish ones. Height and density owed nothing to defence'.

Perhaps though, the steep hills that rise quickly behind most Scottish cities put flat land at a premium and perhaps tenement-based city design in Europe had already impressed generations of Scottish architects thanks to pre-union trade predominantly with North European ports. But then English merchants traded with Hanseatic ports too.

No-one is certain about the rationale, though the influence of feudal tenure is most convincing, but the Scots generally built up while the English built out.

According to English historian Simon Schama, the front and back door of the English terraced house expressed the desire of urbanised workers to reconnect with the river-based country idyll from which they had been removed during industrialisation.[3] This building type, with its symbolic bit of individual land, together with cottage-style cornices and farm-style front-and-back access, was perhaps a form of compensation for workers who had to be wooed into cities. And why did they have to be wooed, not forced? Many were freeholders with some legal title over land. In other words, they had a choice – perhaps not much of a choice, but some.

Scottish rural tenants, however, typically owned neither land nor home and had little choice over what they did, where they went or what type of housing they inhabited in the city. In countries where peasants enjoyed land rights, the need to compensate workers for loss of rural amenity was evident. Norwegian and Danish workers were offered city allotments to grow vegetables and built summer cabins – a workers' version of the out-of-town summer houses enjoyed by the wealthy. Over time, Norwegian society ensured such social goods were within the range of all. In Scotland, workers were offered nothing by way of compensation. They couldn't escape back to the land – so why should anyone bother? As Norwegian ethnologist Professor Ottar Brox puts it, 'The Scottish working classes were treated poorly in cities because they had nowhere else to go. Norwegians did.'

At the time, those tenement flats, including the single ends, represented a huge improvement on cottages in the countryside and, volumetrically, offered more space than English terraced houses thanks to the higher ceilings. For most inhabitants in the 1870s, Scotland's tenement actually represented a great advance.

In the early 20th century, the most important voice on retaining tenements was Patrick Geddes – not an architect but a botanist, and the father of Town Planning. Geddes advocated Garden Cities in his influential 1915 book *Cities in Evolution* but was entirely opposed to the anti-city approach of Ebenezer Howard at Letchworth in England. Geddes thought cities could be restored from within and like any good botanist and gardener, he was wary of the effects of wholesale pruning

---

3   Simson Schama, *Landscape and Memory* (London: HarperCollins, 1995).

on organisms like city centre communities. In the 1890s he moved into Edinburgh's Old Town and began to improve it using a philosophy of 'conservative surgery' which removed only the 'incurable parts' of built heritage and encouraged university professors to come back to the Old Town by developing Ramsay Gardens up by the castle.[4]

In Glasgow though, 'conservative surgery' didn't happen and a century-long, fruitless detour into other housing types took place. The 1918 Ministry of Reconstruction report banned tenements and required new housing to be 12 houses to the acre, no more than two storeys tall, laid out on garden city principles with back drying greens.[5] This was a signal to developers that tenements were a doomed housing type and private investment dried up, leading (in part) to housing shortages on the eve of war as shipbuilding, engineering and munitions workers poured into Glasgow and Clydeside towns. Rents rose and rent strikes resulted in statutory rent restrictions (lifted after the war but resumed in 1920).

It became clear that only a municipal building programme could end the problem of undersupply and high rents. The first phase (1918–24) was on the ladder principle – building cottages for the skilled to free up accommodation further down the scale. It was too expensive and stopped in 1924. Then prefabricated houses were tried – that stopped in 1926. Slum clearance began in 1933 and reintroduced tenements 'in the most threadbare and unpleasant form', like the concrete block three-storey inner slum suburb of Blackhill. By 1977, half of the flat-fronted, unadorned tenements there were demolished as unfit – more went with the construction of the M8 motorway.

Nonetheless, the new low-rise 'Garden City' style was popular. Raymond Young observes:

> The Garden suburbs were primarily designed for skilled and white collar workers. Cheaper developments, including poorer quality tenements, were used for slum clearance. They attracted a social stigma early in their life from which they never recovered. The social stratification of the poor was reflected in housing allocation policy.[6]

---

4   C. McKean, *The Glasgow Story:* http://www.theglasgowstory.com/story.php? id=TGSEF10.
5   Ibid.
6   R. Young, *Annie's Loo: the Govan origins of Scotland's Community based Housing Organisations* (Argyll, 2013).

In 1945 housing need was massive. In Glasgow, a quarter of a million people were on the council house waiting list, and the humble tenement was once again under attack as the 'Battle of Glasgow' commenced. The Government wanted a quarter of a million people to be moved out of Glasgow, but the City Engineer argued they should stay and live in 29 'Comprehensive Development Areas' (nicknamed comprehensive demolition areas) in a flattened, cleared city centre full of modern, high-rise blocks circled by a new ring road. The resulting compromise saw (partial) construction of the ring road, demolition of substandard tenements and the construction of new modern blocks, like the infamous 20-storey tower blocks that made up Hutchesontown C in the Gorbals, designed by the celebrated architect Sir Basil Spence.

A 'six-star hotel on stilts', was how former resident Eddie McConnell remembered it in a recent documentary for BBC Scotland, called *Rebuilding Basil Spence*. 'When you grew up in a one-roomed tenement, you appreciated having a living room, separate bedrooms, a bathroom and a veranda.' The balconies jutted from each floor on a scale designed to offer space and fresh air, and somewhere to hang the washing. Unfortunately, the enthusiasm of former tenement dwellers waned quickly. Gorbals resident Jimmy Mutter, 73, was a member of Glasgow's housing committee at the time. 'Apart from condensation... there was a problem with rain leaking into the lift shafts and causing power failures,' he says:

> In the mid-'80s, we put on a pitched roof and closed in an area which had become a wind tunnel. But by the end of the decade it was obvious the blocks needed complete recladding and new windows. The chief planning officer had a public meeting with tenants and the majority said they'd rather be moved out.[7]

The Hutchie C flats were eventually blown up by a controlled explosion in 1993. One woman died after being hit by flying rubble and the council had to rehouse about 400 people. Building in a hurry, failing to maintain and demolishing in a hurry – a vicious cycle Glasgow has struggled to escape.

'Glasgow city council always had a thing about spending more than other councils on building flats with higher specifications, and

---

7 A *Guardian* reappraisal of Sir Basil Spence's career: http://www.guardian.co. uk/society/2008/jun/11/basil. spence.architecture.

then not maintaining them properly,' claims Miles Glendinning of the Scottish Centre for Conservation Studies. He cites Spence's two blocks as a typical example. 'They were clearly of a very elaborate and unusual style, with many untested aspects.' Interestingly, the architect's low-rise development in Edinburgh's Canongate has proven far more durable.[8] Huge out of town estates like Drumchapel, Easterhouse and Castlemilk were hurriedly built on the city's periphery and large numbers of Glaswegians were shifted to New Towns like East Kilbride and Cumbernauld.

Tenements, particularly those in Partick and Govan owned by large landowners, just kept slipping further and further down the priority list. As Raymond Young observes, the 'idea that any "working-class" tenements should be improved was political anathema.' So they weren't.

The grim result is described by William McIlvanney in *Docherty*:

> High Street, its tenement windows gutted by shadows, closes gaping like abandoned burrows, seemed as dead as Pompeii, a destination where people were frozen into the sordid postures of their grovelling lives.

Until the 1960s, the connection between poverty and tenements was hard to shake – even though many tenements were built for the middle classes. So the pursuit of profit, geology, and industrialisation gave urban Scots the tenement. But the Great Storm of January 1968 gave it a second chance.

The original Hurricane Bawbag

In Northern Ireland 1968, Bernadette Devlin was defying the authorities in a Civil Rights March and I was facing a traumatic move from a little feeder primary to the enormous mixed-denomination school of Strandtown, less than a mile from Van Morrison's famous Cyprus Avenue.

So I was really too young to remember the hurricane-force winds which must have ripped across the Irish Sea before hitting Glasgow

---

8   Ibid.

– stripping off slates, chimney heads and whole roof sections. Cars were crushed by falling debris, 20,000 homes were damaged, people were killed and Glasgow was a blitzed landscape. Storm repairs took months – even years. But a few years later, when local government reform created Glasgow District Council and the mighty Strathclyde Region and armed them with new powers in the Housing (Scotland) Act 1974, Glasgow already had an administrative infrastructure and a housing repairs workforce in place – thanks to the hurricane. Thanks to the backlog, many tenements had escaped demolition and received only interim repairs like re-roofing – which prompted tenants to ask 'why not repair the whole building?'[9] Thanks to an influential report from Strathclyde University, the mood to refurbish, not demolish, tenements was given academic backing. Thanks to Prime Minister Ted Heath, Britain had entered Europe, making slum areas of Glasgow eligible for hefty housing repair grants. And thanks to architects like Raymond Young, who moved into a Govan tenement to help administer one of the first improvement schemes installing indoor toilets, ordinary Glaswegians headed the renovation drive.[10] Ordinary (or maybe extraordinary) Glaswegians like Dorothy Henderson.

One evening in 1974 this 'well-rounded, good-humoured but determined lady'[11] attended a residents meeting to hear Glasgow City Council plans for improvement in the Woodlands area of Glasgow. Heading home, she dropped in on Angela Petrie to tell her the bad news. Tenements in their neighbourhood had been given a life expectancy of just seven years. Sadly, neither woman is alive today – so we can only guess how that conversation galvanised the two friends. Within days they had rounded up all 109 other occupiers in neighbouring tenements to form Woodlands Residents' Association. They won an improvement grant of £36,000, had their buildings cleaned and watched as the stonework came up a gleaming, warm, honey-ochre yellow. The Association also put new doors on closes (common central stone staircases) which stopped the wind howling in and (later) door entry systems which stopped their passing use as

---

9   C. McKean, *Fight Blight* (England: Littlehampton, 1977).

10   Raymond Young's Govan experience was central to Glasgow's great decade of community-led housing. Later he became Director Scotland for the Housing Corporation which financed the tenant-led schemes.

11   H. Diamond, *Can You Get My Name in the Papers?* (Glasgow: Neil Wilson Publishing, 1996).

Before and after renovation Murano Street, Firhill, Glasgow mid-'70s.
Courtesy of Peter Robinson

unofficial urinals. They cleaned up front gardens too hard to manage for elderly ground floor residents and tidied the sprawling jumble of bins and debris in back courts. Neighbours came to see what Woodlands had achieved, and started similar improvement projects. Over the next decade, most of Glasgow's century-old tenements were stone-cleaned and refurbished (see photos p.131). Businesses followed suit. Soon the spectacular City Chambers was transformed from a bleak Dickensian black to a clear, blonde sandstone and the Kelvingrove Museum re-emerged a warm Ayers rock red.

While other cities remained static and unchanging, a new part of Glasgow emerged every few days from scaffolding, protective plastic sheeting and high pressure water jets. Like skin scrubbed clean, like a child's flushed cheeks, like brightly coloured sandstone pebbles after high tide, Glasgow emerged blushing, bashful and utterly beautiful. I remember distinctly the air of general surprise, anticipation and occasional disappointment when a deficiency in the original stone or chemical cleaning solution left mottled marks on the finished building. A collective thought bubble was almost visible over Glasgow: there was nothing wrong with these tenements all along. And by association: there was nothing wrong with us either. The rise in city confidence was perceptible.

Ironically though, that meant the relatively self-contained triangle of 23 street blocks in Woodlands suddenly became a desirable and slightly bohemian destination for research staff at the nearby BBC. Remaining tenements were refurbished into desirable accommodation. So much so that tenement flats attracted professional singletons who unwittingly edged out working-class families. Perhaps if the flats had been co-operatively owned, like tenements in Norway or Denmark, things might have been different. But as prices rose, the original residents faded out and old patterns of tenement life began to change.

Tenements had once been vertical streets with extended families.

An STV film about the Clydebank Blitz, made to mark the 70th anniversary in 2011, featured one elderly survivor who recalled his best friend, playmate and tenement neighbour, Tommy. The lad died with the rest of his family of 13 that terrible night in 1941. 'Tommy's sisters should have married my brothers. My sisters should have married his brothers. The future we should have had was lost that night.'

Such was the closeness amongst tenement neighbours – under-pinned by a council allocations policy that awarded extra points for local family connection. Thus the average Scottish mother lived less than five minutes from her own mother. That had benefits of informal childcare and easy socialising (perhaps the tradition of 'first footing' at Hogmanay lasted so long in Glasgow because there was no lengthy, freezing walk home). People helped people survive.

And that forged strong bonds of loyalty. William McIlvanney writes:

> Where so little was owned, sharing became a precautionary reflex. The only security they could have was one another. Most things were borrowable from a copper for the gas to a black suit for funerals. Wives looked in on one another without ceremony. The men, gathered compulsively each night at the street corner, became variously a pitch-and-toss school, a subdued male-voice choir, a parliament without powers.
>
> Underpinning the anarchy of their social lives... was a code of conduct complex enough to baffle the most perceptive outsider yet tacitly understood by even the youngest citizens of High Street from the time they started to think. One of its first principles was tolerance.[12]

Claims about wellbeing that arise from this sense of connection and understanding of human frailty are often dismissed as sentimentality. In an entirely different context though, Professor Stephen Reicher of St Andrews has studied the surprisingly positive effects on mental and physical health produced by participation in the outwardly chaotic *Kumbh Mela* festival in India – one of the largest makeshift cities on earth where millions of people gather to bathe twice daily in the Ganges. Many aspects of his description ring bells:

> It is intensely crowded. It is noisy – competing loudspeakers blast out distorted sounds day and night. It is polluted – there are only the most rudimentary waste disposal facilities and sanitation... [and] little or no heating at a time of year when temperatures regularly fall to near zero during the night.
>
> People cease to see their fellow *kalpwasi* (pilgrims) as 'other', but rather share the same perspectives and goals. They expect to agree

---

12   William McIlvanney, *Docherty* (London: Allen & Unwin, 1975).

with others, to have their views validated by others and to receive support from others. All this makes social interaction smoother and social relations more rewarding.

What our work demonstrates is the power of identity in transforming collective experience and the power of collective experience in transforming everyday life. It shows how a sense of shared identity provides the underpinning for a sense of community and civility. And, perhaps most remarkably, it suggests that shared identity also improves our physical wellbeing, with symptoms of ill health less apparent after the Mela than before.[13]

Prof Reicher talks about the 'collective self-realisation' of the Mela crowd. Of course it's a temporary phenomenon experienced by religious devotees sharing a faith who've made a positive decision to attend. The same could hardly be said for the random bunch thrown together in the mêlée of the average tenement. And yet.

Maybe the 'tenement crowd' has untapped potential and, as yet unmeasured, health and social advantages as well.

The Tenement Shop

From 1996 until devolution in 1999, I lived in Scotland but commuted to London, opting to stay in a cheap, Slovakian-run hotel in Soho for three days a week presenting *You and Yours* on Radio 4 and the *Midnight Hour* on BBC2. Anything to avoid the panic and depression that kicked in when I tried to stay in the vast anonymous swathes of Acton or the windswept, people-free corridor that was Holloway Road. For me, the most depressing urban habitat has always been endless suburbia with unprepossessing, straggling rows of homes fringed by unusable tiny patches of individual garden – unless of course they were the straggling rows and tiny patches of Belfast. Cities cannot be very large low-rise villages without losing civic focus. They need density to function. Tenements grasp the nettle by offering less kerb parking space per resident (and thus deterring multiple car ownership) whilst bringing bus and train stops closer to more people. In the UK, Scotland alone has the building blocks (literally) upon which modern, well-connected, co-operative European-style cities can be built. And yet the dynamic potential of the tenement is roundly ignored. Next to nothing can be bought off the shelf to fit Scotland's most distinctive housing type.

The average Scottish tenement has a room height of 14 feet with long sash windows that need curtains of 120 inches in length. Since most ready-made soft furnishing is aimed at the lower ceilings and smaller windows of two-storey English terraced houses, maisonettes and semis, nothing from national shop chains like Harveys, B&Q, Homebase or M&S actually fits. So it's common to see curtains in an elegant tenement room dangling at half-mast just past the window sill without quite reaching the floor. Equally, light fittings with short cords look like smoke-alarms glued to the ceiling. Standard lamps look more like table lamps unaccountably planted on the floor. The shortage of furnishings fit for tenement scale and design meant most young flat owners like myself made regular trips to architectural salvage yards, and places like Paddy's Market and the Barras' – several miles of second-hand clothes, furniture, dubiously acquired videos and vast tables of cheap mince sold from market stalls every weekend in the East End of the city.

I even started to think of setting up a business to provide furnishings that fitted tenement-style proportions. But some tentative and unscientific research amongst neighbours suggested native Scots didn't think they had a problem: 'Och aye – nae curtains ever drap aw the way doon below the windaes. But that makes it easier tae hoover. Aye, overhead lights are a bit useless tae – but ye dinnae need to use them. We use standard lamps and pit them on wee boxes tae raise them up a bit. Naebody notices'.

Years later I recognised this frustrating tendency to accept second or even third best in the observations of Dr Samuel Johnson. Whilst touring the Inner Hebrides in 1775 he wrote:

> Scots... have attained the liberal without the manual arts. They have excelled in ornamental knowledge (but)... have wanted not only the elegancies but [also] the conveniences of common life.

How right he was. The Scots national obsession with 'ornamental knowledge' and 'decorating the mind' means higher rates of newspaper and book reading here than any other part of the UK. But creature comforts – until recently – have been far further down the pecking order except for 'those and such as those'. I didn't really want the headache of running a business. So the Tenement Shop idea went no further.

Nonetheless, visiting friends from England and Wales always marvelled at the sheer quality of my Glasgow tenement flat. Not only were rooms larger, stairways wider and walls sufficiently thick and permanent to prevent accidental damage (a friend once fell through a plywood partition in London prompting a year of legal wrangling about liability). The shared close in my Partick tenement was certainly ornamental – with burnished red and green tiles all the way up the stone staircase, and matching tiled fireplaces in every room of the flat (once draught-excluding boards fitted in the '50s had been removed). No-one had the cheek to say it. But looks spoke volumes. How the hell have you got a better flat in Glasgow than we have in London?

I still don't know. I have never seen the worst of the tenement slums – they were demolished before I was born. But I've grown to love what the remaining tenements have done for Scottish cities. And I've realised the compact, vibrant, viable urban environment they create is increasingly under threat as native Scots head for the suburbs in search of tiny private gardens for children to play in – just like suburban England.

The ultimate irony is that the English are finally heading in our direction. I once interviewed a man called Harley Sherlock whose 1980s book *Cities are Good for You* argued that higher housing densities could actually create better British cities. How would that be done, I asked. Well, Harley wasn't sure. Maybe blocks of purpose-built flats with separate staircases to the street.

How about one shared staircase used by all the flat-owners?

No, that would never catch on.

Had Harley ever been to Scotland?

No, but he hoped to make it to the Edinburgh Festival soon.

Right.

Decades later the idea of desirable density also occurred to the redoubtable Germaine Greer. I was chairing a session during Edinburgh's 2009 Festival of Politics when the outspoken Australian-born feminist expanded on her controversial idea that old women in particular were better off in flatted communities with shared mod cons than in large, lonely suburban terraced and detached houses. Before we went on I asked if she had ever heard of tenements and described them to make sure it wasn't just a terminological problem.

No she hadn't.

Scots are used to adapting well-meant English observations of so-called British life to fit some semblance of our own experience. It seemed churlish to tell Germaine she was preaching not just to the converted but to the nation that could have converted England to her own higher density cause.

Stone-built, four-storey tenements are also green. Four times as many people are within five minutes of a bus, tram or train stop (the average distance a UK city dweller is prepared to walk to access public transport). So bus and train networks are more focused and effective (just don't mention the Edinburgh trams). Flats can be hard to insulate on external walls but are effectively insulated by neighbours' flats above, below and on either side. It's also easier to install tenement flats with a single system of district heating.

In fact, since I've recently spent a lot of time in Norwegian cities, I'm struck by two big similarities with Scotland. First, we share a social democratic political outlook. Second, we share stone-built tenements. It's strange that so few folk have put the politics and the tenements together. But then, seeing is believing (see comparison overleaf).

Avril Paton's wonderful portrait of Saltoun Street in Partick reached second place in a poll for Scotland's favourite painting in 2010 (Salvador Dali was first).[14] This cosy scene shows real-life characters, including the writer Bernard MacLaverty and journalist Roddy Forsyth. Children are playing, food is being prepared and people are arriving home. It's a well-proportioned, self-contained little world within a world.

Maybe it's an idealised view and unquestionably there is a lot of sentimentalising life in tenements – where income levels, personal behaviour and social circumstance have a lot more to do with creating a happy close than the standard of wall tiles. And yet, there is nothing more reassuring to the senses than entering a busy, functioning com-

14   http://www.intermezzo-arts.co.uk/blog/?p=63.

Tenement in Oslo, 2012.

Avril Paton's *Windows in the West*, 1993. The painting is on display at
Kelvingrove Art Gallery and Museum.

munal close at teatime. You may not have children, but tiny wellington boots sit outside family front doors. You might not be cooking, but the comforting smell of mince and tatties fills the air as you climb the communal stairs. You may not play the pipes or the fiddle but maybe someone somewhere in the tenement does. You might not have a manual job but there, on the middle of each stone step – worn through the weight of footsteps over centuries – is a tiny deposit of brown-red earth. And finally on the second floor you spot the explanation – a pair of heavy men's boots sitting beside a half open storm door.

When the ground floor tenant goes out for a smoke, we all smell it. When someone comes back singing after a late night, we all hear it. And when someone's embittered ex-boyfriend once set a fire in the ground floor cleaning cupboard the rest of my tenement all suffered the effects of smoke inhalation. When the council came to inspect the damage and insist on structural repairs, we all had to contribute an equal eighth share of the costs – so expensive for some home owners they had to sell up and leave. Eight households agreed to install and pay for a main door entry system – and eight people chose the colour of the paint for redecoration (not surprisingly, it ended up grey).

It's a little thing called society. It's the thing Margaret Thatcher tried to deny in her audacious 1980s 'Sermon on The Mound' when she came to lecture Ministers in the Church of Scotland about the Christian merits of a property owning democracy. They heard her without applause, in stony silence.

If one sentence sealed the fate of the Conservatives in Scotland for decades afterwards it was this perceived attack on Scotland's social glue. For better and for worse, every tenement dweller knows that society does exist. It's all around.

Of course there are downsides – but they just need sensible management. Noisy neighbours are a nightmare – sound insulation between floors is notoriously poor. But that knowledge prompts most people to become more considerate. I realised – before my first Glasgow party – the entire tenement would have to be invited or I'd live with the threat of a phonecall to the police all night and bad vibes for the rest of the year. The gatekeepers of the close – an elderly couple in the ground floor flat – requested gin and Irn-Bru, and surveyed the young dancing journalists and 20-somethings with the open curiosity of adults at a zoo.

In those distant days, groups of hopeful youngsters cruised the streets of Glasgow with 'carry outs', listening for telltale signs of music floating out of open upper floor windows. Gate crashing simply involved walking up the stairs and producing a bottle to gain entry.

In short, modern life tugs us all apart, but the Scottish tenement tugs us back together again. Not to the levels of umbilical closeness known in the good/bad old days when neighbouring families lived in one another's homes. But relative to the rest of our modern, atomised world, life in a Scottish tenement still involves sharing and exchange. It demands and develops social skills to handle occasional flare-ups of hostility and annoyance. At its best, tenement life is like living within a very varied and extended family. At its worst it's like living on a prison wing populated by repeat ASBO offenders – though once again much of that friction has been down to new council allocation policies, not the simple fact of living in a tenement. Older tenement dwellers bemoan the passing of days when every neighbour was an Aunty and informal child-minding arrangements let many women go out to work. The days of the mandatory stair-cleaning rota may be past. But compared to other housing types, tenement flats are still hugely popular. They still involve more regular contact and space-sharing than any other housing type in the UK – and with some imagination they could act as a basis for all sorts of future co-operation.

All stairs could be made accessible with a retro-fitted lift programme like Denmark. Back closes could be used for bicycle parks, polytunnels, or allotment gardens. Bottom floor flats could be bought over by 'stair co-operatives' and turned into a storage space, recycling centre, communal laundry, wood-pellet based district heating system or a meeting space for older residents.

Scotland has a unique society-supporting asset in its stock of tenements. That should be precious. It isn't.

Only the majority experience prevails in a centralised state like Britain, and so the English experience of housing has become the British default. And that's a problem – because tenemental cities must develop or die. City dwellers in Holland who want gardens for their families build them on rooftops – they don't move out to the suburbs. In Germany, rooftop gardens are a compulsory part of planning regulations for new office and residential developments – there's even a formula for the amount of parkland that must be built per urban resident and the square acreage of outdoor play area needed per urban child. In Scotland, there is no similar formula or clarity about the need to make dense tenement-living more attractive in the 21st century. Instead Scots are subconsciously copying southern housing types paraded nightly on series like *Location, Location, Location* (which is made by a Glasgow based production company, ironically enough). As a result, we have clogged up Scottish cities with semi-detached houses and maisonettes to match southern aspirations for status through density-destroying, low-rise housing types. But it's not too late for Scots to reconnect with our own housing tradition – and look east and south for inspiration.Barcelona, with the highest urban density in Europe of 400 homes per hectare, is also regularly voted Europe's best city to live in. Glasgow's 170 homes per hectare is the highest density in the UK – by contrast London has just 55 homes per hectare and recommended a ban in 2006 on any more low-rise, terraced housing construction in the inner city.[15] Sadly, it may be too late for English cities to reshape – or rethink. But Scotland has the right building blocks for city scale. Tenements in Scotland are popular, flats are normal and English terraced housing is Europe's odd relation. That of course is not the view in Albert Square, Coronation Street, Westminster, Number Ten or Broadcasting House. Size matters – and 50 million people can't be wrong. Perhaps though, five million people can beg to differ and get on with resurrecting and developing our own distinctive and sustainable housing heritage.

---

15   Mayor of London's 2006 Density Matrix Review.

CHAPTER FIVE

Land, Land Everywhere but not an Inch for Sale

MY MEMORY IS NO CALENDAR. But there are ways to calculate the date of Maruma's arrival on Eigg – an event that breathed new life into the land reform movement and opened the final chapter in Scotland's history of feudal landownership.

Not that any of us present on the tiny Inner Hebridean isle that day knew it. And not that the final chapter has yet closed.

The mysterious 'fire artist' from Stuttgart became the last private landlord of Eigg, 16 miles west of Mallaig, after persuading the previous owner, Keith Schellenberg, to sell. Professor Marlin Eckhart – to give Maruma his Sunday name – or Gotthilf Christian Eckhard Oesterle to give him his real name – first appeared a few months afterwards, convinced journalists had been put off the scent by a press conference in Edinburgh, cunningly cancelled at the last minute. No journalist would now be able to race five hours to Mallaig, board a ferry and catch him *in situ*. He was safe. At that very last minute however, I was nowhere near the furious press pack, but on board a Cal Mac ferry en route to Eigg from Mallaig. And that scores off some dates on the calendar. If it was summer, I'd be on the privately owned *Shearwater* with its direct crossing from Arisaig – or direct until Ronnie the irrepressibly curious skipper spotted a minke whale, basking shark or school of porpoises en route. The conversation with Ronnie and the generally faster crossing time meant no islander or regular visitor used Cal Mac when he was sailing. So my presence on a Cal Mac boat meant Maruma must have landed in spring or winter when the *Shearwater* was out of the water for seasonal repairs. The rhythms of island life are that predictable and dependable.

Aboard the ferry, I was sitting in the cafeteria with island farmer Colin Carr and the enigmatic Donald MacLean – an intense, lean Scotsman rumoured to have served in the SAS. Given the length of the journey, we embarked on a bottle of Highland Park to the disgust

The old pier at Eigg, the welcoming party and the Sgurr.

of mothers who tugged their children away from our occasionally raucous corner. And that places the year in the mid-'90s when, two unlucky days a week, Eigg could only be reached after a five hour trip via every other Small Isle first. Far simpler though, it was the day after the birthday of islander Maggie Fyffe. Which means *Maruma* landed at 11am on 9 April 1995.

Any lesser event in the Eigg social calendar would not have pulled me from sleep at 6am into pitch darkness and torrential rain. But I'd made the trip dozens of times since I first encountered the Eiggachs in 1992 and became a Trustee of the Isle of Eigg Trust. The trick was to get up and jump straight into the car before the mind had a chance to waken properly and assess the length of the journey ahead. The way-markers soon became familiar. West through Crieff and Comrie listening to the earliest part of *Good Morning Scotland*, losing the signal at St Fillans, weaving round Loch Earn and slowing down for another amused keek at the Clachan Cottage Hotel where I worked as a receptionist one eye-opening summer after leaving school. Climbing up to Lix Toll and along to Crianlarich, where the inevitable hard to pass lorries join the road from Glasgow till Tyndrum and the point where

I imagine all hesitant drivers wilt before the wall of Munros and head west to Oban instead. Then the freedom of Rannoch Moor – past the takeaway on the Black Mount (shut at 8am), past the iconic rowan in the enormous boulder (growing at 8am) and past clumps of road-hugging deer in Glencoe with its waterfalls and brooding darkness. On across the bridge at Ballachulish (a favourite '70s ferry crossing during particularly erratic summer holiday Riddoch family drives from Belfast to Wick). Then behind the inevitable tourist on the winding road past Corran Ferry where time stands still till Fort William. Past the pierhouse that used to hire rowing boats (now a fish restaurant). Round the town on the dual carriageway with glimpses of unlovely bins and back courts never intended to be seen by anything but boats (that'll teach them for ignoring the aesthetic sensibilities of sailors). On through the string of Ben Nevis related B&Bs to the turnoff for the Road to the Isles and the certain knowledge the Mallaig ferry is now attainable in one hour, barring roadworks, tourists, or boats lifting lock gates and blocking traffic across the Caledonian Canal.

On past the Glenfinnan monument, the Harry Potter viaduct, the start of the old single-track road at Arisaig (now an elegant two-way road with overtaking lanes) and the switch to headlights which I always hoped might suggest (and excuse) ferry related urgency to more leisurely traffic ahead.

Past Arisaig pier, the tucked away beach used in the *Local Hero* film just before Morar, into Mallaig, onto the pier, into the office, out again onto the pier, up the passenger gangway (badly packed bags banging everywhere) and onto the first available seat, ticket still in hand, as if such a victory snatched against time, fatigue and distance needed proof.

'What happened to you? Your eyes look like pissholes in the snow.'

'Look who's talking – how many weeks have you been away?'

'Three days – we had a bit of a singsong last night.'

'Which explains the voice. And the hair and the shirt and the...'

'OK, we all look rough. How are you anyway?'

And then the hugs and stories since last time, and the drams and long trip round the isles till the ancient, crumbling Eigg pier was finally in sight, tucked safely behind the outlier, Castle Island – a great place to say there were sheep in the old days, when newly arrived subsidy inspectors could hardly face getting straight back on the boat to check.

By 2pm on 8 April 1995, the weather had improved dramatically and when people, luggage and island provisions were finally decanted from the large ferry to the small flit boat person by person, rucksack by rucksack, box by box and case by case, half the island had gathered on the pier to assess the amusement new people and provisions might add to entertainment. A fixed link means supply containers can be driven off these days – but for long decades, in all weathers, everything islanders needed was subject to this dodgy seaborne juggling act.

That day, after the communal lifting, passing, stretching and unloading was complete, Colin Carr, Camille Dressler and myself led a posse of kids up the Sgurr – the mountainous outcrop that gives the island its name of edge or notch in Gaelic, Norwegian and Icelandic – and its distinctive tilted cap profile from the mainland. Over the long buyout years I must have climbed that Sphinx-like lump of pitchstone lava several dozen times – and its cliff-face became a metaphor for the islanders' dilemma. From one direction, an unscalable cliff: from another, a long saddle with a safe access point halfway along its two mile length. Impossible or relatively easy – depending on location and perspective.

The reward for tackling the climb however, was always the same. A truly stunning vista. On a clear day, Muck sits low beneath the Sgurr like a sponge in a bath and beyond sit the tiny but distinctive Dutchman's Cap off Mull and the brown Paps of Jura.

To the West, the mountainous spikes of volcanic Rum rise sheer from the sea like igneous turrets of a Narnian castle. Beyond that the tortured outline of the Cuillin, the high cliffs of Waterstein Head and beyond them all the dreamy, winking outline of Barra and the Uist. North sits the fat mountain clumps of Applecross, Torridon, Slioch, and An Teallach – the great western sideboard of Scotland – and below them the glinting white sands at Morar and Ardnamurchan. If there is a better view in Europe, I haven't seen it. That spring day the Sgurr's vantage point on the rest of the world seemed glorious – and symbolic.

I got some of the kids to gather dry grasses on the summit and lit them. The breeze took the burning bush a few yards up into the blue sky, twigs crackling and orange sparks flying as the little fireball drifted away from the Sgurr, burning brightly for a few glorious seconds. I stood transfixed, hoping none of the kids were sharing my own perverse urge to jump off after it.

Fire on the Sgurr. I've no idea why that should have happened the day before the fire artist Maruma landed. But the walkers got home, the long preparation for Maggie's party began and finally, around 11pm, two Landrovers set off from the Kildonan side of the island crawling up the single-track road and over to the more populous township of Cleadale. One vehicle was operated by a screwdriver jammed into the ignition (lost key), the other had a door kept shut by binder twine held by the front seat passenger (broken handle). Since there was no car ferry to take island cars onto mainland roads, Eigg vehicles were exempt from MOTs and tax discs. The average speed on the eight miles of hilly single-track road was perhaps 20mph. With official passage on CalMac costing more than the scrap value of most bangers, the most common means of getting cars onto the island was to strap them onto the Shearwater (craning them on and off at either end) and hope for a quiet crossing. Either way, there was little point in running anything but the oldest vehicle on Eigg – though many families also kept a 'proper' licensed car across at Mallaig or Arisaig for mainland excursions.

The party was definitely worth the long journey. Maggie and Wes have always been the perfect hosts, with the island's largest supply of sleeping bags, spare mattresses and sofas. The upstairs floor of the Fyffe's traditional stone crofthouse has long been open house, especially for visiting musicians. Indeed, music was the most powerful unifying force in the story of Eigg. In 1991, Maggie's determination to organise a *Fèis* (Gaelic traditional instrument learning festival) was thwarted by a last minute veto on use of the village hall by the island's (mostly) absentee owner. Keith Schellenberg was a larger than life personality – a member of the 1964 British Olympic bobsleigh team who made his money in shipbuilding, livestock feed and agricultural chemicals.[1]

The Yorkshireman (of Liechtenstein descent) bought Eigg in 1975,

---

[1] Islanders were still bitterly complaining that, as they struggled to eke out a living, Schellenberg entertained scores of chums to motorboat races and 'champers and hampers' weekends. His costumed Jacobite and Hanoverian mock battles did not go down well either. It may have been mere history to Schellenberg, but it was salt in the wounds of some locals. The 1745 Jacobite rebellion and the final defeat of the clans at Culloden sounded the death knell for the ancient Highland way of life in which no-one owned land, not even the clan chiefs – though they would later claim it as their private property. It also heralded the clearance of hundreds of thousands from Eigg and elsewhere to North America and lowland cities to make way for lucrative sheep farming.' Mary Braid, *The Independent* 26/02/1996.

promising leases, jobs and access to land for new residents. The people came, but the promised new dawn never materialised.[2] Perhaps, as one sage observer wrote, 'too many long term leases would diminish the value of the laird's property'.

Fifteen years later, the situation facing tenants without leases and old people without hot water was serious. And yet it was the sense of frustration over that cancelled *Feis* which cemented a real change in island mood. The young folk felt cut off and controlled. The older folk felt basic rules of Highland hospitality were broken when they had to withdraw invitations to musicians, guests and neighbouring islanders. Relations never recovered. Years later Colin Carr resigned as farm manager and Schellenberg issued an eviction notice on Colin, Marie and their family of five on Hogmanay. Yip – seven people facing eviction for no reason. Yip – on Hogmanay. You couldn't make it up. Colin's decision to quit had been a hammer blow for the man who was once the darling of the artists, hippies and free spirits he invited to come and give Hebridean island life a try. By the '90s, though, Keith Schellenberg was so isolated on the island he hardly ever visited.

His second marriage to Margaret Williams had foundered and the jointly owned island had been put up for sale to finance their separation. To general dismay, 'Schellie' immediately bought the island back himself – without the steadying influence of his former wife. That winter he announced the farm tractor could no longer be used for 'other' island purposes. This put Colin Carr as farm manager in the impossible position of watching neighbours struggle with smaller machines or the boots of old cars to hump large drums of diesel around and keep the population of stalwart, independent old native islanders in heat and light.

Despite ideal conditions for hydro and wind power, Eiggachs depended almost completely on expensive and hard to ship diesel for every energy need (apart from a few small pico-hydro schemes).

There were rats round most houses because no land was available for a rubbish tip (and, to be fair, the islanders hadn't chosen to

---

2   Simon and Karen Helliwell uprooted from their home near Norwich... Mr Helliwell was to be employed as the boatman and to repair cottages. But the promised lease never materialised and the boatman work was a disaster. He claimed in court that he was expected to take boats out when he judged they were overloaded and conditions dangerous. After less than two years, he resigned from Mr Schellenberg's employment, eventually building his own house on land bought from a crofter. Anne Campbell, an old lady who lived on the island, described how she used to drown the rats she had caught in her house in the sink. Jamie Wilson *The Guardian* 20/05/1999.

use any of their common grazing for that purpose either). So rubbish could only legally be dumped at the end of each croft.[3] The old people were exceptionally hardy, but most were reduced to living in one room to conserve heat. As Gaelic speakers, they were slightly isolated from their (mostly) English speaking sons and daughters and the mixture of Scots and English incomers Schellie had encouraged onto Eigg. So there were plans to bring 'the oldies' together in sheltered housing and a day centre near the lovely Singing Sands beach at Cleadale – but these came to nought, thanks to the landlord's missing signature.

That missing signature withheld a lot. The majority of families were not crofters, but tenants without leases. No leases meant no access to housing improvement grants for the best part of two decades, no chance of borrowing money against the value of the house for major repairs and every chance repairs might prompt rent rises. There was absolutely no chance of wheedling new land for new build from the Laird. As a result, the degree of overcrowding was phenomenal, and most children lived away from home during the week to attend secondary school in Mallaig, only to return to life in a shared bedroom with other siblings or – like the hardy George Carr – splendid isolation in the top floor of a draughty barn above the dogs and farm machinery. George called it the penthouse – but made visitors promise they would never go up there. Ever.

Nothing in the Eigg story was completely black and white though – Schellie's rents were generally low and, inexplicably, he paid Colin and Marie Carr's eldest son through Gordonstoun. Keith himself – like much of the landowning class – had been bunged off to private boarding school at an early age. Evidently, he was trying to strike an emotional deal, allowing some sort of inclusion in the Carr family. Keith would act as paternal provider and the Carrs would love and respect him like a surrogate dad. The day Colin quit as farm manager, the deal was in tatters and Colin was unemployed for the first time in his life. On an island where the majority of men were often jobless, it took courage to join their number and draw a line in the sand where the cynical, world weary wise-cracking would end and belief in the impossible – local ownership – could quietly begin.

---

3   A croft is an area of land which may or may not have a croft house on it.

From 1994, I was a trustee of the Isle of Eigg Trust (IET), composed mostly of sympathetic outsiders so no islander could be evicted
from a rented house or sacked from an estate job for perceived acts
of defiance. Clearly the tactic was only partly successful and hadn't
managed to protect the Carr family or Scottish Wildlife Trust bird
warden John Chester, whose stout defence of his neighbours at Kildonan earned him a place on Schellenberg's eviction list. I also set up a
group called 'Friends of Eigg' – a well-connected bunch of Central Belt
folk who met every month for several years to support the IET in whatever way was needed. Around a dozen folk, including ecologists like
the late Andrew Raven, were ready to head Eigg-wards at a moment's
notice to help prevent evictions should Schellenberg decide to act.
After several long, nervous months though, the Eiggachs decided the
Laird's threat had passed. But his clumsy threat had an unforeseen
consequence, uniting almost the entire community behind fundraising
for a community buyout.

If the bailiffs had ever arrived at the Kildonan farmhouse, I suspect
they would not have gone quietly. Colin Carr was not an islander by
birth, but came from farming stock in Stirlingshire, an 'inconvenient
truth' playfully lobbed at him by island natives when he was in full

Eigg's penultimate private owner, Keith Schellenberg leaving after the island's sale to
Maruma. *Courtesy of Kenneth Kean*

verbal flight at their expense. But 20 years married to the local Marie Kirk had given Colin a positively Hebridean ear which delighted in unravelling the delicate nuances of island exchange. Colin noticed almost everything – said and unsaid.

One week at the kitchen table in Kildonan, talk was full of the expected arrival of Schellenberg. He was planning to remove sheep after his sudden decision to sell Eigg to the mysterious, foreign and non-agricultural Professor Maruma. He had already rejected a well-crafted bid from islanders. A disputed farming partnership was still being disentangled, so there was general worry that Schellie would arrive unannounced and take sheep that really belonged to islanders. The phone rang. Colin answered, stood up and switched ears, jamming his finger in the other to hear better. Recognising the voice, he smiled and put the call on speakerphone. It was the voice of an old man from the mainland.

'Hello Colin. Maybe you could advise me about a boat that wants to land on the beach at Eigg next Wednesday at about 2pm. Would the tide be right for that, I wonder?'

Colin was the local coastguard as well as the special reserve policeman at the time.

'Well, it depends on the size of the load.'

'Och well it could be taking off 60 to 80 head of sheep. And maybe a large item of furniture.'

'A heavy load, then.'

'Heavy enough.'

'Well, a 2 o'clock landing would give him two hours for gathering safely.'

'That'll be time enough, I think. It's just that the gentleman doesn't want everyone knowing his business.'

'Well you've said nothing. If it was Schellenberg himself we'd be none the wiser.'

'Just so. Well goodnight, Colin, and good luck.'

'Cheerie.'

Colin put the phone down.

'That's it. Schellenberg's coming next Wednesday and he wants the map.'

A ten-foot square framed map of Eigg dating from 1805 was evidently the 'large item of furniture' under discussion. Islanders claimed the map was gifted to them by the pre-war government minister Lord Walter Runciman, who owned Eigg from 1925–1966. Ironically, his Lordship understood island ways so well that gifts were made by verbal agreement and details went unrecorded. The map had never left the island despite changes of landowner, but without a bit of paper to wave, the islanders didn't expect to win a legal wrangle with Schellenberg or his lawyers. So the 'furniture' was moved to a crumbling but watertight hut by the pier, an old transit reversed against the door, its tyres deflated and several old cars parked and locked around it with their keys removed.

The islanders weren't exactly withholding the map but not exactly making it available for collection either. For months afterwards, it was moved from house-to-house as a further precaution.[4]

At midnight on 8 April 1995, Maggie's birthday party was full of such tales.

Songs were sung, dozens of cans of McEwen's beer emptied, whisky measures carefully poured into the bottle cap and shared round, tales of Schellenberg's ignominious exit from the island recited and strategies for the next stage of the island story vaguely formulated.

At 6am, the weather was changing. I walked back to Kildonan before the rain hit and found my way to the attic bedroom in the dark – once the diesel generators were shut off for the night, they didn't come back on till daylight. The wind had got up, so I tied one of my walking boots by its laces to the loop at the base of the skylight and hung a bag from the boot to add weight and minimise the danger of breakage. As usual.

Within minutes I was asleep – and within a few more minutes (it seemed) I was awake again. It sounded like a helicopter.

I looked at my watch. 11am. I turned over to go back to sleep. And suddenly it hit me. A helicopter. Maruma.

The household jumped into action almost simultaneously. Colin was first out the door – wellies on, decent shirt, old jacket and a trip to the pier to top up petrol in the Landrover, and maybe gather breath for that important first meeting. I'd been allowed to chum Colin (with strict instructions to act as a second pair of ears, say nothing and just listen). Colin drove up to the Lodge through the palm tree studded

---

4   Finally though, Schellenberg did remove it and gave it to his close friend, Ranald MacDonald, chief of the largest branch of Clan Donald.

garden and past the mildewed front gate – then hesitated, reversed, parked instead at the back door and knocked on the servant's entrance at the kitchen. A young woman answered, dressed almost as casually as ourselves. Maruma's make-up free girlfriend, Marianne, led us through the damp smelling, Italianate Lodge to the kitchen where Maruma sat. He was one of the oddest looking men I've ever seen – a tall, bulky, inflated and puffy looking 41 year old with long, lank hair beneath a black beret he never removed. His eyes appeared slitty and assessing – his skin was pock-marked and drawn so tightly over his wrists he looked slightly inflated. There were duty-free cartons of Marlboro cigarettes, evaporated milk, coffee and sugar sachets, a few sleeping bags – and that was it.

'Hey, tonight you will in a bed sleep, but Maruma will be on the floor. And Schellenberg has everything including the kitchen sink taken.'

Looking at the rubble-strewn worktop, he was right. The kitchen sink was missing. Eigg's new Laird was playing for sympathy and acting the underdog.

He didn't offer us a coffee or a seat, so we stood awkwardly until his agent Vladi came in and Maruma decided he wanted to see round the island and meet the people. I never got Vladi's first name or saw him without a tie or briefcase. Maruma introduced the well-dressed, dark haired German and explained his brief had been to survey the islands of the world, including the Seychelles and Maldives, to find a suitable place for Maruma's Project (the Prof nearly always referred to himself in the third person). At that point only one thought was going through our minds – aye right.

I said nothing (for once) and took cues from Colin. Minutes after the household was awoken by the helicopter's vibration, he had stopped a visitor trying to find an un-sampled bottle of whisky to present to the new Laird.

'Things are changing here. And that tradition is the first to stop. He needs to get our approval – not the other way round. Not anymore.'

Now Colin was probing gently. Obviously Maruma had enough money to buy the island – but he would need more cash to run and improve it.[5]

---

5 Maruma claimed to have made his money as a 'fire artist', fusing paint onto canvas with a mysterious technique to produce work sought after by conveniently anonymous private dealers and collectors in his native Germany.

'Would Maruma a Rolls Royce buy when he not enough cash for the petrol had?' Gradually we all that day to German sentence structure adjusted.

Davey's transit van (the island bus) appeared outside and we all poured in. The rain was lashing down, the windows steamed up and the excesses of the previous night – well, early morning – were still working on me. I expressed some surprise that Maruma was up for being trailed around the island so soon after he'd stepped out of a helicopter.

'And I was in a survival suit that fitted her,' he beamed, pointing to the diminutive Marianne. It didn't bear thinking about. But it was worth considering that Maruma sat on planes and choppers for the best part of five hours to get from Stuttgart to Eigg. He was a man with a mission. But what was it?

Stop one – the doctor's house, where fellow journalist Maxwell MacLeod caught up with the posse.

Vladi asked Maxwell and myself to stay in the van – funny how a good minder can always spot journalists – and the rest went in. Twenty minutes later, the group emerged and moved on to Dolly's house. Maruma came out furious that an old woman could be left with only cold water and one habitable room. Colin told me later that Maruma had been genuinely angry and spluttered that having no bed was hardly a problem now. He wouldn't have been able to sleep, thinking of her situation – and he couldn't believe Schellie had ignored it.

One hour in, and despite the hangovers, islanders were starting to warm to the 'Prof'. He said and did the right thing – precisely the right thing – everywhere. Earlier, at the doctors', he'd been offered a large Macallan. He accepted it (which was socially correct) but because it was before noon he hadn't drunk it (probably also correct for a serious new Laird). Finally, he rolled into the Fyffe household, where Maruma knew there had been a big party the night before – and despite a hasty morning tidy up, a few cans of McEwen's Export were still visible. Maggie and Wes were sitting beside their display, holding mugs of black tea and roll-ups.

Maruma grinned.

Journalist Rob Edwards discovered he was born near Stuttgart as Gotthilf Christian Eckhard Oesterle and changed his name when he saw the word 'Maruma' reflected in a puddle in Geneva.

'Well, Maruma had plans a distillery on Eigg to build... but perhaps instead it should be a brewery?'

There were almost audible intakes of breath. The guy couldn't speak very good English but he had just spoken fluent island. He had tried to make a joke.

There was no doubt; we were starting to slip under Maruma's spell.

Finally, the minibus crossed the island to Colin's house at Kildonan, where Marie had volunteered to cook an evening meal for everyone. Marie has run a Bed and Breakfast (as well as being island Registrar) for decades and is a fantastic cook. No spindly *haute cuisine*, but steak pie, chicken curry, cakes, homemade bread. Maruma started eating and had polished off two bottles of red wine by the time conversation turned to his Concept and reason for choosing Eigg. It was perhaps one of the most fascinating conversations I've ever heard – the man was a genuine mystery, and yet the lives of 65 people hinged on his intentions. I remember trying to explain the limitations of crofting tenure to him, then to Vladi and then to both in rusty A-level German. The main point I was trying to make was that, although he owned the island, he couldn't just build things anywhere he liked. The apparently empty meadows fringing the beautiful white sands of Cleadale Bay for instance, were common grazing.

'Common what?'

'A common place for cows and sheep to eat.'

'What? And the cows have rights over this land? This is impossible.'

'Not the cows, the crofters.'

'Who is a crofter?'

'Many of the islanders are crofters. It's the way the land has been arranged.'

'But if there are no houses then the land surely belongs to me.'

'Well, not necessarily.'

'But there were no cows there either.'

'That doesn't actually matter...'

'So absent cows have more rights than real life owners? This is very strange.'

I could see he didn't believe me. Jings, listening to myself I didn't believe me. The conversation moved away from legal matters and onto Maruma's reasons for buying the island.

During the day he'd been asked this at every house. His answer was that he admired the spirit of the islanders – defying their bad, feudal landowner. And this kind of spirit showed there was a positive energy that could be harnessed by a different owner to help his own Concept succeed.

And that Concept was actually quite simple. Holiday homes, a distillery, art studios, wind turbines and everyone working together in creative harmony. It sounded good.

It was clear the wine, the day, the fatigue and maybe some form of chemical interference slipped into his giant frame were all tempting Maruma to inch nearer to the truth. Or as we would eventually understand about him (and life in general I suppose), a truth.

'I came here Schellenberg and his dog to visit and I made him an offer. Vladi and I for a walk along the coast went to let him decide. We came to this place you the Massacre Cave call, ja?'

At this point Vladi interrupted forcibly.

'Professor Maruma. I don't think this story is now one to tell.'

'No, no Vladi. This one I will tell.'

'Really, I don't think…'

Maruma droned on over the protesting minder. We were on the edge of our seats.

'So we up to this cave climbed where so many people from one clan have been, you know, smoked up by fire by another clan [400 MacDonalds were burned to death in the cave by rival MacLeods in the 16th century] and I stand there at this hole into the Mother Earth that so deep and narrow is. And I to myself think…'

Vladi's hand covers his face.

'I think this cave is like a uterus where the mother new life pushes out. Und like childbirth there is *viel pain aber auch viel energie*. Both pain and new life in the same place. And I think then this is why I must Eigg buy. You understand?'

And the amazing thing was, we sort of did.

'Aye, right enough.'

'Ach, you could look at it like that.'

'It's an amazing cave, that's for sure.'

Vladi looked between his fingers. The madman had done it again.

The next day, they both disappeared quite early and we were all left piecing together what it all might mean.

'Aye well, he's hardly going to evict anyone is he? I mean, that would affect the positive energy he needs for his Concept.'

'Do you think we're part of his Concept or do we need to develop our own Concept to interact with his?'

'For fecks sake, listen to yourselves!'

Of course it had to be Colin.

'You've all been Maruma'd!'

'No we haven't. I think the guy's quite genuine.'

'He's an actor. He didn't put a foot wrong. Anywhere. That's not normal. We still know nothing about him. Nothing. Where does his money come from? When's he coming back? The guy's a phoney.'

And although a few signatures did finally happen, releasing land for sheltered housing, improvements and a new tea room near the pier, Colin was right. Maruma visited only twice and wound up defaulting on one of two loans he'd taken out to buy the island (from Hong Kong and Liechtenstein). After a false alarm suggesting he had sold the island to the Pavarotti Foundation for an offshore opera school (you really couldn't make it up) and a public appeal that saw £1 notes from kids and £100 cheques from grannies pour into Maggie's home (she was now Secretary of the Island of Eigg Appeal Fund) – it was clear community control was just a matter of time, and finding a million quid.

At that point I was Assistant Editor of *The Scotsman*; a useful position to make sure news about the island got coverage. Quite often the angle selected was a matter of fierce dispute. I remember arguing with then News Editor (now *Scotsman* Editor) Ian Stewart over news that Maruma's Professorship had been awarded by a Mickey Mouse establishment in Louisiana. I insisted the fact he'd failed to issue leases (just like his predecessor) was more important. At the time though, Ian was probably right, because Maruma's fake persona was unravelling fast. Clearly he'd been banking on the fact that years of delayed development would mean a flurry of state-funded infrastructure improvements raising the value of the island without Maruma himself having to spend a red cent. The state would issue housing improvement grants as soon as he issued leases. With the merest hint of stability, they'd also make long overdue improvements to the ferry, roads and electricity supply. All Maruma had to do was build high-class log cabins and a distillery overlooking the bay, and watch the income roll in from dream holidays and island whisky with its unique and now world-famous bolshie brand.

But it all took too long – in no small part because Vladi had never understood the intricacies of Scotland's crofting tenure (and let's face it, that's easily done). Land used and held by crofting families in perpetuity could not be owned by the Laird, but non-crofting land couldn't be developed by the crofters either. The result was an unproductive stalemate. Survival on a remote island was well nigh impossible without the capacity to build, improve housing stock and develop. Eigg needed a political solution. But politicians were woefully and shamefully absent.

The local MP at the time, Russell Johnston, refused to help and political etiquette meant almost no other MPs would then get involved. Thankfully though, Lib Dem Councillor Michael Foxley paid no attention to party rules and was a constant supportive presence during the buyout years along with other individual councillors and staff members at Highland Council. Labour MP Brian Wilson was a regular visitor, though the city-based core of the People's Party in Scotland failed to engage. The strangely biddable Tory Scots Secretary Michael Forsyth arrived a year before the buyout and said he was 'rather appalled' with a situation that was 'pretty shocking and not sustainable'. But he came up with no solutions or cash. The young Nationalist and teacher Angus Brendan MacNeil (now SNP MP for the Western Isles) visited but the SNP leadership didn't.

One of the biggest let-downs came from the National Heritage Memorial Fund (NHMF), after a promising start at a meeting in Glasgow presided over by heid bummer Lord Jacob Rothschild. In the wake of the Churchill papers row (bought for the nation at a knockdown £12million in 1995), the Fund realised they looked like a bunch of toffs buying the accoutrements of toffs. They'd taken a great deal of flak over this and didn't know how to reposition the Fund to dodge more hostile headlines. Sitting round the elegant dinner table at a four-star hotel in Glasgow, neither could I (representing *The Scotsman*) nor any of the other Scottish editors summoned to brainstorm a solution.

There was one big catch. The Fund could spend money only on capital investments like the purchase of an asset – building, artefact or art work – with national significance and historical value. What object that mattered to working-class people could possibly fulfil those criteria? Billy Connolly's Banana Boots? The Townhead Library? The Rottenrow Maternity Hospital? The goalpost from *that* 1977 Home International?

Minutes of head scratching over exquisite starters rolled into hours chewing the minimal fat of seaweed-fed Orkney lamb. By the chocolate mousse it was clear we had come up with... nothing.

Rich people own nice things other rich people rate. Poor people don't.

'What about support for islanders who've raised half a million pounds to buy an asset all of Scotland thinks they should have? It's in rather dodgy hands and in danger of being sold off by a foreign bank.'

Puzzled looks all round.

'The island of Eigg.'

Puzzled looks now limited to the London-based Heritage Team.

'Eigg's an island off the west coast with a disastrous history of private owners – now islanders want to buy it. Land is an asset. So why not help them? It may be stretching the definition a bit but...'

The conversation was swiftly moved on.

I finished the chocolate mousse (come on, chocolate is chocolate) and got my coat to go. Lord Rothschild came after me.

'We can't go into detail in public now, but this is a good idea. We'll be back to you soon.' And to my amazement, they did. Eigg got a case study number. Jemimas and Jeremys from the Lottery Fund travelled to Eigg, met the locals, savoured the views, heard the frustrations and got religion. It was like Bill Forsyth's *Local Hero* all over again (in those days before mobiles the Lottery folk even had to use the island's scenic but solitary red phone box). Things progressed until an offer was ready.

I was working in London at that point and stayed in a hotel near Broadcasting House run (even then) by East Europeans. I'd been staying on a regular basis three nights a week for several years – and had long chats with staff in the wee small hours when I was dropped back after presenting BBC2's aptly named *Midnight Hour*. As a result, I generally got the best room in the place with two windows facing away from the noisy street and, to combat the stifling warmth of summer evenings, a blessed electric fan.

Anyway, Colin Carr arrived in Euston looking strange with no sheepdog at his heel. The NHMF meeting was that same night, and though the man from the Hebrides was smiling, he was clearly a fish out of water. Colin didn't want to take in the Galleries, Buckingham Palace or the shops. We went over the underground route several times but finally booked a taxi and another to get him straight back to the sleeper afterwards.

I left him looking decidedly uneasy – as it turned out, with just cause.

A poisoned chalice was on offer – a million pounds available right then and there *if* Colin agreed public agencies would have a controlling majority stake in Eigg with islanders in the minority. Forty-nine per cent control might have seemed pretty good to a tired man who'd travelled alone for three days to reach the feet of the great and the good. But Colin got up, thanked them for their time and walked out. No way would locals accept less than 51 per cent control, even if that meant losing the million pounds. The offer was removed from the table.

I was furious at the strings attached by lottery bosses but told to shut up. Wiser, calmer heads already realised the buyout would inevitably happen and lottery cash would be useful afterwards for improvement projects waiting in the wings. The Fund would deliver – eventually.

Back home, no-one questioned Colin's decision. Perhaps more wise words were ringing in their ears. The charismatic ringleader of the Assynt crofters, the late Allan MacRae, had visited Eigg just after the historic Sutherland buyout in 1993 – and his advice was simple. Buy everything. Buy all the rights. Don't be fobbed off. Get everything – go for gold.

Colin's decisive response to the NHMF proved Eigg was actually already run by the community – or as human ecologist and fellow Isle of Eigg Trustee Alastair McIntosh put it, 'un-lairdable'. With conventional landowners scared off, it was only a matter of time before the right cheque came through Maggie's door to make that informal reality a formal truth.

And a few months later, it happened. I still don't know the identity of the anonymous female donor from the North of England – Maggie Fyffe insists it wasn't Catherine Cookson – but she coughed up more than £900,000. Deals were done with the Lichtenstein bank and finally, in April, Colin appeared unexpectedly in Edinburgh, saying he was down for a meeting with 'the department' about sheep dip. We got through one course of a lunch before he cracked.

'We've bought the island – there's a press conference in the Caley [Caledonian Hotel] in an hour!'

So with backing from the public, the mystery donor, friends, a few individual politicians, the Highland Council and the Scottish Wildlife Trust, Eigg made history as the first Scottish island to be bought by its inhabitants. Ever.

Why does the Eigg saga matter?

Well, it's a great tale and this is just one tiny part and one person's subjective version.[6]

But it reveals some truths about Scottish society which are both inspiring and downright alarming. In a country that likes to think of itself as a modern democracy, it took 65 people on Eigg an unbelievable eight years and a community buyout just to make sure each island tenant had a lease. Eight solid years of campaigning, organising, focussing on very little else and withstanding every attempt at bad-mouthing, deflection and obstruction. Before that, several generations spent their precious lives learning to dance round the egos of 'great men', second guess their temperaments and hang onto empty promises in the pursuit of security.

So much effort has to be expended in Scotland to reach a level of fairness that's been normal in other neighbouring nations for centuries.

That's why it's important not to leave the story in 1997 at the buyout, when only a point had been made. The Eiggachs real triumph was only possible once they had full control and the chance to make a mess or a miracle. And full control only happened after one final attempt by Keith Schellenberg to rain on the islanders' parade.

In 1999, the aggrieved former landowner took legal action against several journalists, including myself. He tackled the *Guardian* first in the High Court, forcing islanders and supporters to write submissions of evidence and make long expensive journeys south to London for the trial. Mercifully, the defamation case collapsed within days, cementing Schellenberg's reputation as a deluded and bitter man,

---

6 C. Dressler, *Eigg: The Story of an Island* (Edinburgh: Birlinn, 2007) and A. MacIntosh, *Soil and Soul: People Versus Corporate Power* (London: Aurum Press, 2001).

ending the threat of legal action against anyone else and removing the only shadow left hanging over the Eigg buyout.[7]

So what did the Eiggachs do with this new-found freedom? The first action – after a week-long party – was the hardest. Peppercorn rents had to be raised to finance repairs – that wasn't universally popular. Valuable contracts for housing repairs had to be drawn up and awarded – bad feeling could easily have been generated if contracts had gone to one local builder or an off-island firm. Instead the Eigg men decided to work together, not in competition, and formed the Isle of Eigg Building Co-operative, sharing contracts, income and employment opportunities. Within a few years the Co-operative had acquired considerable expertise and Eigg had full male employment – though of course activity ebbed and flowed.

New tenants had to be chosen for the renovated housing. Freed from the council allocations policy, which of the shortlisted applicants would Eiggachs favour? George Carr – the young, local, single farmer and occupant of the aforementioned draughty 'penthouse'; an elderly woman and Eigg native living near Mallaig, or Grace and Tasha, the 20-something daughters of two Eigg families? Shrewdly, the Trust gave the first renovated house to the two gals sharing, echoing a Norwegian study of the same year which showed that depopulation generally starts with disaffected young women – not men.

Norway's first female Minister of Agriculture, Gunhild Øyangen, had surveyed areas losing people and discovered that contrary to local mythology it was local women who were leaving first:

> The young girl dreams of another life than her mother's. A professional career may be easier to obtain in the cities. The small villages are felt to be narrow-minded with no space for untraditional or unconventional behaviour. The girls lack relevant female role models, and few local jobs fit with their future plans. Many social and cultural activities are those that men favour, like hunting and fishing, and this does not necessarily attract younger women.

---

7 On three occasions, Mr Justice Morland, the trial judge, suggested to the wealthy businessman he should speak to his QC about the status of his case. 'If I were trying this case on my own, without a jury, it is likely I would already have come to the conclusion that sufficient facts had been proved to be true to justify the comments made about you.' Throughout the five-week trial, a picture emerged of Keith Schellenberg as a 'Toad of Toad Hall' character: racing around the island in his Rolls Royce, wearing a tweed jacket and goggles, his scarf flapping in the wind and with little regard for anybody else. Jamie Wilson, *The Guardian* 20/05/1999.

The Norwegian solution was truly radical. They introduced quotas to get women into local planning and politics – 'women can be a vitamin injection in the democratic process.' They paid remote mums or dads who wanted to bring up their children full time. They gave special funding to women setting up businesses in remote areas on the grounds that 'women's ventures add value to the raw materials produced by male labour.' They backed places for socialising other than the sheep fank. They put public money into creating challenging indoor jobs not just more jobs at fish farms. And they paid for good public transport to stop women feeling trapped without access to boats or cars.[8] Without even reading the report, the Eigg islanders had intuitively reached the same conclusion and made an inspired departure from the usual social housing priorities. Grace and Tasha were friends back then – today they are both young mums living on Eigg with their own children. George left to study agriculture and came back to run Lagg Farm with his partner Saira and their young daughter. Putting young women first, putting friendship on a par with marriage and keeping young folk on the island has been Eigg's greatest achievement.

'Eiggtricity' came along in 2008 when expensive, polluting diesel was finally replaced with a mini-grid integrating solar, wind and hydro energy and a unique system of 'demand management' – islanders cannot use more than 5KW without tripping their house and businesses have a 10KW limit. The system was chosen by Eiggachs and to date no-one's been disconnected – switching off one device before switching another on is embedded island behaviour. House building is now relatively easy as long as newcomers stick to preselected plots where land's contributed at a discounted rate so young folk can afford to build and stay. As a result, Eigg's population is rising in contrast to her privately and quango-owned island neighbours of Muck, Rum and Canna.

Eiggtricity meant affordable energy security at long last, international publicity and a winning entry to the NESTA challenge (beating 100 other shortlisted communities across the UK) after islanders managed to cut emissions by a third in 2009.

---

8   L. Riddoch, *Riddoch on the Outer Hebrides*, Luath 2006.

Eigg energy before (diesel generator) and after (homemade solar panel).

Of course, Eigg is no Nirvana. There are disagreements. A few folk still remain opposed to the buyout. Under-employment is a worry. Volunteer burnout is a constant risk. And isolation is a big problem – especially in winter. In 2012, the GP of more than a decade, Rachel Weldon, took her own life – no-one had been aware of the near-permanent pressure that came with being the only health professional and on-call GP serving four island communities. The danger of trying to demonstrate success on Eigg is to suggest island life is perfect. It's not.

On Eigg, as in life, success is measured by the way problems are tackled not their improbable absence. The island's fate is now squarely in the hands of the people who live there. Quangos, councils, government departments and passing millionaires must all deal with islanders as equals – not easy to ignore, disposable locals. That's a big result for islanders – and of course the ripples have spread far wider.

Eigg ensured that a Land Reform Act – including a Community Right to Buy and legal rights of access – became the first substantial piece of legislation passed by the new Scottish Parliament in 2003.[9]

---

9   The Community Right to Buy (CRtB) allows Scottish communities with less than 10,000 people to register an interest in land and have the opportunity to buy when it comes up for sale… after which the community body will be given six months to conclude the purchase: Outlaw.com 26/07/2012.

Since then, 17 land buyouts have taken place and a 2011 report shows those communities are measurably more resilient than they were as private fiefdoms. In Stòras Uibhist on South Uist, turnover is ten times higher than it was in 2006, when Scotland's largest community buyout took place. In general, school rolls have almost doubled, population has increased, energy supply systems have improved, local land ownership has prompted young people to build homes and start families and old people don't face the unpalatable choice of living locally without heat or in a distant old folk's home without company. Historian Professor Jim Hunter has calculated that all the community buyouts and associated improvement grants have probably cost the public purse £100 million – roughly equivalent to eight weeks of agricultural subsidy.[10] Do many other public realm projects show anything like such a healthy return on investment – in human or monetary terms?

And yet, there's still scepticism – about buyouts, community control and the long term capacity of people managing their own land. Amazingly, the first time I witnessed such naked hostility towards the viability of Eigg was amongst their nearest mainland neighbours on 'Independence Day' itself. Colin Carr, Maxwell MacLeod and I were waiting at Arisaig for the Doctor's boat to make a triumphant crossing to the island after that heady day in Edinburgh. We decided to have a 'hair of the dog' and went into the hotel bar. A local man stood with his pint, one foot on the rail, one elbow on the counter. He glanced up at Colin.

'You'll be pleased with yourselves,' he said.

Colin nodded and picked up his pint.

'We are.' News of Eigg was audible on a radio somewhere in the background. The well-wisher cleared his throat.

'I give you five weeks.' I was quietly appalled but Colin just smiled: 'That long?'

In the days, weeks, months and years that followed, the Arisaig doubter was not alone in predicting and even inciting disaster for the plucky, over-confident islanders. Some Scots seem to have a deep-seated emotional need for all who challenge the status quo to meet with ignominious failure. Issy MacPhail experienced the same reac-

---

10 J. Hunter, *From the Low Tide of the Sea to the Highest Mountain Top* (Scotland: Islands Book Trust, 2012).

tion to the success of the Assynt Crofters and developed her 'crabs in the bucket' theory to explain it. Apparently if one crab tries to crawl out, the rest will pull it back in. The message seems to be, 'If we're going down, we're all going down together.'

That day in 1997, the Eiggachs were finally on a fast-track to community development, leaving others to follow in their wake, stuck forever in the feudal slow lane. Their new perspective had allowed the Eiggachs to look at what was once an insurmountable obstacle and find a route to the summit – a bit like the route up the rocky Sgurr itself.

It would be easier for similarly disadvantaged communities to believe there was no alternative to the status quo but now the damned Eigg folk had visibly demonstrated otherwise. And the closer folk lived, the better they knew that the islanders were no super humans but ordinary west coasters like themselves. There was no escaping the truth and that really hurt.

Of course, for every lukewarm response there were three or four ecstatic messages of congratulations and goodwill. In the end though, Eigg's victory did not prompt a tidal rush of communities competing to repeat their declaration of UDI – despite funding from the newly established Scottish Land Fund. Why not?

The Sgurr – a steep cliff face from one angle but an accessible summit
(and great wind energy site) from another.

For one thing, the inspiring human story of triumph over adversity on Eigg was all too quickly subsumed into a complex legal, political and historical case for land reform – absolutely necessary, but alienating for non-specialists. Broadcasters like the BBC were wary about 'taking sides' and urban Scots were unable to see parallels between dramatic land battles 'in the sticks' and city problems of land scarcity and high prices on their own doorsteps. Few small mainland communities were well-enough organised to take advantage of the new buyout legislation. And relatively few estates came onto the market anyway, giving locals little chance to make pre-emptive bids.

All in all, the community buyouts of the nineties and noughties started a slow burn on neighbouring Hebridean islands, but failed to set the mainland heather alight. Now – a decade after Scotland's historic land reform legislation – fewer than one in ten communities that registered a desire to buy land actually managed to do it, and only 142 communities out of tens of thousands even tried. That could mean all in the garden is rosy... or it could mean the community buyout model is too daunting for all but the most thrawn island communities like Eigg.

I'd plump for the latter explanation. Despite the challenge posed by Eigg, Gigha, Knoydart, Stòras Uibhist and North Harris, it's generally been business as usual for Scotland's landowners – buoyed by new revenue streams from wind turbines, conservation agreements agricultural subsidies and forestry grants.

Scotland still has one of the most concentrated patterns of land-ownership in Europe.[11] The government cannot finance more than a few buyouts and individuals still cannot get their hands on small, affordable parcels of land. The ball is still in the court of the large land-owner.

Working together and flat-out for eight long years, the Eigg folk did manage to deter any rival bidder, raised more money in a public appeal than the combined value of all their own homes and turned the tide of Scottish history.[12] But the Eiggachs also quietly tolerated impos-

---

11   To date, 142 applications to register a community interest in land have been submitted under the provisions in the Land Reform Act, of which 95 have been approved. Of these, 33 have had the chance to go ahead and purchase land and 11 have been successful in doing so, according to Scottish Government figures: Outlaw.com 26/07/2012.

12   Eigg was purchased on 12 June 1997 for £1.75 million by the Isle of Eigg Heritage Trust (which took over from the Isle of Eigg Trust), a partnership in which Eigg residents have the majority of trustees along with representatives from Highland Council & the Scottish Wildlife Trust.

sible circumstances for decades before making a public fuss or daring to believe they could do better than absentee landowners. Which says two things: the dead hand of disempowerment isn't dislodged fast and if you stand around expecting formal help from any part of the Scottish political establishment, you'll wait forever.

Eigg demonstrated that land reform is about people not soil, the present not the past and relevant to every Scottish community, not just remote ones. And yet an Eigg-style buyout is still a giant leap from a standing start for most communities. As a result, the chain of (largely Hebridean) one-offs is an ever-growing exception to a still dominant rule of quasi-feudal land ownership. Which means stultifying 'Old Eigg'-style situations are being tolerated by people across Scotland right now, as help is focused on those local fighting forces able to bid successfully for limited public cash.

Why is that?

Put simply, almost everyone in authority still has more faith in the capacity of tweed-jacketed, well-spoken self-made millionaires than in local people. It was the unpalatable truth in 1997 – and it's the unpalatable truth today.

Certainly Land Reform legislation has helped communities buy land, islands, bridges, pubs, wind turbines, libraries, orchards, woodlands and even farms and these ventures have been life-changing for all involved. But there isn't enough cash in Christendom to fund the purchase of very parcel of land, forest or water, nor the energy amongst unpaid volunteers with day jobs. And actually, why should there be?

Community buyouts alone will not reverse the disempowerment experienced all over Scotland today. The community on Eigg is now one of Scotland's most capable – tackling everything from depopulation and climate change to saving the corncrake. I've visited the island more than sixty times over two decades. Without frequent visits and strong friendships there it may be impossible to appreciate the degree of change. But it's been empowerment the very hard way.

In more democratic countries with no feudal landownership there have been no community buyouts. In Norway, for example, land has been owned or rented on long secure leases by tens of thousands of individual Norwegians for centuries. All rural communities also own common land – often planted with trees and co-operatively managed to yield a local income and steady supply of wood – and exercise control through small municipal councils.

Here, community activists get marginalised unless they join a political party, become a councillor and travel to distant council meetings where they learn to micro-manage other communities they have no time to visit. There, the small size of municipal councils allows activists to stay at home but still get involved in the formal business of local self government – without having to spend millions taking over massive estates.

Widespread land ownership, land taxes and local control in Norway mean communities don't need to buy what individuals already own and voters democratically control. The community buyout is a typically piecemeal, Scottish solution to a larger problem we don't have the will to tackle universally, systematically or at source.Those who work hardest may escape the blight of feudal-style landownership. Those who can't, must bide their time. Don't get me wrong. The amount of money involved in community buyouts has produced amazing returns from relatively small investments. But the wider system remains intact with no prospect of an end to the overall shortage of available land. Cash is easier to pledge than change.

The easy way to transform Scotland overnight is to swap our current property-based Council Tax for a Land Tax so large landowners and speculators would have a financial incentive to 'divest' fallow acres and unused buildings or face eye-watering tax demands. The Scottish Parliament could legislate to give all children (not just the eldest son) the legal right to inherit land – the main way large estates elsewhere were 'naturally' broken into manageable, diverse blocks. Holyrood could make 'sporting estates' pay business rates – currently they don't – and could replace toothless community councils with tax-raising parish councils as an 'ultra-local' tier of democratic control and service delivery.

Almost all of these changes could be made today and could be recommended by the Scottish Government's Land Review Group. They could – but I'm not holding my breath.

Land reform still sounds too remote and too radical, there are still too many vested interests to annoy, and there's too little political belief in the capacity of Scotland's people to manage their own communities – whether they own them or not.

In his seminal book *Who Owns Scotland,* Andy Wightman obs-erved that 25 per cent of large estates have been held by the same family for over four centuries, and the majority of aristocratic families who owned land in 1872 still own it today.[13]

Indeed, there was more open challenge to Scotland's concentrated pattern of landownership in the Victorian era. Tom Johnston, born in 1882, wrote an exposé of the Scottish aristocracy in *Our Scots Noble Families* which became a controversial bestseller in 1909.[14] He noted with outrage that miners and salt workers till 1799 were 'bought and sold as part and parcel of the pits in which they were condemned to work for life,' and recounted Hugh Miller's description of a 'slave village' at Niddrie Mill near Edinburgh where the collier women, 'poor, over-toiled creatures,' carried coal up a long stair inserted in one of the shafts, shifting a hundredweight from sea level to the top of Ben Lomond with each day's labour. The young journalist then 'exposed' the people he blamed for such exploitation – every noble family in the land:

> The Scott's of Buccleugh, [sic] descended from border thieves, land pirates and freebooters, still boast their pedigree. The blood of knaves and moonlighters has by process of snobbery become blue blood; lands raped from the weak and unfortunate now support arrogance in luxury.

And Johnston famously concludes:

> Today in Scotland our artisans and peasants appear to believe that these ancient noble families hold their privileges and lands at the behest of Divine Providence; that their wealth has been justly earned and that their titles are but rewards for honest service to the state.
>
> The first step in reform... is to destroy those superstitions. Show the people that our old nobility is not noble; that's its lands are stolen lands – stolen either by force or fraud. So long as half a dozen families own one-half of Scotland, so long will countless families own none of it.

This angry revolutionary went on to become the outstanding secretary of state for Scotland in the wartime coalition under Churchill, who brought Hydro Electricity to the Highlands. And yet even with such

---

13   Over 1,000 acres in size.
14   Brian Osborne in the introduction to Thomas Johnston, *Our Scots Noble Families.*

formidable powers, the exceptional Tom Johnston could not push any further against landed power. So, the force of history has still not been undone. Scotland's law and tax systems still encourage vast estates and absent landowners. Stifled, frustrated communities like pre-buy-out Eigg exist across Scotland. This should be one of Scotland's most urgent concerns.

Instead, questions about the way land is owned are regarded as rude, personal gripes against upstanding people or an irrelevance in this modern age. Yet we are physical creatures who experience the world first and foremost via the patch of earth that supports and surrounds us. To ask who owns it is simply to pose a basic question about democracy and human development.

A nation has no greater asset than its people and yet the energy of many Scots is being wasted, in a mass of uneven battles for basic human rights, even as we speak. It took 65 people on Eigg eight years and a community buyout to give each island tenant a lease. No wonder Scots have been ground down. No wonder a grim air of defiance is all many have inherited. No wonder people have left. The miracle is that so many have stayed. Those people have self-selected as stoic beyond belief and thoroughly adapted to their environments. To lose them now would be to lose an essential building block in a delicate human ecosystem. And yet, those precious people are still leaving rural communities for the age-old reasons – no land, no housing and no prospects.

The good news is that after everything, Eigg is now thriving in its own co-operative, creative, eco-friendly way and the buds of development are present in the population of each thwarted community. The job of a democracy is simply to shift heaven and earth to put those people first.

In Scotland, it still isn't happening.

CHAPTER SIX

Scotland's Natural Assets – Look, But Don't Touch

DIRECTLY ACROSS THE Minch from Eigg lies the tiny village of Arisaig. I was first shown round more than twenty years ago by a local woman living in her car at the time. Even with the comparatively good wage of a hotel housekeeper, Rosemarie MacEachen couldn't buy or even rent local summer accommodation. That seemed quite unbelievable – hence our late evening stroll through the village as Rosie listed the ownership credentials of each house. It turned out most of the quaint, traditional white-washed cottages in the picturesque, loch-side village were second homes. A few had been council houses (till the Right to Buy removed them from the social rented sector) and new building was simply impossible. A vast 8,320 acres lay empty beyond the village, owned by the Arisaig Estate, which was owned by Amphill Investments, which was owned in turn by Xavier Namy.[1] And Xavier didn't want to sell any land back then – at least not cheaply.

Eventually the French landowner did make a tidy sum from land sales, when the route for an improved double-track road to the Isles between Lochailort and Morar was finally approved. But while those protracted negotiations were taking place, no new housing or investment in Mallaig's lucrative prawn fishing could take place. Rosemarie left, like many other young locals, and drivers of massive, Mallaig-based, articulated lorries spent another decade weaving in and out of passing places on Britain's last bit of mainland single-track trunk road.

Of course, that was some time ago. Now the A830 has been upgraded, the Land Reform Act has been passed, feudal tenure has been abolished and the government is committed to empowering local communities. But the feudal spirit lives on. Local landowners still block and delay local initiatives, as Arisaig Community Trust's 2011 Development Plan demonstrates:

---

1   Andy Wightman, *Who Owns Scotland* (Edinburgh: Canongate, 1996).

Our previous playing field became a casualty of the new A830 road construction. The village was offered a piece of ground by a local landowner, and protracted negotiations began to acquire a long-term lease (the landowner did not want to sell the land). We have at last finalised a 50-year lease on the field and are slowly beginning to improve the playing surface.

A new pier seems to be impossible:

It is unlikely that the community will be able to realise this ambition, given the current ownership of the Arisaig Estate, which controls the foreshore surrounding the village. If the Estate were to change hands, then such a project might become feasible.

Getting land for vegetables, allotments and poly tunnels is another impossible dream:

A site alongside the new playing field had been identified for garden plots and the landowner was willing to lease the land, but this, unfortunately, became a casualty of protracted lease negotiations. We are actively looking for other sites.

But if you go to Arisaig today, all will probably seem hunky dory. You won't hear anti-landowner remarks. You won't encounter resentment. You won't see insecurity. And you won't witness depopulation. There will be no sign over one home saying 'securely owned by happy people' and another saying 'stressed out tenants in a winter let hoping to find a caravan for the summer soon'. Buildings are mute. They don't readily confess to being tied houses (where tenants are set for eviction once working lives or job contracts are over). They don't clype about dampness or bad landlords. You can't tell which home has been lovingly chosen and which is simply a last resort.

But you can gaze out on mile after empty mile around Arisaig and find it impossible to believe local people have no ownership of such an abundant land resource. It's even harder to imagine how much that thwarts democratic spirit and entrepreneurial muscle.

So think about it now. Who is generous when they are uncertain? Who invests when improvement might only result in higher rents? Who plans under such circumstances? And when it's been like this for generations, who irritates others with the naïve Pollyanna-like belief that things might suddenly improve?

Quiet, real quiet, too quiet

Sociologists and other academics have observed the phenomenon of 'learned silence' amongst disempowered communities all over the world. Paolo Freire analysed it in his ground-breaking book, *Pedagogy of the Oppressed.*[2]

Every reader seems to take something different from that 1970s classic, but I was struck by Freire's discussion of inferiorism – a set of learned beliefs, outlooks and behaviours which constitute vital survival skills for the dispossessed. Pessimism, wariness and low expectations, for example, all protect the poor against constant disappointment. Those most skilled will bite their lip and walk away from confrontations with authority, knowing they cannot win. They will discourage the rebellious, defiant and ambitious – for everyone's sake. That way at least, all will survive.

None of these are skills in the minds of successful Scots. But for those in the weakest situations, where warm words mask endless and chronic inequality, the ability to suppress high expectations is a useful skill in the art of getting by. The trouble is that these attitudes – the emotional legacy of disempowerment – don't disappear overnight even when conditions finally improve.

Freire maintains marginalised people must consciously 'unlearn' what they still regard (deep down) as life skills, traditions and legacies inherited from respected forebears. That's hard.

For those who don't unlearn old, ultra-cautious ways, the effort involved in community activity will seem overwhelming and threatening. For all sorts of reasons, the people who most need change may be the last to seek it out and will generally have had least experience of managing any local assets before a 'big opportunity' suddenly arises and their mettle is suddenly tested.

Mercifully, though, there are exceptions.

One was the Assynt buyout. When Lord Vestey carved the North Lochinver Estate out of his massive northern domain and put it up for sale in 1989 – provocatively advertising the populated land as 'an

---

2 'There is no such thing as a neutral education process. Education either functions as an instrument which is used to facilitate the integration of generations into the logic of the present system and bring about conformity to it, or it becomes the "practice of freedom", the means by which men and women deal critically with reality and discover how to participate in the transformation of their world.' Richard Shaull, drawing on Paulo Freire in Gramsci, Freire and Peter Mayo, *Adult Education: Possibilities for Transformative Action* (London: Macmillan, 1999).

unspoilt wilderness' – he drew boundaries already used by the local Crofters Union branch. The estate was bought by Scandinavian Property Services Ltd but when that company went bust in 1992, the Assynt Crofters Trust didn't hesitate to acquire it from the liquidator. Crofters living on this 'new' parcel of land already knew and trusted one another and had a shared history of practical deeds, land management, complaint mediation and action. If Vestey had doubled the acreage, he might easily have weakened the crofters' resolve by requiring them to bond with relatively unknown, distant neighbours. As it was, the only real obstacle the Assynt crofters faced was themselves, and that negative inner voice constantly muttering – *dinnae get above yourselves.*

Sociology has something useful to say about that too.

Frenchman Pierre Bourdieu devised the concept of 'cultural capital' – the knowledge, skills, education, and outlooks which combine to determine what people like to do, see, wear, listen to, eat and drink. 'Taste' or 'habitus' may seem individual, but according to Bourdieu, cultural preferences are chosen, even preset by the social or class group we belong to.

Anyone can buy a painting, for example, but no-one can buy the ability to appreciate it. Cultural capital is not a commodity that can be bought or traded but generally arises from membership of a certain group or class. That may sound unduly determinist. But in 2013, the 'Great British Class Survey' effectively acknowledged Bourdieu by adding economic, social and cultural capital[3] as new dimensions to Britains 'old' class divisions of working, middle and upper class. But how does habitus work?

Habitus means working-class Scots will not adopt double-barrelled names after marriage in case they sound pretentious and middle-class, young folk will not listen to classical music lest they seem prematurely aged and serious-minded people will not even accidentally know the names of *X Factor* finalists lest they lose credibility with friends. 'Each to their own', you might say – but if poor Scots feel somehow 'honour bound' to reject the mind-set and cultural preferences of middle-class managers, then self-improving behaviour like eating well, quitting cigarettes or running at lunchtime will feel like forbidden fruit or acts of betrayal.

---

3   http://www.bbc.co.uk/news/uk-22007058.

If Bourdieu is right, this is potent and dangerous stuff. Cultural preferences feel natural and instinctive, so individuals feel they are betraying roots and letting their 'side' down by adopting the habits of other classes. Poor Scots may even feel compelled to avoid healthy living altogether if that's seen as the preserve the wealthy and privileged. Preserving group identity matters more – so actions that appear self-defeating to 'right-thinking people', can still serve to maintain a place in the group.

So 'choice' is often not choice at all. Loyalty and fear of siding with the opposition are powerful dynamics in Scottish society. Perhaps Bourdieu's theory helps explain why.

In my own case, like the descendant of many other cleared Highland families, I cannot fish, ski, sail or hunt. That always seemed perfectly normal in my world until I went to Norway, where only the disabled or seriously overweight don't regularly do some of these activities. Over there the habitus is different. 'Country sports' are not the preserve of an elite. Hunting has nothing to do with wearing plus fours and a deerstalker, skiing doesn't mean you have *au pairs* to mind the kids, fishing doesn't mark you out as a friend of the landed gentry and sailing doesn't automatically connect you with the well-heeled, summer visitors of the county set.

Now I'll grant you these are all clichéd views of sports (particularly fishing) which are actually enjoyed by a wide range of humanity – even in Scotland. But habitus doesn't depend on reality – just on the way activities are perceived.

If your group thinks sailing is elitist, it wouldn't matter if you were skelping along on a boat made by the great-great-grandson of Robert Burns with Nelson Mandela at the helm fundraising for Oxfam. It would still feel wrong.

Of course all of this is my subjective interpretation of a sociological theory whose academic masters rarely depart from their own high-falutin habitus of complex language to provide comprehensible examples. Habitus is also nigh on impossible to measure or prove. That doesn't make Bourdieu's theory any less powerful.

So how does it apply to the fraught world of land ownership?

Well, if the dispossessed don't want to share any characteristics with the landowning class, they won't want to own land, manage the countryside, hunt, fish, own any kind of second home, exhibit knowl-edge of nature or mix with heavily accented people who do.

More than that, if land and the countryside appear to belong exclu-sively to the wealthy, then Bourdieu's theory suggests the urban dis-possessed will shun all knowledge of that domain and all experience of the great outdoors to maintain group cohesion and their own dis-tinct identity. Imagine Marvin from *The Scheme* sailing on the Clyde, joining a mass clean-up of Kilmarnock, going to see a play (even with a 100 per cent discount for the unemployed), watching a 'how to quit smoking' video by a well-spoken member of the Scottish Rugby squad, eating lettuce, reading a book or even wearing glasses – it's not going to happen. Such a self-styled wild man would rather be seen dead than consciously taking care of himself (his girlfriend or the planet).

Of course, Red Clydeside produced a host of exceptions. But hardy 'Men of the Mountains' like Jock Nimlin, Tom Weir and Hamish MacInnes walked miles, rowed even further and slept in caves, bothies and even under bridges in the rain – to distinguish themselves from the soft, feather-bedded, deer-shooting elite whose louche enjoyment of the land had to look completely different in character.

According to Bourdieu, the essential desire for social solidarity creates taste and demands conformity – so for tens of thousands of working-class Scots who weren't as hardy as Jock Nimlin, it's been simpler to regard the land and countryside as 'out of bounds.'

Perhaps I'm laying it on a bit thick. Perhaps I have misinterpreted Bourdieu (though I wouldn't be the first). Or perhaps this matters hugely.

Perhaps excluded Scots have no confidence problem at all but a habitus that effectively stops them joining in 'healthy' and 'out-doorsy' activities associated with natural resources because they have traditionally been the preserve of the upper classes. To stretch the point further, perhaps such a profoundly unequal nation isn't really a nation at all – just a clutch of wary groups for whom maintaining group iden-tity and class cohesion is more important than any new, larger loyalty. Put absolutely bluntly, such a divided, unequal nation is unlikely to push wholeheartedly for a cause like Scottish independence. Why bother when folk have got far smaller fish to fry?

As the redoubtable Sinead O'Connor once put it – 'I do not want what I haven't got.'

If ordinary Scots haven't got access to land without kow-towing, ingratiation, spending a small fortune or marrying a Duke or Countess, then ordinary Scots may quickly decide they don't really want access to land, or any of the 'fancy' activities that occur upon it. This may seem like a self-limiting ordinance – but in the face of systematic exclusion, group solidarity is more important to maintain. Even when times change, wealthier group members will continue the boycott. To paraphrase Sinead, 'I still do not want what others haven't got'.

This kind of cold-shouldering undoubtedly wounds sensitive landowners with access to land resources which aren't generally shared. Being resented, held at a distance and even despised is not a chosen part of anyone's habitus. That, for example, was what eventually happened to Keith Schellenberg on Eigg – and it must have been a miserable experience. But an inevitable one, given his near total control over island life and readily articulated perception of his own superior status.

Resolving the land problem in Scotland would remove nature from the exclusive habitus of a wealthy elite. It could soften the hurt-hardened, 'couldn't give a toss' reflex of the underclass at the epicentre of the Scottish Effect, re-establish connection and produce engagement. We know easy access to land does all these things – it's why estate-owning families have hung onto their land against all comers for centuries.

And they have. If this all sounds too complex to unravel, too airy-fairy to bother with or too much like hard emotional work, then bear this in mind:

One thousand landowners still own more than 60 per cent of privately owned rural land in Scotland.[4]

Locals have no right to shoot deer or fish from rivers they've lived beside for generations. Nor until 1992 had tenants the right to plant trees, even on crofting land.[5]

These manifestations of feudalism's icy grip are extraordinary, and yet for the majority of urban Scots, also meaningless because of their sheer lack of familiarity with our land.

This is how deeply landlessness is embedded in the Scottish psyche. After all, how many times has the average Joe (or Josephine)

---

4   Wightman A, The Poor Had No Lawyers Birlinn (2012)
5   Scottish Executive, Crofting Reform - Proposals for Legislation, SE/2002/105, Edinburgh, 2002.

wanted to fell a tree? How many folk have walked beyond a car park
or picnic spot in the Scottish countryside, let alone from coast to coast?
Who can fish? Who amongst Scotland's city and town-dwelling majority knows a member of Scotland's landowning aristocracy, a crofter, a
tenant farmer or indeed anyone who lives on the land? Who can ski
(and who learned that skill in Scotland, not the Alps)? Who can sail
(even though our country is surrounded by sea and studded with lochs
and rivers)? Who can visualise 241,887 acres -- the size of Scotland's
largest privately owned estate? Is that a truly vast amount of land or
just a lot? Actually, the Buccleuch estate in the Borders is bigger than
137,000 football pitches or the landmass of Islay and Jura combined
– but who knows those west coast whisky islands well enough to be
aided by the comparison? Who feels instead that I have just heaped
unknown world upon unknown world?

Familiarity with land is not in the habitus of the average Scot.

City-dwellers can cheerfully go for years without setting foot on
heather moor, wheat field, seaside, riverbank or forest path. Munro
baggers can happily access mountain summits every weekend without
wondering why the country around them is so utterly empty. Rural Scots
can be certain there's not a hope in hell of coaxing a small, affordable
parcel of land from the average hereditary landowner. As a result, Scots'
experience of land and nature is full of looking not touching; passing not
stopping; watching not acting and renting not owning.

But you don't miss what you've never had. Indeed, if Bourdieu is
right, you can't miss what your class or family has never had without
feeling you have abandoned their values. Ordinary Scots have lived for
so long without the expectation of more than temporary and conditional access to land, the whole vexed issue of 'Who Owns Scotland?'
has become rather academic. Statistics fail to move us. If they did, the
combined lifetimes of research produced by Professor Jim Hunter and
Andy Wightman would have created political change within days.[6]

Land needs to be hauled up from the distant past, out of the dusty
Sassine Register and put back on the tips of our tongues. We should size
it up. Lust after it. Fantasise about it. Bid for it. Plan on it. Break the rules
and build on it. Bide on it. Talk about it – and above all – want it.

---

6   I don't propose to repeat the excellent and definitive work by Professor Jim Hunter and Andy Wightman laying
    out the roots and dimensions of Scotland's land problems in Andy's *The Poor Had no Lawyers*, and Jim's *The
    Making of the Crofting Community*.

A 'normal country' would have a welter of ideas about how people could use land – mono-cultural Scotland, by contrast, has just a few: the sporting estate, the fenced-off forest and the fenced-off farm. If nature abhors a vacuum and detests straight lines, I'd guess she'd also feel twitchy about the dull conformity of that. And yet, Scots apparently do not. Empty is normal. Forlorn is natural. Hierarchy is traditional. Privacy is paramount. Development is problematic. And better use of natural resources is none of our business. It could be otherwise – as these young Scottish architects have demonstrated.

The Spaces of Labour project emerged in 2009 from a design studio directed by Dr Jonathan Charley at the University of Strathclyde's Department of Architecture. 'Reimagining a productive Landscape for Scotland' looked at the fate of Scotland's industrial built

Figure 11: Spaces of Labour – Mixed use on a Scottish loch; Madden & Thomson

Figure 12: Spaces of Labour – Mixed use in a Scottish glen; Madden & Thomson

heritage and imagined what possible new forms of production and architecture might emerge in the 21st century. The two images above, produced by students Liam Madden and Iain Thomson, 'contradict the idealised vision of the Highlands and instead playfully render it as a highly productive landscape producing everything from fish, to energy, textiles and plants for pharmaceuticals'.

This – or a variation of this – is how Scotland could be. But if empty, 'pristine' land and lochs can't be imagined differently, change will never happen.

If Scots can't see the link between land scarcity, housing costs, poor health, disempowerment and economic under-performance, land reform will go no further. No matter what the latest Land Reform Review Panel recommends. Change only comes when people can visualise things being otherwise.

It's a terrible irony. Our foremothers and fathers were so dependent on land that they named, fenced, drained, coaxed, seaweed-fertilised and wanted it, agitated for it, joined British armies through the false promise of maybe having it, and finally left Scotland altogether over the enduring want of it. All that pain, hope, love and sorrow – over land. Such emotional attachment is incomprehensible, even mildly embarrassing to those from a world in which land has become a mere commodity. It's like the boring but vital base board in Lego, or the table upon which computers sit – the featureless, characterless stuff that lies beneath houses, factories, shops, roads, museums, airports, supermarkets, railways and parliaments. It's the stuff beneath things that really matter – objects you can move, sell, watch, eat, or wear. Land is thought valuable these days only because of what's built there. Not because of what can grow on it, or who has security to live on it, or how communities can harness the resources of it, or what ideas and whose dreams can be made tangible upon it.

Most Scots agree the Clearances were destructive but are left wondering if it actually matters these days? We ask ourselves – very quietly because we know this is wrong – what else could be done with the vast, empty, desolate acres that make up most of Scotland? We ask if squabbling locals could find the cash and sense of purpose to run remote areas as the Lairds did for centuries. We believe that few ordinary Scots really want the responsibility and hassle that ownership brings. We whisper to ourselves the doubting, self-limiting language of our excluded habitus. And because of all these thoughts, we doubt deep down that land ownership makes that much of a difference.

The thing is, it really does.

The A9 Lupin Patrol

The Scottish Government website tells us that 'invasive non-native species are the second biggest threat to native species worldwide – after habitat destruction.'

I'd humbly suggest that is wrong. The biggest threat to Scotland's diverse habitat are the people who believe Scotland is 'naturally' a barren wilderness where nothing grows except heather moorland (for grouse shooting) and rows of tightly-packed, diversity-defeating conifers (for sale). Our land is capable of much, much more.

Broad-leaved trees can grow almost anywhere sheep and deer are largely excluded. You can see natural regrowth on sheep-free hills, hard to reach verges and central motorway reservations where deer fear to tread. But excluding tiny teeth is not enough. After a century of overgrazing, soil needs a revival. When that's done, a lush flower, herb and insect-rich woodland habitat can be recreated very easily – given vision, patience, wire fencing... and some lupins. The proof lies in six areas of woodland off the A9, on the barren wasteland of Dalnaspidal by Loch Garry.

Twenty-five years ago, local ecologists Ron Greer and Derek Pretswell used a 'succession planting' technique – mixing lupins and broom with broad-leaved saplings. There was method in their madness. Lupins and Scotch Broom fixed nitrogen in the soil, provided shelter in high winds for growing plants and raised micro-temperatures at soil level so the trees could finally flourish. Sheep and deer were fenced out, but two years into the experiment it looked like the lupins and broom had taken over. Today though, those first protective species have mostly gone, replaced by wild raspberries, insects, herbs and flowers blossoming under tree species which provide daylight beneath open canopies and leaf litter for bigger, healthier fish in the neighbouring loch. Exotic grey, red and green Alders have added more nitrogen to the soil. Larch allow blueberries and heather to grow beneath them and also make excellent wood for fuel. Ditto Norwegian Maple, which provides a source of glorious colour in the autumn. They are all non-native trees and yet utterly effective in transforming this part of the man and sheep-made desert that flanks the highest parts of the A9.

Once again, seeing is believing (see photo below). The contrast between the rich, improved, verdant woodland the two friends patiently created and the barren, overgrazed desert outside is striking, utterly beautiful... and completely depressing.

Ron Greer (foreground) & Derek Pretswell at the A9 wilderness woodland.

Ron and Derek pulled together an ambitious £100 million buyout plan which would have extended their successful regeneration method to thousands of acres in upland Perthshire. They were supported all the way by Scottish Enterprise, and then... a safer, less disruptive bet just looked easier. It was mentioned that neither of them possessed the right academic qualifications. They were self-taught, instinctive ecologists – a bit disruptive (especially Ron, for whom there is no greater compliment) and a bit brilliant. Who knows the real reason they got no backing. It is the old, old Scottish story. Now they count themselves lucky that a new landowner has agreed not to fell 'their' forest. It must be heartbreaking.

Why is the creation of such lush, productive woodland not a higher priority for someone like Forestry Commission Scotland? Why do councils like Argyll not consider strategic tree planting to prevent landslides in areas like the Rest and Be Thankful at a fraction of the cost of concrete engineering? Why do Scots not demand leaf-litter-producing trees round lochs to double the size of fish? Is it because none but paying customers and friends of the landowner currently sees or tastes the products of our lochs and rivers? Ah, but we need wood. Lots of it – and fast. Scotland currently has 17.8 per cent forest cover – the government wants that to be 25 per cent by 2050. A recent agreement means more farmland will be planted – probably with more 'classic' densely packed, non-native, shade-creating species like Sitka Spruce, Lodgepole Pine and Douglas Fir, whose competition-suffocating growth creates the arid, cellulose factories that are the modern forests of Scotland.

Ironically, it's these state-sponsored forest monocultures that could yet destroy Scotland's greatest natural asset – its glorious diversity. As the ash dieback disease demonstrates, native trees which once succeeded in a former Scottish climate may not work well now. Currently Scotland's Highlands are either overgrown with densely packed conifers or barren, overgrazed and empty. How would our landscape change if its ownership changed?

Ron Greer estimates the current mixed woodlands of Perthshire's enormous Atholl Estate could keep the towns of Pitlochry, Blair Atholl, Dunkeld and Rannoch supplied with wood for heat in perpetuity… if locals resumed the practice of pollarding (harvesting some wood but allowing the tree to keep growing) and had any democratic say over use of land.

With oil and gas prices hitting the roof, why isn't this home-grown solution even discussed? Because our forests, like our land, are off-limits.

The biggest threat to a diverse, peopled, productive forest is not the humble Rhododendron ponticum – it is the monoculture-favouring, people-excluding private landowner or public forest manager.

Forestry Commission Scotland could plan people into forests, not just as day trippers but as weekend and summer hut owners too, as state-owned forest managers do in most other countries at our latitude. As it is, a long-standing hutting community at Barry Downs near Carnoustie closed in 2012 after evictions, and the largest hutting community left – scattered in woodland around Carbeth, 12 miles

One of sixty huts vandalised at Barry Downs in 2012, after tenants were evicted.

north of Glasgow – has only avoided mass eviction by achieving a community buyout.[7]

Is it any coincidence the Scots have such a perilously passive, sedentary and indoor culture while our Norwegian neighbours (with 368,000 basic wooden weekend cabins against Scotland's 568) are outside every available hour in all weathers?

Attempts to enjoy the Great Outdoors in Scotland are fraught with difficulty. An outdoor nursery in Fife was almost closed by over-zealous health and safety bosses in 2010 who demanded constant access to clean running water – not wipes, as the World Health Organisation recommends. Happily, that threat was seen off. But lack of easy familiarity with land has made nature seem dangerous and threatening. It's only a hop, skip and a jump from there to entirely indoor primary school careers which produce yet more generations of nature averse Scots.

Landowners still have such indirect power to shape the lives of everyone else.

If they are co-operative, long distance paths can be developed, if they are not (as they are not in the 'Far North' of Scotland) – a tourism-dependent local population will miss out. If they are willing to rent out small plots of land, then weekend cabins or caravans can be berthed to allow working people the luxury of an affordable weekend

---

7   http://www.guardian.co.uk/uk/scotland-blog/2013/mar/20/scotland-carbeth-hutters-buyout.

escape. Just such a weekend cabin near Dunkeld accommodated the Dundee family of the late songwriter Michael Marra and led to his friendship with local boy Dougie MacLean, which in turn prompted the marvellous song 'Niel Gow's Apprentice'.

If landowners won't rent out small, affordable pockets of land (and that's the majority), caravans can only be parked in large coastal parks where van owners have no protection against arbitrary eviction or sudden price hikes.

The patterns of landownership and power in the countryside have morphed into a rigid, paternalistic template that still casts a long shadow over Scotland – like ripples spreading long after the pebble has sunk. And the physical dispossession of an entire nation is no small pebble.

The Africans say it takes a village to raise a child. I'd say we need to raise some real villages fast – and by that I mean powerful, active, self-determining, local communities, not passive, inactive dormitory towns on land owned lock, stock and barrel by one man, one government department, one quango or one insurance company. 'Post-feudal' landowner control in the 21st century has become a very subtle, private thing. So the reformers challenge to convention, habit, tradition, custom and the integrity of pleasant people with large estates may seem rude, unnecessary and exaggerated.

Why cause such a ruckus? Why impute Machiavellian motive to highly respected men like the UK's largest private landowner, the Duke of Buccleuch? After all, the (current) 10th Duke has been a District Councillor, a Director of Border Television, a Regimental Trustee of the Kings Own Scottish Borderers and Chairman, South West, of Scottish Natural Heritage, a National Member for Scotland of the Independent Television Commission, a Millennium Commissioner and a Trustee of the National Heritage Memorial Fund. He is a Fellow of the UHI Millennium Institute, a Fellow of the Royal Society of Edinburgh and Royal Geographical Society. He was made a KBE in 2000 and President of the National Trust for Scotland until the equally busy Earl of Lindsay took over that role in 2012.

Hereditary landowners like the Duke of Buccleuch are visible, promoted and active within Scottish society. The disempowered, by contrast, are not.

Indeed, dipping further into the Buccleuch's history, the ninth Duke (descended from the eldest illegitimate son of King Charles II) left a personal fortune of £320 million when he died in 2007, putting his personal wealth on a par with the Queen.[8] It was reported at the time that the 54-year-old Richard, 10th Duke of Buccleuch, received shares worth £1.6 million, woodlands valued at £1.3 million and inherited the £224 million Buccleuch Heritage Trust, comprising jewellery, furniture and his father's art collection (including the £50 million Da Vinci masterpiece 'Madonna with the Yarnwinder') when his mother died in 2011. Each of his three siblings, Lord John, Lord Damian Scott and Lady Charlotte-Anne, reportedly received just £50,000 each.

Wow.

According to the Carlisle-based *North West Evening Mail*:

> A friend of the close-knit Buccleuch family told a Sunday newspaper it was unlikely there would be any fall-out from the comparatively small sums awarded to the Duke's immediate relatives because they all had an interest in the estate and were well provided for. If he had left them £100 million each, bits of the Buccleuch Estate would have had to be sold to fund that. The Duke would have hated that to happen.

Well, maybe. But what if Scotland needed that to happen?

If each of Richard's siblings had inherited an equal share of the Buccleuch estate, change might finally have crept into Borders life. One sibling might have cashed in, moved out and sold some smaller parcels of land. The villagers of Newcastleton – currently surrounded by 'not for sale' acres – might have been able to build affordable new houses for their children. Tenant farmers might have been able to live in farmhouses they could own and improve. Heavens – one Buccleuch might have had a total rush of blood to the head and given land to the local community free as a gesture of good will.

As it is, the business of oldest sons inheriting all land (primogeniture) at the 'top' of Scottish society has conveniently stopped locals getting a look-in by halting the natural process of fragmentation in Scotland's big estates. The Succession to the Crown Act 2013 ensures gender equality in accession to the throne so any first-born daughter

---

8   According to the *North West Evening Mail*, 'the Duke's personal fortune did not take into account that of Buccleuch Estates, a separate business, of which he was chairman.'

will inherit ahead of any younger brothers. I suppose that's progress. And yet, Prince Charles rattled a dull sabre at even this 'well-meaning' reform, saying he worried about its effect on dukedoms and the hereditary peerage.

How can the self-interest of a small, privileged elite still matter so much? Why has the Scottish Parliament still failed to give all children equal legal rights to inherit land as families throughout Europe have had for centuries? Do politicians fear the end of landowner privilege would split up estates, herald chaos on the land or prompt a Robespierre-like revolutionary bloodbath? Of course not. And yet there was next to no critique of Prince Charles's very public remarks.[9]

In Scotland, son still follows father as the single landowner of a vast sporting estate as surely as night follows day, thanks to a practice every other part of the developed world has long since abandoned.

It's neither fair nor modern and has created a society where natural assets seem to be out of reach for the vast majority of its people.

The Crofting Acts of 1886 did give greater access and security of tenure to some Highland Scots – within a host of constraints. After a ban on Highlanders leaving Scotland in the early 19th century, when landowners needed labour for the profitable kelp harvest,[10] eviction, forcible ejection and 'aided passage' were all deployed when the kelp market and potato harvest failed and deer or sheep looked more profitable. The Crofting Acts finally let crofters use and own their small patch of land and hand it down through their family (but not sell it unless the land is 'de-crofted' first). Even so, the Big House still loomed large over townships in the crofting counties visited by the 1883 Napier Commission. Landowners retained control of the best land (from which crofters were generally cleared) infrastructure (or lack of it), employment patterns, land-use and pretty much every aspect of life outside the patch of crofting land itself, deliberately drawn too small for self-sufficiency. This semi-autonomy, this guarded-freedom, this bounded liberty, this conditional control, this 'bonsai' democracy could not – over centuries – generate the deep-rooted, long-lasting experience of security and fairness that has helped to produce high

---

9   http://www.guardian.co.uk/uk/2013/jan/07/prince-charles-worried-succession-laws.

10 The Passenger Vessels Act (1803) was established under humanitarian pretences, but the practical effect was to treble the cost of passage to prevent as many as possible leaving Scotland for Canada. Landlords who feared the emigration of their population lobbied extensively for this piece of legislation, and just as extensively for its repeal after the market for kelp crashed in 1826.

levels of resilience, local control and mutual trust amongst our Nordic neighbours.

Eventually these intangible issues are the only important ones – the last remaining indicators of past hurts and enduring unfairness. Optimism, expectation, resilience, active citizenship – these are attributes money cannot buy and only a changed reality can create.

The Nordic nations did not emerge with silver spoons in their mouths – far from it. The average male life expectancy of Norwegians when they voted for independence at the turn of the last century was 48. Rural Swedes were so poor around the same time that they made alcohol out of the starchy wash from pulp mills. Many centuries ago, Icelanders exposed weak babies to preserve meagre food supplies for the living and volunteer Finnish troops defeated the mighty Red Army in 1939 helped by doctors who stored anaesthetics in their oxsters to stop them freezing. Life for the Nordic nations has been far from a doddle. And yet all their peoples seem to share varying degrees of confidence in the innate capacity and resourcefulness of people and a plucky combativeness towards difficulty (man-made or natural).

Such resilience is the gold standard of all outlooks. But like any precious material, it arises from a process, a past and a reality – not government diktat, health board posters or drink-fuelled bravado. Resilience has traditionally been ascribed to religion, education, and even national temperament. It has also arisen from control over land and the stability, security, fairness and predictability that has allowed Nordic people to invest their time, labour, cash and hope productively. To paraphrase medical sociologist Aaron Antonovsky, communities with democratic control over natural assets experience life as comprehensible, manageable and meaningful and this sense of coherence about life helps them endure difficulty and stress.[11] To paraphrase the naturopath James C Thomson and modern food activists like Mike Small who devised the Fife Diet, people need access to land to grow wholesome food.

Of course, Scotland industrialised and urbanised much earlier than

---

11   A 'sense of coherence' is defined as: 'the extent to which one has a pervasive, enduring though dynamic, feeling of confidence that one's environment is predictable and things will work out as well as can reasonably be expected.' In other words, it's a mixture of optimism and control. A. Antonovsky, Health, Stress and Coping (San Francisco: Jossey-Bass, 1979).

Norway. But each country's exploitation of its considerable natural resources has differed in ways that reflect underlying ownership patterns.

The development of cheap hydro-electric power from the late 19th century gave Norway a comparative advantage and created a precedent of public ownership and a template for the modern Oil Fund. Cheap hydro-electricity allowed the development of Norway's mineral resources. Norske Hydro was founded in 1905 to produce artificial fertilisers and the company remains 40 per cent state owned. In the Victorian era, foreign capitalists – many English – had bought up rivers and natural resources and there was great disquiet in the newly independent nation about the impact on Norway's industrial and social development. As a result, the Concession Laws of 1906–09 restricted foreign and private ownership, allowing Norway's central and local governments to retain a stake in all its key natural resources, and to use them productively so people could stay on the land.[12]

Not here. The Crown Estates Commission kept people from control of the beach and foreshore, and landowners managed to oppose most hydro development until the redoubtable radical Tom Johnston was able to use the demands of wartime (and the swift removal of all remaining editions of *Our Scots Noble Families*) to force change. Still many lochs are not used for more than 'ornamental' fishing, rivers are timeshared and hunting is still the preserve of a titled social class.

Colin Ward has speculated that the cheapness of land between the wars led to the boom of hutting communities in the countryside outside cities like London and Glasgow and this in turn led to the first planning legislation (1947 Town and Country Planning Act), as the countryside gentry sought to protect their acres from the scourge of the working classes.[13] Certainly the Act 'provided the means for urban containment, safeguarding the countryside for the production of food' by large-scale farming rather than small-scale, local food producers on plots and allotments.[14]

The concentration of social and health problems in 'dark satanic mills' seemed to confirm the wisdom of sparing the countryside from

---

12   E. Lange, 'The Concession Laws of 1906–09 and Norwegian Industrial Development', *Scandinavian Journal of History* 2, 1997). pp. 311–330.

13   Ward C and Hardy D, Arcadia for All: the Legacy of a Makeshift Landscape. Mansell. London (1984)

14   Ian Hodge, 'Countryside Planning' in Barry Cullingworth, ed. *British Planning* (London: Athlone Press, 1999).

housing and industrial development. But perhaps the reverse was true. Perhaps inner city and suburban housing estate ills arose in part from their physical containment; from lack of contact with a rural environment that could offer sanity-restoring connections with informal work and nature – the kind of contact sought after by healthier nations and post-war politicians who found rural retreats for themselves whilst passing the 1947 Act that raised the planning bar too high for a viable hut culture in Britain and delivered camps instead for the masses at Butlins.

Nordic cabins are largely in forests which do not compete with agricultural land – possible because Norwegian forestry is usually locally owned and provides a resource for the entire community. In Scotland, nationalisation of forestry land removed any expectation of connection and use by the wider local community.

It is the ultimate irony. Many of the losing families during the Clearances left Scotland and built large houses and prosperous small ranches in the New World where they still own land, fish rivers, escape to log cabins and go hunting. Many of the 'winning' families who stayed have endured the same substandard housing stock as they did centuries back, dare not venture beyond their small plots to fish a trout and face a greater scramble for land today than their forebears did 150 years ago. The outlook of the lairds has somehow become enshrined in the planning philosophy of today's local authorities. The enduring aesthetic of emptiness means cleared glens are considered too beautiful to be marred with basic homes or the static caravans locals can actually afford. The historic absence of services like mains water and electricity means the price of house building is prohibitively expensive anyway. It's as if Scotland's Victorian landowners are having the last laugh. Their massive estates are largely intact and would-be house-builders are still fighting for tiny parcels of overpriced land – unable to compete with crofters for their common grazing, unable to fight topography for what remains, unable to challenge habitat designations of special scientific interest, and unable to compete with wealthier incomers for the occasional house plots that do become available.

Scotland's land reform legislation, which has transformed ownership patterns across the Western Isles, has failed to bite in the most extensively cleared areas – because there are no communities left to exercise a community Right to Buy. And failed to bite on the mainland, in small towns or in Scotland's big cities where councils have swiped land owned by Common Good Funds which should belong to the people. Of the parties in the Scottish Parliament, only the Greens have proposed a Land Value Tax to end land speculation in cities. Somehow the prominence of Eigg has persuaded Scots that land reform is a problem at the margins of Scotland, not at its unavailable, over-priced urban core. And a problem now fixed by Land Reform legislation anyway.

People are still at the bottom of a pecking order that puts landowning interests first, factory style farms and forests second, protected plants, habitats and animals third and indigenous people a poor fourth. The only way for locals to have some say is to take complete control. That suits some defined, close-knit, island communities – but it doesn't suit everyone.

Eigg laid bare the lie of Grannie's Hieland Hame. Much of Scotland looks wild, empty and barren. But it didn't get like that on its own and it doesn't stay like that on its own either.

Eigg proved the high-handed treatment of locals by feudal landowners isn't ancient history and involves much more than a dry, academic argument about title deeds. Land ownership is about the release of human potential. It's as big and as simple as that.

There are four big things to say about the cloak of feudal land ownership that has lain across Scotland longer than anywhere else in the developed world. First and foremost – it limits people, families, development, wealth and confidence – not just who plants tatties where. Second – it's still there – even though feudal land tenure was abolished in 2000. Third – it could be otherwise. Finally, it will not disappear on its own.

The solution must be to release the chained up forces that impede the natural, organic break-up of large estates into more manageable, affordable, varied and accessible land parcels. It's time to change the law so that all children have the right to inherit land and change the tax system so that landowners can't avoid paying tax on their landed wealth.

Just as roughly broken, ploughed land breaks down in Scotland's frosty winters – so the large estates of feudal Scotland will break down once exposed to the processes of democracy.

Processes from which they have been shielded for far too long.

CHAPTER SEVEN

Supersized councils
– Disempowered Communities

IT WAS 1.30am on 11 July 2006 – a time and date arrived at by precise calculation. My archaeo-astronomer friend Dougie Scott had assured me this was the best time to view the lunar standstill which 'activates' the Standing Stones of Callanish on the Hebridean island of Lewis. This part of the moon's cycle happens once every 18.6 years. And tonight was the night.

So I was hurtling in a transit from Atlantic-facing Uig on the remote west coast towards the 5,000-year-old stone circle. The van was driven by Maxwell MacLeod, my friend and support driver who'd been accompanying me while I (mostly) cycled up the Western Isles recording a 13-part series about Hebridean life for BBC Radio Scotland.

What has any of this got to do with localism? Bear with me.

Dougie believes Scotland's key stone circles are set out like calendars to mark the lowest and highest orbits of the sun and the moon. He thinks our forebears believed the sun and moon 'impregnated' Mother Earth with energy, bringing forth crops and new life. And he's spent enough early mornings measuring celestial alignments in remote sites to prove it. His theory seems fair enough to me, but has apparently caused irritation among 'proper' scientists, who say no such inferences can be drawn, even though so many sites are oriented precisely to key positions of the sun and moon thousands of years ago.

Anyway, Callanish is the Mother of all lunar sites, and 1.30am on 11 July 2006 was the precise moment Dougie's theory would be put to the test. Then the moon would emerge from behind the mountain known as the *Cailleach na Mointeach* (Old Woman of the Moors) and 'walk' along her undulating shape before sending shafts of moonlight down the stone flanked avenue at Callanish, briefly illuminating her two tall, central stones. Fairly reproductive sounding, if you ask me.

Anyway, 18.6 years earlier, when the lunar standstill last occurred, folk came from all over the world to witness the 'Moon walking at Callanish', including a group of Japanese tourists who had hired a jet and travelled to each archaeological treasure with lunar orientation around the world, collecting small bags of earth which they carefully deposited at the next site in the kind of makey-uppey, yet purposeful, ritual I wish I'd thought of (and could finance) myself. Every self-respecting hippie, New Age traveller and Waterboys fan for miles around was expected to be there – in short, the pagan nature of this celestial event promised an entertaining evening – as long as we had all calculated the same kick-off time.

Even if Dougie Scott was right we might see the moon but not the masses if calculations differed. And it was people I had come to record. We hummed and hawed. 'Let's just go,' said Max at midnight.

So we did – and headed for Callanish with clouds building and excitement growing. At the car park, there were only seven cars. Hardly evidence of a lunar stampede. Fearing the worst, I wandered up the path. Suddenly ethereal chanting filled the air. Sure enough, silhouetted against an iridescent sky was the shape of druid-type gowns. Seconds later, the steady beat of drums and scent of incense were unmistakable.

I already had the tape recorder running, in case our own remarks were the only sounds I managed to record – just as well. Out of the darkness, we bumped into a bearded Jethro Tull lookalike carrying a set of bagpipes. We asked if the big moon moment had already happened. He wasn't sure.

'Something happened half an hour ago and all the pagans started howling – you know that ululating thing they do. Then this Free Church choir started singing in Gaelic, and for a crazy moment they seemed to be trying to outdo one another. I mean it's nothing to me, eh. I'm fae Fife. But I thought, this is crap. If this moon thing means something, then don't fight over it – just let it happen. But they were all still singing at each other, so I thought the pipes will sort this out and started playing 'Amazing Grace' over the lot of them. It was so loud it drowned them all out – so they gave up and started to sing along. Magic.'

'So that's you away home now?'

'Aye, that's enough. I've been here for the past two nights as well. Time to get back to Cumbernauld.'

'I thought you said you were from Fife?'

'I am – my God, I'm not from Cumbernauld. I just have to stay there. But I'm in it, not of it. Know what I mean? In it, not of it.'

Bizarre as that night proved to be – culminating in a stand-off between a 70-year-old shamanic astrologer from Louisiana and a local Free Church ensemble – it was the piper's description of his erstwhile home that stayed with me longest.

In it, not of it.

How could the Pied Piper of Callanish have such a thoroughly disconnected life back 'home'? Admittedly the dated-looking collection of roundabouts and dual carriageways that's earned the New Town 'Plook on the Plinth' status is not easy to love. And who knows what personal sorrows may be associated in the piper's memory with that single word, Cumbernauld?

Still. *In it, not of it.* Like a man inhabiting a prison cell. The phrase stayed with me, because it summed up a remoteness and apparent contempt towards place that's common in Scotland and yet entirely at odds with the kind of people using it.

The bearded bagpiper was no slouch. He'd learned to play an instrument, chosen to travel hundreds of miles to an empty moor, intervened with a spot of bagpipe diplomacy when unseemly quarrels erupted and finally exercised the common sense to leave once the clouds (and midges) descended. This Fifer was clearly an outgoing, active and capable man who might be expected to respond positively to everything around him. Not Pollyanna perhaps, but no shrinking violet either.

And yet he actively disliked the place he lived and wanted everyone to know it.

In it, not of it. Such a lack of belonging is commonplace in Scotland. Is that because we don't value place or because we lack control over the community, land, buildings, society and nature that must come together to create it? I suspect it's the latter.

Take the classic west of Scotland greeting – 'Where do you stay?'

Not where do you live – but where do you stay? The dictionary tells us that 'to stay' means to be fixed, immobile, inert, immovable, motionless, riveted, sedentary, stationary, transfixed. None of these words convey a cheery, active or positive life experience. So what does it mean when Scots describe where they stay? Is it a slip of the tongue, a meaningless way of speaking, a small semantic point one shouldn't exaggerate? Or a bit of a giveaway? Well-trained dogs stay. Inanimate objects stay. Rabbits in hutches stay. Books on library shelves stay. But people in places 'live' – don't they?

People put down roots, explore surroundings, customise their environment, get to know neighbours, attend school, go to the doctor, hang around street corners, acquire accents, catch the bus, miss the bus, get bored, visit friends, collect prescriptions, use the post office and grunt hello to people in the street. All of this happens locally.

That's why place matters. Education, housing, language, friendship and play happen on the doorstep, not further afield. Early ideas of fairness, fun, danger and acceptable behaviour are also developed under our noses.

When we are young, life is completely local. Adventure is the little wall you finally have the courage to walk along alone. Nature is the small patch of dandelions halfway home from school. Posh is the tennis club where people play with their own rackets. Huge is the Goliath crane. And loud is the sound that wakes you from sleep in the middle of the night. OK – my early ideas were deeply coloured by growing up in Belfast. But that's the point. That's the power of locality. It creates a sense of normality – even in abnormal situations – through deep, subconscious attachment.

People are increasingly understanding the power of early years to shape children and their lifelong outlooks and capacities. By the age of three, children have acquired (or failed to acquire) half their adult vocabulary, learned teamwork, acquired negotiating skills and bonded strongly with the people and ways of life around them. They do that – or fail to do that – in particular places. If Jesuits believed they owned a young life by directing it until the age of seven, how much more powerful is the place that forms us until our late teenage years?

And yet 'normal' life in Scottish places disempowers local communities and denies citizens an effective and organised way to pour energy into that most important place – their own backyard.

Why? Because Scots have the biggest councils with the lowest levels of local democratic activity, the biggest and most remote landowners and the weakest community councils in Europe.

In it, not of it Scotland – we all live there.

The land we see, the streets we walk on, the rivers we walk beside, the problems we witness – they're all there for someone else to fix. It's why we pay our council tax, isn't it? For someone else to bag problems and take them away? Except they can't.

The average population of a Scottish council is a whopping 163,000 people (the median is 115,000 people – see Figure 13). Most of our European neighbours have county councils this size. But they also have a smaller, more loved, more vigorously contested and more vibrant 'delivery tier' of community-sized local councils as well. Scotland, along with the rest of the UK, doesn't. Our 32 enormous councils try to do everything – the strategic co-ordination work of a county council and the truly local delivery work of a parish council. It's an impossible task and it's the community level that suffers. Genuinely local simply doesn't exist in Scotland – except where hard-pressed, determined, unfunded, voluntary groups have decided to act and pump life back into their communities. I sense raised eyebrows.

How does this picture square with the Scotland of a hundred High-

Country	Number of councils/ municipalities	Median Population	Median Size (km square)
France	36,781	380	11
Spain	8,112	564	35
Italy	8,100	2,343	22
Norway	431	4,439	465
Germany	12,013	6,844	15
Belgium	589	11,265	40
Sweden	290	15,039	672
Scotland	32	115,000	990

Local council size across Europe[1]

---

1   Andy Wightman, 'Scottish Six Lectures', Edinburgh Festival Fringe, 2012.

land Games, several dozen *Feisean* (Gaelic learning festivals), night schools, sports clubs and folk nights? Surely Scotland is full of particular places – distinct, fiercely defended by their inhabitants and loved. That's all true. But it's true despite the official structures – not because of them. Even the keenest volunteers who make life vibrant and interesting don't run the places they light up – 'local' units of governance are too large and election is too dominated by political parties. Towns, villages, islands and communities are all run by council HQs in larger settlements elsewhere.

And it's been like that for a while.

The democratic heart of 'small town' Scotland was ripped out in 1996, when 32 unitary authorities replaced 65 old style councils – nine regions, 53 districts and three island councils. Mind you, the big local downsizing had already occurred. In 1975, a mixter-maxter of more than 400 counties, counties of cities, large burghs and small burghs was swept away and before that in 1930, 871 parish councils were axed as democratic structures (though they still exist for census purposes).

That's quite a change. In my own village in Fife, for example, rents paid in the village for council housing were once used to employ 'the drain man' who went round unblocking drains, gutters, roans and pipes. Now we are part of Fife council, with headquarters 40 minutes distant, there is no local 'drain man' and flooding is so common, flood alert road signs are stashed all the way along main routes into Perth – 'for convenience'. Meaningful village control largely disappeared in the 1930s. Meaningful town control went in 1975. And after 1996 many places became non-existent – in the eyes of the authorities at least.

The 1996 reforms probably saved money. Undoubtedly the smaller system looked more efficient on paper. But it also severed the vital link between people and place in Scotland.

So this is where the 'best wee country in the world' is currently run – somewhere else.

In Norway, Finland, Denmark, France, Germany, Holland and Belgium, towns like St Andrews, Saltcoats, Kirkcaldy, Fort William, Kelso, Pitlochry or Methil and islands like Barra, North Uist, Westray and Unst have their own councils.

But in Scotland today, big is efficient and efficient is beautiful. So Scots inhabit the least locally empowered country (perhaps) in the developed world and tend to look higher (to national policy) or lower (to micromanaged families) for solving problems – even when the answer lies in between at community level. The absence of genuine local control is Scotland's enduring blind spot.

Take three towns; Wick, Fort William and Linlithgow.

Wick used to be one of the largest herring ports in Europe, the county town of Caithness (sorry, Thurso) and a royal burgh. Now it's run from council headquarters a three hour rail journey away in Inverness. Meanwhile, 1,200 miles further north sits Hammerfest – the world's northernmost town and the county town of Finnmark. In 1900, Wick and Hammerfest were both busy North Sea ports. Today both have around 9,000 inhabitants – but one is thriving and one is struggling.

Hammerfest was the first place in Northern Europe to have street lighting powered by river hydros and funded by a local tax on beer in 1897. Townspeople went on to experiment with that turbine technology in the fast running straits at nearby Kvalsund. Years of relatively hassle-free access to their own waters helped the local energy company Hammerfest Strom become experts in tidal turbine technology and now the company is providing the kit for Scottish Power to make Islay the world's first tidal-powered island in 2015. The Hammerfest firm now called Andritz Hydro Hammerfest – has also won the tender to exploit the mother of all tidal stream sites off Duncansby Head in the Pentland Firth – 16 miles north of declining Wick, which lost its official port status a decade back.

It's the ultimate irony. Wick's inhabitants (including my own family) survived centuries of pummelling by the North Sea aboard fishing boats, lifeboats, oil supply boats and pilot ships. But Wickers didn't have easy access, local control, cash, investment or sufficient local belief to turn their intimate knowledge of a cruel sea into energy harnessing technology.

Today the ports look very different – one is constantly busy, the other is very quiet. One has been raising its own taxes and deciding how to spend them for centuries. One hasn't.

I'll grant you, other factors are also at play.

But the Wickers' frustration at being forced to tackle decline with both hands tied behind their backs is palpable. And Wick is not alone.

A few years back, I was asked to speak at a Rotary event in Fort

Wick 1900s, from the Johnston Collection.[2]

Hammerfest, 1900s.

2   http://www.johnstoncollection.net.

Wick and Hammerfest 2012 (Hammerfest courtesy of Johan Wilhagen – Visitnorway.com).

William. As the crowd gathered in the reception area, conversation was downbeat. High rates bills meant shops were closing and boarded up windows, Poundstretcher chain stores and a legion of charity shops had begun to dominate the High Street. The ring road, built decades earlier, meant most people bypassed the town. The crumbling 1960s facades of many buildings needed repair and, despite the innovation of the Mountain Film Festival, mountain biking, the ski lift at nearby Aonach Mor and the enduring natural spectacle of Ben Nevis, Fort William itself seemed shabby – a disappointment at the end of the West Highland Way.

Once spoken about, it was a situation that plunged the entire banqueting suite of retired town planners, retailers, secretaries, shop owners, lorry drivers, council officials and civil engineers into almost unshakeable gloom. So I ditched my speech. Asking for a show of hands to demonstrate the level of expertise sitting in that function room alone, I suggested they had more than enough experience, commitment and affection to resurrect Fort William themselves. The mood lifted. There was a momentary buzz. Folk looked around like chefs planning a complicated, ambitious menu. Yes – all the raw ingredients are to hand. Yes, we could easily work together and put the time in. We could fix everything here. We could raise money, hold ceilidhs, get the young folk involved and… then something visibly knocked the wind from their collective sails. *It's not our place to do this. We aren't councillors. It's too hard to get involved. Anything we do will be against some rule. And there's no love lost for well-meaning amateurs.* The moment passed.

So it is in communities across Scotland. Local places are run by Europe's smallest councillor cohort who make decisions about villages, towns and cities they hardly know and can rarely visit. And while they vainly try to micromanage distant lives, local people are freed from the burden and responsibility of fixing what's around them but also robbed of the powerful feelings of rootedness and attachment that come from improving places, not just 'staying' in them.

There is only one thing at which any place excels – being itself. And there is only one set of people who fully understand that – the people who live there. Right now, capable people all across Scotland can only stand and survey the failing public façades of their local lives.

At a meeting set up to counter decline in historic Linlithgow, I was again urging self-help. A businessman told me local efforts had got nowhere – symbolised by a non-functioning light bulb in a nearby underpass.

'The council say they fix it, but every time I walk home, the light's not working. Maybe it's kids. Maybe they don't even change the bulb. When I complain, they say it costs too much to send a workman out. So what happens? Nothing! Why do I pay council tax if the council can't even keep an underpass lit?'

'So why don't you change the bulb yourself?'

'What!'

'Change it yourself if it annoys you so much.'

'It's not my job – why should I?'

'Listen to yourself. You are consumed with anger over a £1 light bulb. Change it, act, do something, take charge.'

There was laughter, a release of tension and then a resigned shake of the head.

'I can't. They'll prosecute me for interfering with council property.' Mr Light Bulb was probably right. This is the simmering rage and wasted energy that lies at the heart of almost every local community. Little things cannot be fixed by capable local people. New ideas cannot be tried out. The people elected and employed to make decisions about the most important and intimate aspects of life are generally strangers.

There could be few more vivid depictions of the infantilisation caused by disempowering and distant 'local' governance than grown men infuriated by broken light bulbs they feel unable to change. Where does that frustration and fury go? Think of Einstein's famous maxim: 'Energy cannot be created or destroyed, it can only be changed from one form to another.'

So what happens to the desire to fix when it cannot find an outlet? Where does that energy go? Thwarted goodwill is eventually transformed into cynicism and civic detachment – amongst some folk it may even manifest as vandalising rage. Disempowerment is a volatile state.

So welcome to Scotland – a country full of local places where most inhabitants are marking time. A place randomly chosen to suit convenience, habit, or proximity to work. Places which do not want your input – just your council tax. Places Scots must thole.

'I'm not from Cumbernauld – I just stay there.' Those words conjure up all the weary passivity and stultifying boredom that characterises life in small-town Scotland. The conclusion is inescapable.

The 'best wee country in the world' is run in units that are far too big.

The mountain village of Crianlarich, for example, is overlooked by Munros from whose summits you can look west to the Atlantic. Yet it is run by Stirling Council, whose headquarters almost lap the North Sea on Scotland's east coast. The tiny Hebridean island of Barra is run by councillors six islands distant. Massive Easterhouse – which could be the 19th largest town in Scotland by population size – is just another part of Glasgow Council.

In a way, this human-scale-defying 'bigness' mirrors the vast size and remote management of many Scottish landholdings. Some lairds and pinstriped gents from the Crown Estates Commission run the land and coastal waters from miles even continents away. Is it really any surprise that our towns, villages, islands, housing estates, suburbs and cities are also run at a distance? The political and social consequences of distant democracy are profound. According to the latest Scottish Household Survey, only 22 per cent of Scots think they can have any impact on the way their local area functions. That's a terrible condemnation of Scottish democracy. Local should be the most important dimension in our lives. And yet almost four-fifths of Scots think their neck of the woods is run by other people – not folk like themselves. And they're absolutely right. Let's return to Fife. Between 1894 and 1930, the Kingdom had 82 councils. Until 1975, it had 33. Now it has just one. I'm grateful to Andy Wightman, land reformer campaigner and erstwhile co-performer in our Edinburgh Festival Fringe show the *Scottish Six*, for 'doing the maths' (Figure 15). He showed that if Scotland returned to its old pre-1930 parish council structure it would sit mid-way in the European league table of local democracy between the Norwegians and Germans – not a bad place to be.

Putting it the other way round, becoming 'normally local' in a European context would change Scotland's council map back from the current reality (left) to pre-1930 boundaries (right, in Figure 16 below). This is how atypical Scotland has become. But preoccupied with almost equally oversized England and cut off from our ultra-local European neighbours – we have failed to notice.

Our super-sized democracy is completely out of kilter with the rest of Europe. Admittedly, the French are almost crazily local – their smallest commune has just 89 people. But the average unit of local government in Europe is closer to the population size served in Scotland by toothless community councils. Deliberately shorn of power, each community council has an average budget of just £400 a year. A recent attempt to raise interest by limiting the number of seats – thereby triggering elections – didn't happen because the legislation wasn't authorised by higher tiers of governance. So it's true. Community councils are full of virtually

Country	Number of municipalities	Median population	Sq km
France	36,781	380	11
Germany	12,013	6,844	15
Spain	8,112	564	35
Italy	8,100	2,343	22
Scotland	871	4,998	45
Belgium	589	4,998	45
Norway	431	4,439	465
Sweden	290	15,039	372
Scotland	32	115,000	990

Figure 15: European Municipal Government with Scottish parish councils restored.

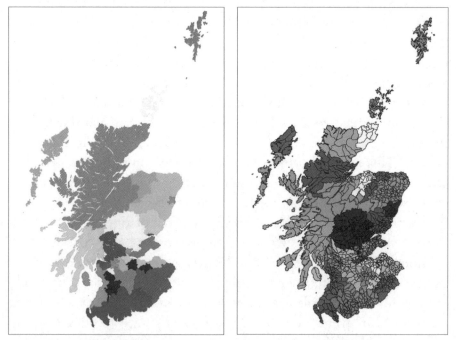

Figure 16: Scottish Councils 2012 (left) and 1929 (right).

self-nominated people with time on their hands. Given deliberate efforts to make them that way, it's a miracle any function properly at all.

No matter what any Scottish politician says about the importance of community, no matter how much anyone praises 'vital voluntary effort', no matter how many fetes, roups, fairs, Highland games and car boot sales are opened by hand-pumping councillors, MSPs and MPs, no matter how many 'planning for real' 'consultation exercises' are conducted with 'the grassroots' – remember that £400. That's how much structural community democracy in Scotland really matters.

But is anyone really bothered? Well, I suppose we don't miss what we've never had – truly local democracy and effective community delivery.

Turnout and participation

If a 38 per cent turnout at the 2012 Scottish local government election is not a mandate to transform local government – then what is?

Strangely, even Tories (almost) agree. The Tory MEP Daniel Hannan made this case for localism:

'Give councils more power and you will attract a higher calibre of candidate as well as boosting participation at local elections. In Britain, local authorities raise 25 per cent of their budgets and turnout is typically around 30 per cent. In France, those figures are, respectively, 50 and 55 per cent; in Switzerland 85 and 90 per cent.' It's an interesting comparison – and not just because French councils raise more cash and enjoy higher voter turnout. They also have the tiniest units of local governance – 36,000 communes with an average population of just 380 – compared to Scotland's 32 councils with an average population of 165,000. Likewise the Swiss, Austrians, Finns and Germans (see figure 17). Norway – with the same population as Scotland – has local election turnouts of more than 70 per cent amongst 431 municipalities which run primary and secondary education, outpatient health, senior citizen and social services, unemployment, planning, economic development, and roads. Scottish council elections in 2011 had a 38 per cent turnout amongst 32 councils. Coincidence? Local government across Europe means decision-making by people like your mum, neighbour or other 'weel kent' faces. In Scotland, it means control by people you don't know. Could that be why Scots don't vote?

	Average Population Size	Average Geographical Size (sq km)	Turnout at Local Election	Number of sub-national governments			Ratio of Councillors to Citizens
				Local	County	Regional	
Austria	3,560	36	73%	2,357	99	9	1 : 200
Denmark	56,590	440	69%	98	5	-	1 : 2,000
Finland	15,960	1,006	61%	336	2	-	1 : 500
France	1,770	17	64%	36,697	101	27	1 : 125
Germany	7,080	31	60%	11,553	301	16	1 : 400
Italy	7,470	37	75%	8,094	110	20	1 : 600
Spain	5,680	62	73%	8,116	52	17	1 : 700
UK	152,680	601	39%	406	28	3	1 : 2,860
Scotland	163,200	2,461	54%*	32	-	-	1 : 4,270
EU Average	5,630	49	-	-	-	-	-

Figure 17: International comparison of council size and voter turnout.[3]

The recent Silent Crisis report by the Jimmy Reid Foundation (summary above) demonstrates Scotland's unhealthy place in the democratic league table of Europe. Feast your eyes and think it through a bit. In Austria, the ratio of councillors to citizens is one councillor per 200 people. In Scotland, it's one councillor per 4,270 people.

Put it another way. In Norway, one in 81 people stands for election in their community. In Scotland, it's one in 2,071.

Or look at it this way: in Sweden, 4.4 people contest each seat. In Scotland, it's 2.1.

Using every indicator available to identify the health of local democracy, Scotland performs worse than any other comparable northern nation. That's what led the report's authors to conclude that 'Scotland is the least democratic country in the European Union'.

North or South, Baltic or Mediterranean – most European states are micro-sized at their local tier, which means more grassroots connection, traction, trust, effective service delivery and involvement than

3   Jimmy Reid Foundation, Silent Crisis Report 2012.

Scots can ever hope to generate. Instead decisions and services are shipped in from remote authorities elsewhere.

What does that mean in practice?

In the most powerfully municipal Nordic nations, levels of 'social trust' amongst citizens and between citizens and government are the highest in the world.[4] That has tangible benefits. According to the *Economist*:

> High levels of trust result in lower transaction costs – there is no need to resort to American-style lawsuits or Italian-style quid-pro-quo deals in order to get things done. But its virtues go beyond that. Trust means that high-quality people join the civil service. Citizens pay their taxes and play by the rules. Government decisions are widely accepted.[5]

Perhaps that's because more Norwegians ARE the government and know they are trusted by neighbours to manage spending and life decisions locally. As Britain's many crises of trust demonstrate, you can't put a price on democratically regulated, high levels of mutual confidence.

What happens when proximity and involvement in political decisions are missing from communities?

A 2013 report by the Federation of Small Business and the Centre for Local Economic Strategies revealed Scottish councils spend less of their budget with local firms (27 per cent) than the UK average (31 per cent).[6] And such UK local spending is already at the lowest levels in Northern Europe.

In their defence, councils insist that rules about 'best value' and European procurement procedures stop them preferring local suppliers. Strange that other EU members seem to manage. Perhaps the truth is that Scottish council chiefs are far closer to their own staff (especially legal officers) in the ivory towers of large remote council offices than council chiefs in nations with much smaller units of local government. Perhaps being physically close, accessible, responsive and responsible to a small number of people makes it harder to prioritise legal compliance over local livelihoods.

The vast majority of Nordic MPs started life in dynamic municipal

---

4   The World Values Survey has been monitoring values in over 100 countries since 1981.

5   http://www.economist.com/news/special-report/21570835-nordic-countries-are-probably-best-governed-world-secret-their.

6   http://www.scotsman.com/news/politics/top-stories/councils-in-scotland-spend-less-on-local-firms-1-2992710.

government so they plan with an expectation of local capacity and factor that dimension into every policy. The opposite is true in Britain. Politicians of all parties like the sound of involving local people but in practice, most MSPs and MPs wouldn't trust communities to run the proverbial in a brewery. They 'know' because they've been there. And so the vicious circle continues. Local remains an unimportant backwater in the eyes of national politicians instead of a powerhouse for social and economic change.

So we are stuck with the biggest 'local' government in Europe – too large to really connect with people and yet too small to achieve maximum efficiencies of scale. Kind of the mummy-sized bowl in *Goldilocks and the Three Bears* – betwixt and between and going nowhere fast. The logic of the current direction is inescapable. Why do we need any local councils at all?

None of this is meant to criticise councillors. Structures are to blame, not individuals. Most councillors make a huge effort to be all things to all people, tackling strategy at council HQ and trying to engage with community activists too. Some councillors are obstacles to community growth, and behave defensively if anyone tries to 'interfere' – but I'm sure that happens the world over.

Highland Council covers an area the size of Belgium, with a population the size of Belfast. Councillors regularly drive hundreds of thousands of miles a year to create a sense of connection through meetings, surgeries and local events. Despite such superhuman efforts, many remote communities still feel excluded – reduced to questioning, suspecting and vetoing whatever emanates from the centre. Meanwhile, Europe's fastest growing city also lacks a dedicated council of its own – although a pilot resurrection of old area committees by the newly elected Highland Council may help.

Those who run Scotland's overlarge authorities are on big salaries and a losing wicket. Many struggle valiantly to keep their ears to the ground. But the ground is simply too large. Ironically, this just means more money spent on consultation, resulting in a low response rate and yet further erosion of councillor confidence in community capacity. So what will change?

If self-determination is good enough for Scotland, it's good enough for Scotland's communities too. If power and responsibility can renew

Scotland, then a democratic stimulus can also give a leg up to capable, active communities. Instead they are being micro-managed badly from on high while politicians bemoan punter apathy. Wrong-sized layers of governance allow power to be hoovered upwards by the nearest quango or distant council not devolved downwards to the nearest competent community unit. Scotland needs smaller, more meaningful, democratically accountable units of organisation before big policy gains will follow.

Better lives await

In the absence of truly local councils, development trusts have become the most effective vehicles for communities that want control of their own destinies. There's a legal question mark over community councils owning assets. So development trusts have been set up to own and manage orchards, housing, land buyouts, lochs, pubs, libraries, bridges, libraries, community centres, wind turbines, shops, transport and even a hospital – and in the process a very practical, capable and focused set of people has been gathered together.

Some of the poorest Glaswegians worked together to restore Govanhill Baths – a decade-long campaign to retain a swimming pool against the wishes of Glasgow Council. The project has produced much more than a beautiful set of Victorian Baths – the people of Govanhill are now purposefully organised in their own development trust and are taking on responsibility for their own health and well-being. The more services that can be channelled through this popular, community-driven vehicle, the better.

And yet the vast bulk of social and welfare spending in Govanhill and elsewhere is channelled through local offices of large councils whose paid staff often live elsewhere. The present council setup delivers a clear message to local, active, capable Scots. Your job is to stand still while we fix you. Happily most folk in development trusts aren't listening.

West Kilbride in Ayrshire is another sparkling example of successful, community-driven regeneration where conventional 'top down' policy had drawn a blank. This 19th century former weaving town suffered from high unemployment and competition from out-of-town shopping centres. At one point, half the local shops were boarded up.

In 1998, the West Kilbride Community Initiative (WKCI) was set up by locals with one craft shop opening on the High Street. Other skilled craftspeople took over derelict shops and profits were ploughed back into the town. In 2006, West Kilbride won the Enterprising Britain competition. Now eight artists' studios, an exhibition gallery, a delicatessen, a photography business, a clock and watch repairer, a bridal shop and a graphic design business have opened and the existing butcher, baker and greengrocer have been able to stay put. In 2001, the Trust bought the old Barony Church in the heart of the town, which was in desperate need of repair. I was an *Any Questions* panellist there in 2012 on the opening night of the London Olympics. We wondered why such a lively crowd had turned out despite competition from the biggest TV experience of the decade. We didn't realise we were sitting inside a labour of love. Further along West Kilbride's main street, an outdoor theatre's being developed on the site of an old Corn Mill and a scheme's under way in a disused quarry to recycle the village's domestic organic waste through composting and vermi-composting (worms) financed through a Landfill Tax credit scheme. These guys may be good at compost – they're better at filling out forms and applying for grants and awards. And even better at drumming up trade and selling local goods and services to fellow locals.

None of this is formal council activity. If local people had not decided to take action in a voluntary development trust, West Kilbride might today be dead as a dodo – or as lifeless as many other neighbouring towns without the same level of community control. Elsewhere wind farms owned by Development Trusts will soon be netting millions, whilst 'normal' communities receive peanuts, and community benefit payments are often siphoned off by councils. Already in Fintry near Glasgow, community wind cash has paid to insulate homes and replace axed bus services. It's a silent revolution. There isn't a more optimistic, can-do, practical bunch of people anywhere in Scotland. And yet hardly any are elected councillors. There's too much to do closer to home.

Capable, connected, powerful communities – based on the kind of dynamism demonstrated by development trusts – could generate energy, supply district heating, find work for unemployed young people, tackle local flooding problems, fix derelict buildings, build and manage housing and keep an eye on old folk, helping them stay out of hospital and the personal care budget stay under control.

This kind of social transformation is already happening via the development trust that runs the island of Eigg – and the West Whitlawburn housing co-operative.

There's a lesson and a challenge here for the Scottish Government. As councils face the task of saving millions from budgets, hundreds of land and wind-energy rich community development trusts are deciding how to spend their dividends. Should they treat the cash as 'extra money' – providing window boxes, traffic calming or other marginal improvements when roads are pot-holed, energy costs are through the roof, old folk need carers and young parents need affordable child-care? Or, if they spend money on core council services, will they prompt local authorities to pull-out altogether and end up as DIY communities where residents pay council tax for next-to-nothing? The solution might be to transfer some council tax income to self-governing communities. I can hear the howls of protest already. But what's the alternative? Do we just pat successful communities on the head and continue to fund municipal failure?

There are around 200 development trusts in Scotland – community led, multiple activity, enterprising, partnership oriented and keen to move away from reliance on grants. Could they help run Scotland?

Actually, they already are. Cost-cutting councils are already closing libraries and village halls. The SNP government does not appear to smile upon our over-large councils. Nor does it want community-sized councils to take over. Development Trusts may seem to be an ideal intermediate solution.But can this ad hoc situation work in the long term when all involved are un-elected volunteers and councils still expect council tax bills to be paid regardless of local service provision?

The Municipal Nordics

The difference in democratic vitality across the North Sea has to be seen to be believed.

Five summers ago I visited the small town of Seyðisfjörður in northeast Iceland (population 668) and was impressed to see gangs of youngsters mending fences, mowing grass, and painting walls at the local hospital. 'Yes, the municipality decided to pay them a small amount to fix the town every summer. The older kids guide the young ones, they don't get bored, they learn to earn money, work as a team and we get everything ready for the tourist season.' It made so much sense. They were even fixing fences in the hospital grounds.

'Doesn't the hospital have to employ unionised labour for work like that?'

'Well, along with two neighbouring municipalities, we run the hospital too.'

Gobsmacked was too small a word.

Three years ago, in snow so deep it would have brought Scotland grinding to a halt, I visited the Medas Outdoor Kindergarten in Arctic Norway.

The national Norwegian government had called for farmers to diversify and for children to have at least one full day outside per week. So the local municipality backed a bright idea by local farmers Jostein and Anita Hunstad – a farm kindergarten where the children feed and care for the animals, make hay, grow vegetables and sell eggs and tomatoes in local villages at the weekends to raise funds for school trips. There are now 100 similar farm kindergartens across northern Norway. Did health and safety people from Oslo have concerns?

'No, I think we are all happy here. Why would outside agencies get involved?'

Why indeed?

Some winters ago, on the Swedish island of Gotland (pop 57,000), I met Development Director Bertil Klintbom, who invited me to the opening of a new pier. For centuries, Gotland was a vital stepping stone in Baltic trade until the Cold War ended ferry travel and the port status of Slite.

So the municipality struck on an ambitious and controversial plan. In 2008 they gave the Russian government permission to lay a new trans-continental gas pipeline within Gotland's territorial waters in exchange for the use of Slite as the Russian's Baltic pipe-laying base, an (upfront) payment for its refurbishment and a contribution to the cost of a new hydrogen-powered trans-Baltic ferry.

Did the Swedish government have a say?

'Why should they?'

In Sweden, only those earning above £30,000 per annum pay any tax to central government. Income tax is paid to relatively tiny municipalities which in turn deliver most of the services used by citizens. Only corporation tax and higher earner income tax goes straight to the centre. Describe the Scottish system, where all taxes are sucked into Westminster and grudgingly farmed back out again, and the Swedes are astonished. 'Why do you do that?'

Who knows?

Of course, people in Nordic communities do grumble, moan about taxes and support mergers amongst the smallest municipalities. But they view councillors as respected neighbours, not ill-informed strangers, and expect the bulk of day-to-day decisions about their lives to be taken by people they know. And mergers still leave Nordic municipalities small – a tenth of the Scottish average council by population size.

Why doesn't the left care?

What is it about 'local' that the traditional left seems to find mildly embarrassing? Place has shape, history, limits and baggage which can produce sentimentality – but it also provides the small, compact scale and grounding particularity that facilitated radical change in Eigg, Assynt, Gigha and Storas Uist. Karl Marx shaped the thinking of generations by suggesting the urban proletariat would be the inevitable agents of transformational change – surprising then to find that a bunch of Highlanders could seize the moment and turn the tide of history without a high-rise block, pub, office or the other trappings of urbanism in sight. In the local domain you need personality (or relations) not a clipboard. It's a place with quirks not rules; subjectivity not objectivity and attachment not cool, professional detachment. Community cannot be established by wild-eyed radicals with abstract theories but is built slowly by stories, memories, first names, being there and knowing people. For some whose reforming zeal arises from a deep-seated uneasiness around people – and in my experience there are a few very shy souls who've turned that personal temperamental issue into the centrepiece of their politics without even knowing it – the local sphere is an uncomfortably informal, low key arena whose modest aspirations for change invite parody and ridicule. For such people, 'local' is broken... Local is broken pavements and a politics of dogs' dirt, populism and litter. It's nimbyism – Alan Partridge stuck forever inflicting the hits of yesteryear on people who are off the pace and behind the times. That's the stereotype – and sometimes it's true for the very political reason that rural councils have often been controlled by the landed gentry.

The Duke of Buccleuch and the Duke of Roxburghe between them held the convenorship of Roxburgh County Council for 43 years between 1900 and 1975. The great Borders landowners were able to exercise influence directly in this way but also indirectly through the offices of Sheriff Depute, Commissioners of Supply, Lord-Lieutenants of the counties and Commissioners of Peace. In 1918 the convenor of Roxburgh County Council was the Duke of Roxburghe; his Vice-Convenor was the Duke of Buccleuch. Half a century later in 1975 when the County Council was abolished, the Convenor was the Duke of Roxburghe; the Duke of Buccleuch and Baronness Elliot were also on the council. Nothing much had apparently changed.[7]

> In the Scottish countryside lairds kept a firm grasp of local politics until the reorganisation of local government in 1974.[8]

Even then, the kind of people selected as candidates often echoed the status of the landowner. In the 1970s, Highland councils had the highest proportion of ministers and churchmen standing as councillors, the highest proportion of men elected and the highest proportion of councillors elected unopposed. Not a radical environment– that's perfectly true. But some cities historically were not much more militant:

In late 19th century Edinburgh, for example, the lawyers and professional men withdrew from local, political affairs, leaving the Town Council to be run by small landlords and shopkeepers.

> The kind of politics they indulged in were largely defensive and negative. Because local revenues were raised by property taxes – the rates – many small property owners only got themselves elected to the local council to control the level of public spending (Dickson and Treble, 1992).

---

7   Ibid.
8   A. Morris, 'Patrimony and Power', Unpublished DPhil Thesis (Edinburgh: Edinburgh University, 1989).

In short, local councils have often been fiefdoms for the great and the good – the most effective arena for domination of less powerful Scots by more powerful Scots. Not a place where genuine democracy has thrived. So the call for parish-sized democracy is not a return to the 'good old days'. It would be a new beginning for Scots who for centuries, have become active citizens in other countries – ensuring local democracy is nothing like the feudal places in Scotland that shaped them.

Is the progressive answer to keep running off to a larger place where the wearisome gridlines of ownership, control and permission are a little less clearly laid down? Is the answer to downgrade the local dimension of life – or to fix it, so the formative years of the next generation are not spent learning all the things that cannot be done in Scotland because...

Now it's true that many communities at present are not mini nirvanas. All too often, in the absence of real democracy, gatekeepers and cabals have taken over. There's no clear idea of what community development is for since it seems to duplicate what councils should be doing. Many community radio stations find retired incomers have taken over. And whilst Development Trusts are thriving, they make huge demands on time and voluntary resources.

Local is haphazard because it exists in the nation's collective blind-spot – not because place is irrelevant and community impossible.

The answer is more structure, more democracy, more functions, more expectation, more asset transfers, more connection, more grass-roots integration and more power – not less.

Government leaders and distant bureaucrats cannot act endlessly as our absent mentors and proxies. Communities need to do some light, medium and eventually heavy lifting themselves. But no athlete ever started a long race without a warm up. Currently communities who want a share of the action must run the equivalent of a democratic marathon after decades struggling to run for the bus. Scots have such a slender grasp on local power that participation in the community often means no more than buying a paper.

And that too has political ramifications. Surveys find professionals have fewer local attachments, go less frequently (if at all) to local pubs and shops and socialise less with neighbours. 'A life less local' describes the governing class who spend their lives devising services, frameworks, health messages and desirable realities for everyone else. That's problematic.

Some say a plethora of small municipal councils would cause waste, duplication, jobs for the boys, postcode lotteries, chaos and soaring expenses claims from second-rate interfering amateurs. Of course, there would be problems with radical decentralisation – we're all out of democratic practice. But the evidence from development trusts and other countries is that we can pick up the ropes pretty quickly.

It's time for the Scottish Government to admit that scale hasn't ended the scourge of poverty and disadvantage – it's just meant decision makers don't bump into it.

In Scotland, places are dying because of remote, wrong-sized governance despite being full of human talent, capacity, problem-solving energy, history and natural resources.

And yet place is revolutionary because place is where people are. And empowerment and self-determination are principles for everyday life – not just the independence referendum.

CHAPTER EIGHT

Language – Many Mither Tongues

TAVISH SCOTT MSP, his advisor Andy Myles and I were standing in the chalky sunlight of a corridor in Daliburgh School on South Uist, 15 miles from the end of the Outer Hebridean island chain. It was the venue for Ceolas – Gaeldom's annual knees-up with the Canadians of Cape Breton – and we were preparing to enter Angus Peter Campbell's advanced Gaelic class. It was 2006 and Tavish (then Scottish Transport Minister) was keen to show he took Hebridean culture seriously through this fleeting immersion in the Gaelic language. And just as keen to rebut suggestions the (then) Executive was anti-cyclist by chumming me on the bike for 20 miles as part of a Radio Scotland series I was recording.[1]

'So before we go in, what's the festival and who is Angus?'

Tavish oriented himself impressively before every meeting or chat.

'Angus Peter – don't shorten it – is probably the spikiest poet in Gaeldom and the festival is a Hebridean/Canadian cultural love-in swapping songs, arguing about piping methods, drinking, and doing most of it in Gaelic...'

'Right. How do I say hello in Gaelic?'

'*Ciamar a tha sibh* (kimera ha sheeve). Only don't say *sibh* to Angus Peter. It's like *vous* in French or *sie* in German – it implies age and respect and he doesn't like it.'

'What?'

'Try *cimara tha thu* (kimera ha oo). It's more familiar.'

'What?'

We knocked and went in. From the second that familiar hush descended – ten Gaels silenced by the mere presence of three English speakers – I knew we were dead meat.

Angus Peter had been kept waiting too long, the suspension of fluent Gaelic conversation was too irritating and being recorded too

<hr />

1   The 13-part BBC series *On the Bike* prompted a book: *Riddoch on the Outer Hebrides* (Luath 2008), from which this little exchange is an extract.

stifling to be tolerated for very long. Having said all that, I was still hoping for a little forbearance to stuff some words of Gaelic into an important islander's head. It struck me then that without intending it, Gaels and Scots seem to effortlessly antagonise one another.

Try suggesting to a room of Scots struggling for belated, formal acceptance of their own 'Mither Tongue' that their forebears probably spoke Gaelic and that names like *Scotstoun* are proof – Scots speaking towns adrift in a sea of Gaelic – suggest it and stand well back. Some folk are fascinated, others mightily irritated by the sheer presumption of a minority linguistic community that will not learn its place. 'Who dura who dura helicopter – Gaelic isn't even a proper language,' goes the familiar taunt.

In a calmer mood, any rational person will concede helicopter is a foreign word in English too – but somehow the occasional Greek borrowing doesn't undermine the validity of the 'world language'. Perhaps the real difficulty is that Gaelic sentences bear absolutely no resemblance to anything the average Scot can understand. Scotland's 'national' greeting is famously *ceud mìle fàilte* – a hundred thousand welcomes. But few Scots can pronounce it with confidence. Complex rules also mean words like Mhairi are pronounced with a 'v' in certain circumstances to sound like Vairi. So without a grounding in Gaelic grammar, the average Scot cannot confidently pronounce a common girls' name either. What does a majority population do when it tries to use a minority language and is instantly corrected? I'll tell you what it does. It doesn't like it. This is not spite – it's human nature. I wonder how many Gaels would respond well to the notion that everything culturally significant originates in a language they cannot understand without effectively going back to school.

Of course, many have done just that – learning Gaelic at night school. I was one, until the combined effects of an overheated Perth High School, a long day and a long drive home from work in Glasgow meant I fell asleep consistently after 40 minutes – slumping (and possibly dribbling) on the next guy's shoulder. That and a complete failure to do any of the homework meant that after nine weeks I did a Captain Oates and wandered off into the overheated corridors to stop slowing down the rest.

But during that short, steep learning curve, I did make some discoveries. Welsh, Irish and Scots Gaelic do not have words for yes and no. Gaels simply use the verb employed by the questioner and do the same in English.

Thus, 'Did you go to church?' is answered 'I did' or 'I did not' – yes and no are entirely missing. Irish comedy used to hinge on this practice, emphasis being delivered by repetition – 'You will, you will, you will. You did, you did, you did.'

I was hugely intrigued and encouraged in my language struggle by these little discoveries – for another few weeks at least. I felt I actually had a tiny experience of Gaelic's strange thinking – albeit secondhand through English. I could also see how Gaelic words like *brog* for shoe had crept to or from Scots along with *briogais* (pronounced breeks) for trousers. This cheered me up almost as much as learning years later that the Norwegian for cow is *ku*.

And yet, even in a few months, I could see that Gaelic isn't just a bare translation of words – its vocabulary describes a different way of seeing the world. And that raises a new level of intrigue and difficulty for the learner. Take colours.

Gaelic names are applied to the spectrum in a subtly different way to English names. *Gorm* (blue) is the word used to describe the colour of grass but *uaine* also means green. *Dearg* (red) covers scarlet to orange. *Ruadh* is a reddish brown, *donn* is a dark brown. *Liath* (grey) can also cover light blue. *Glas* is a dark grey which also covers grey-green. It's no wonder Gaels recommend immersion in learning centres like Sabhal Mòr Ostaig on Skye. The language is at times so particular to the landscape of the islands, it's hard to see how it could be learned and applied properly outside them.

But the night class experience did at least make me curious and sympathetic towards Gaelic. Usage of a language always does. When Brits go to Greece, the Greeks have the common sense, commercial savvy and confidence to let us stumble along in their language without correction, explanation, reference or historical lecture. That's why people like the Greeks.

If Angus Peter Campbell could encourage repetition of a few similarly basic Gaelic phrases, I reasoned, an important mind might warm towards Gaelic as well. So despite the growing tension in Angus Peter's Daliburgh classroom, I tried to coax a few beginner's words from him to repeat and ram home during the course of the bike ride and radio broadcasts. He made a valiant attempt. *Madainn mhath* [matin vah] is simple enough – it sounds like the French word for morning, *matin*. *Feasgar math* [fesker ma] sounds like the day is starting to fester – which by the afternoon it generally is. *Oidhche mhath* [oyche va] is the one we have all heard Gaels use for goodnight– and the three give Scots a confident trio of greetings.

But Angus Peter – the dangerously honest soul that he is – simply could not pretend that these Anglophone greetings had any home in his Gaelic head.

'I wouldn't say to my wife "good morning" in Gaelic. I would say something like "there you are – how are you feeling today" – and that isn't *madainn mhath*. This isn't real Gaelic. This is English Gaelic. Your ancestors have taken the words from our mouths. Now you are taking the time from our lives. Get out.'

I was actually impressed by Angus Peter's single-mindedness, unbiddable bluntness and complete lack of interest in our stumbling efforts at token Gaelic. But then, as one Gaelic proverb puts it, 'if you want to be praised, die.'

Five minutes later we weren't exactly dead, but out on our ears. Told kindly but firmly that Gaelic speakers had so little time together, we shouldn't waste theirs with half-hearted learning efforts. Even if 'we' did include a government minister.

Back in the corridor, Tavish was completely unruffled and happily practised the Gaelic words for ferry, plane and bus. 'John Farquhar Munro *will* be impressed.'[2]

It wasn't the gentlest immersion into Gaelic, but my stranger's curiosity about the language and culture grew during the next two weeks 'in the saddle'.

Take names, for example. I was called Lesley after competing pressures from the two families prompted my parents to go wild and name their firstborn after the winner of a local Beautiful Baby competition. A wee boy won. Lesley describes nothing about my family, appearance or place of origin. In Gaelic nothing is that random.

Some names are descriptive, like Catriona Ruadh (red-haired Catherine); patronymic like Màiri Sheumais (James's Mary or Mary

---

2   John Farquhar Munro was a Liberal Democrat Gaelic speaking Highland MSP until 2011.

of James); occupational like Dòmhnall Cìobair (Donald the Shepherd) occupational and patronymic, like Màiri a Ghoba (Mary of the Black-smith); geographic like Ràghnall a Bhràighe (Ronald of/from Braes); origin-based like Ruairidh Leòdhasach (Roderick of Lewis), or the whole shebang like Calum Dubh a Chlachain (Black haired Calum from Clachan).

Gaels have different ways of conceptualising objects as well. Many still talk about a trouser and a scissor in English because the objects in Gaelic are not thought of as plural. The Scots practice of pronouncing the word film more like 'filum' is because of a Gaelic rule which commonly inserts a vowel between certain consonants (hence the otherwise baffling pronunciation of BBC Al(a)ba and Ardnamur(a)chan). There's a Gaelic origin, too, for the 'continuing present' in phrases like 'are you wanting your tea?' or 'is he needing to go?' rather than the more abrupt 'do you want tea?' and 'does he need to go?'

Gaelic has probably also given Glaswegians the glottal stop, which results in words like Paterson being pronounced Pa-erson. In Gaelic, consonants like 'g', 'm' and 't' are often silent. Thus the word for father, *athair* is pronounced 'aher' – as if no 't' was present.

Such a wheen of grammatical rules imported from one language into another is technically called 'macaronic.' So perhaps Gaelic heritage explains the perceived grammatical 'mistakes' of modern working-class Glaswegians. And perhaps that's a matter of considerable social importance. Tommy Sheridan's political career may be over but his insistence on not allowing his speech to be 'corrected' for the official Holyrood record was a small victory for vast numbers of (publicly) silenced Glaswegians. How much more confidence might West Coast Scots speakers have if academic research clearly established a formal link between Gaelic grammar and Glasgow patter? And who knows, in some obscure journal, perhaps it has.

In any case, Gaelic has long had its own separate battle to fight.

Gaels endured shocking treatment at the hands of Scots-speaking monarchs like King James VI. Official documents during his reign described Highlanders as 'void of the knawledge and feir of God' and prone to 'all kynd of barbarous and bestile cruelties'. The Gaelic language, spoken fluently by James IV, became known in the time of James VI as 'Erse' or Irish, implying it was foreign in nature. The Scottish

Parliament decided it had become a principal cause of the Highlanders' stubborn refusal to be assimilated into the Lowland Scottish state
and tried to abolish it.

In 1598 James VI authorised the 'Gentleman Adventurers of Fife'
to civilise the 'most barbarous Isle of Lewis... not by agreement but
by extirpation of thame'. The Gentlemen were sent packing at first
but finally prevailed in 1607. Two years later the Statutes of Iona
were enacted, banning bards and other bearers of traditional culture,
forcing clan chiefs to send their heirs to Lowland Scotland for education in English-speaking Protestant schools and providing support for
Protestant ministers in Highland Parishes. So began a process 'specifically aimed at the extirpation of the Gaelic language, the destruction
of its traditional culture and the suppression of its bearers.'[3]

The Hanoverian clampdown after Culloden – banning Gaelic,
wearing tartan and clan association – in many ways just tried to finish
what Lowland Scots had already begun.

In his Hebridean tour of 1773, Dr Johnson remarked:

> The clans retain little now of their original character... of what they
> had before the conquest of their country there remain only their lan-
> guage and their poverty. Their language is attacked on every side.[4]

Despite opinion polls demonstrating a steady 70–80 per cent support
for Gaelic, a noisy minority still begrudges every penny spent. In a
way it's not surprising some 'modern' Scots are in two minds about
the Gaels. If they could shear off the sorrow, sentimentality and
nostalgia that has beset their society for generations, the Gaels could
yet re-emerge as Scotland's radicals – grasping that crown from their
jumped up descendants, the Glaswegians. But radical is not how most
Scots see the Gaels. Nor do they respect the Gaels stamina, feel guilt
about their betrayal, or shame about their repression. The thing Scots
identify most strongly about the Gaels is their sense of superiority.

Put bluntly, the values Gaels have espoused for centuries make the
Scots wrong. Wrong to grab the deal from England 300 years ago.
Wrong to put the removal of small comforts before ornamentation
of the mind. Wrong to become materialist, wrong to become secular,

---

3   K. MacKinnon, *Gaelic – A past and Future Prospect* (Edinburgh: The Saltire Society, 1991).
4   Samuel Johnson and John Boswell, *Journey to the Hebrides* (Edinburgh: Canongate, 1996).

wrong to become big, wrong to question the primacy of family and wrong to become remote from nature and spiritual lives.

Gaels know they should have led Scotland in a different direction (whether it would have been the 'right' direction is of course debatable.) But they couldn't do it. And the great fear – the elephant in the room – is that in failing to lead with old values or develop new ones, Gaelic culture has collapsed inwards to stifle natives and deter incomers.

All this complex heritage leans heavily on young 'tradition bearers'. Amazingly though, some have proved more than equal to the daunting task.

Mòd winning singer Arthur Cormack was the driving force behind the grassroots *Fèisean* movement which kicked off on Barra in 1981. Now the week-long, local volunteer-led festivals teach traditional instruments to local children through the medium of Gaelic all year round in 45 parts of Scotland. Indeed some *fèisean* like Aberdeen lie well beyond the conventional *Gàdhealtachd*. The Blas Music Festival across the Highland and Islands every September is also expanding, the traditional Gaelic Mòd with its more formal structures is still popular and BBC Alba has added a TV channel to the pivotal BBC Radio nan Gàidheal, which was set up in 1985 through the happy coincidence of Gaelic-taught Alasdair Milne as Director General of the BBC and Neil Fraser as head of Gaelic and then of Radio Scotland.

Indeed, in his obituary after Milne's recent death, that other influential Gaelic-learner Brian Wilson – the founder of the bilingual *West Highland Free Press*, former MP and Minister for Gaelic – paid this tribute to Milne's stubborn support for the Gaelic language and culture:

> Alasdair Milne could have lived a very comfortable life within the BBC and done none of this. Indeed, when the knives were out for him in the 1980s, his commitments to Gaelic and piping were sneered at by those who wished to patronise him and portray a feckless misfit in the job of Director General. There was never the slightest chance of Milne being deterred by such prejudices. He not only had a fine sense of his own worth but the values and friendships associated with his cultural affinities represented a treasured dimension in his life. Away from the power struggles of the BBC, he loved the camaraderie of his sojourns to the West Highlands and Islands.[5]

---

5 *West Highland Free Press* 2013: http://www.whfp.com/index.php?option=com_ content&task=view&id=1148.

It seems fitting that it took a Madras-born Scot to understand British-ness as something bigger than Englishness writ large.

But Milne paid the price for his attempt to house the many differ-ent cultures and languages of Britishness within the one British Broad-casting Corporation – 'enjoying the melancholy distinction of being the first Director General of the BBC to be dismissed from office', and therefore the first not to receive a knighthood. It may be stretching the point somewhat, but more than a century earlier the same fate befell the Orcadian John Rae – the only notable Arctic explorer not to receive a knighthood. He was acknowledged by Canadians as the man who found the final link in the North-West passage during a search for the remains of Sir John Franklin's expedition in 1845 but failed to master the language of diplomatic half-truths and straightforwardly reported evidence of cannibalism in the wreckage. Rae was effec-tively ostracised from horrified London society and blackballed by the English Establishment.[6]

This may seem to have little to do with the current state of Scots Gaelic – 65,000 speakers and dwindling.

But speakers of any tongue, like members of any cultural minor-ity, quickly learn the ways of advancement and deter or encourage their children accordingly. Alasdair Milne was sufficiently thrawn to withstand monoglots, Establishment voices and little Englanders for a while, but many Gaelic speaking parents on the islands are less self-as-sured. So ironically, Glasgow is building a second Gaelic school, as research demonstrates better overall outcomes for bilingual children, while the Western Isles itself has Gaelic streams in almost all schools but not one single school that teaches all subjects through the medium of Gaelic. It's a Catch 22 situation. Gaelic's unequal chances of sur-vival motivate language activists and doubting parents in almost equal measure.

The activists know any successful language needs the same 'surround sound' that English enjoys – popular use in the playground, school shop, walking home, arguing, fighting, chatting up and texting. But beyond the school gates, Gaelic isn't a popular language within the communities young people frequent – the home, the internet, the sec-ondary school and the TV.

---

6   K. McGoogan, *Fatal Passage: The True Story of John Rae* (New York: Carroll & Graf, 2002).

Does that make Gaelic a 'loser language'?

Well there isn't much of a queue to have primary school children taught in Chinese languages instead – even though fluent speakers can probably expect jobs for life.

In fact, Gaelic is another language where fluency almost guarantees a good job in Scotland. Fluent graduates are in great demand in the media – so sought after that few trickle beyond the relatively high pay and bright lights of broadcasting, to the education system that is crying out for their specialist expertise.

And there's the rub.

A few fluent Gaels have great scarcity value, and are unlikely to opt for teaching. But if they shun teaching, the language will become so marginal their own prestige jobs will dry up or appear economically unjustifiable.

And yet as long as Gaelic medium remains such a minority interest, objecting parents can't be blamed for feeling wary. After all, if immersion in a second language was such a great educational opportunity, why wouldn't the Scottish Government order compulsory immersion in primary schools everywhere? And of course Gaelic is not an easy language to master so non-speakers project this difficulty onto small, child-sized minds and wonder if the effort of learning Gaelic and English will simply exhaust them for all the other tough learning work that lies ahead.

These are all understandable concerns. But they have no grounding in fact.

Children under six can learn up to three languages easily. And their improved language skills make them better general communicators. Even boys. The Welsh have proved it.

Roughly a quarter of Welsh kids are in Welsh-medium schools learning everything from English to Maths and cookery in the Welsh language. In Gwynedd, 90 per cent of children are in Welsh medium primaries and incoming children are offered intensive Welsh courses at special centres before joining in local Welsh schools. In (generally) English speaking Rhondda, 40 per cent of kids are in Welsh primaries – almost all have non-Welsh speaking parents.

Their motives are simple. Parents know the Welsh schools get better results, view the language as an important asset for children in a competitive job market and buy the educationists' line that learning two languages improves almost every aspect of linguistic ability. The fact Welsh medium schools also tend to possess enthusiastic teachers and a self-selecting group of parents who make sure the little darlings do their homework is icing on the Welsh cake.

Scots Gaelic today is where the Welsh were 40 years ago. A decade of rebellious activism by the Welsh Language Society brought the cash and control to establish Welsh medium education. And what they've achieved since then is astonishing.

In 2001, 184,000 kids aged 3–15 spoke Welsh – just 7,000 spoke Gaelic. Which puts Welsh well above language-group reproduction levels – and Gaelic well below.

Even in Wales, though fluency peters out fast – at GCSE and A level only six per cent and five per cent of students are fluent in Welsh. The figure drops to 1.6 per cent at university. In short, Welsh for Welsh speakers is a language more like French or German – not the native tongue of the hearth, or the heart. The biggest selling Welsh language book in 2007 shifted only 5,000 copies. Welsh, like Gaelic, will probably not survive the century because, according to Welsh veteran, Geraint H. Jenkins, 'a language network is not a community. And a language which is not a community language will die'.

But then, we all die. It's not a reason to rule out learning the big, beautiful, frustrating thing called Gaelic.

So something else is holding Gaelic back – maybe it's best explained by a closer keek at its country cousin, Scots.

Anyone looking at the vast number of crabbit, sleekit, dreich and carnaptious emblazoned coffee cups and tea towels would think Scots must be in rude health. Likewise Burns Suppers celebrating drouthy neebors, wee sleekit, cowrin, tim'rous beasties and auld lang syne. Those of us who live outside cities or in working-class urban communities can testify Scots is alive and kicking. But it's rarely used by anyone in positions of authority – from newsreaders to politicians or judges. Indeed certain court authorities have ruled that use of the Scots word 'aye' is a form of contempt for the whole legal system.[7]

---

7 In December 1993, a witness in a Scottish court who had answered 'aye' to confirm he was the person summoned was told by the Sheriff that he must answer either 'yes' or 'no'. When his name was read again and he was asked to confirm it, he answered 'aye' again, and was imprisoned for 90 minutes for contempt of court. On his release he said 'I genuinely thought I was answering him'. *The Times*, 11/12/1993.

Compared to the levels of Scots spoken in the 18th century, the language is in decline. Nonetheless a 2009 survey conducted for the Scottish Government found 85 per cent of people living in Scotland think they speak Scots, 86 per cent think Scots is important for local identity and Scottish culture, 69 per cent use Scots when socialising with friends, 63 per cent when home with the family but only 31 per cent use it 'out and about' and just 25 per cent at work.[8]

The good news from this survey is that Scots is still a language of the hearth and the playground. The bad news is that Scots speakers (like Gaels) stop using the Mither Tongue when non-speakers might be present. That's a puzzle. If the survey figures are correct, almost everyone speaks Scots. So why the self-censorship?

You can (almost) see why Gaels jump out of their own language when a non-speaker is present. Non-Gaels generally cannot under-stand a single word of Gaelic. Not so with Scots. And yet speakers evidently abandon Scots in public. If a whopping 85 per cent of Scots really do speak Scots, why haud back?

Perhaps it's feared the 15 per cent non-speakers constitute a power-ful minority of managers whose perceptions of being snubbed could make or mar employment prospects. Evidently some Scots – like some Gaels – fear their language is perceived as a 'loser' language by the winners and have internalised those values. But most of our European neighbours speak several languages and dialects and simply switch between them as appropriate. Why is Scots never deemed appropriate in public?

The belief that one Scots dialect is incomprehensible to others is sometimes cited – but that also fails to ring true. Most Scots speakers understand one another perfectly well, savour local variations on the general theme and revel in exchanging vocabulary.

Perhaps occasional speakers fear they are not Scots enough, not the 'real deal' amongst those who speak Scots as an involuntary default. I know from living in North Fife that the fairmers, former lino workers, fishermen, quarry workers and aipple growers who populate the toons of the Tay Estuary do mair than slot pithy Scots words into English – they use Scots as their constant Mither Tongue.

8   http://www.scotland.gov.uk/Publications/2010/01/06105123/1.

They divide fowk (not people) intae lassies and laddies, tak their time with yin anither, coont the beasts and kye (not cattle) and are hugely entertained when speakers fae furth o the parish roll in and yaise their ain tongues.

By contrast, I speak Scots as I speak German – selectively. I generally don't use either until the need arises and the situation seems right – 'real' Scots speakers don't pick and choose because they can't.

So are we all really in the same linguistic boat? Or do 'part-time' speakers of a 'Step-Mither tongue' feel inauthentic the minute they are up against the real McCoy?

Is watching *Gary Tank Commander* enough to claim 'I understand Scots'– or is explaining 'Tam O' Shanter' line by line a better benchmark? Is 'gonnae no dae that' guid Scots or bad English? Is Stanley Baxter's *Parliamo Glasgow* slang? Is using 'aye' not 'yes' and 'scunnered' not 'disgusted' enough to qualify – and does reading the above prove that you read and I write Scots?

Hardly.

Without agreement on its vital signs, it's no wonder there's disagreement about the current health of Scots.

Billy Kay's book *The Mither Tongue* is a comprehensive account of Scots and its publication was a landmark moment for the Scots language. Author James Robertson said:

> Never before had (Scots speakers) been told, on the BBC no less, that what they spoke – far from being 'the language of the gutter' or debased English – had an 800-year pedigree, two multi-volume dictionaries describing it, a vast and glorious literature, and a whole set of dialects of its own. This was a life-affirming, emotionally and intellectually liberating message, and it took courage and conviction to be the messenger.

In 2010 Billy Kay produced a radio programme, *The Bonnie Broukit Bairn*, to accompany a report on the Scots language for the Scottish Government. Huv a shufty. Even for native speakers, the Scots part of this text takes concentration:

> *The Bonnie Broukit Bairn* spiers whit the future hauds for the mither tongue o ower a million an a hauf Scots fowk in the 21st centurie, fowk like you that micht speak the leid ilkae day, but hae nae kennin

o ocht belangin the braw leiterature or gowden history o the langage. I wad be gleg tae haud forrit scrievin tae ye in Scots, but jalouse that maist o ye wad finnd it a sair chave tae follae whit I am threapin on aboot, as gey few Scots are leiterate in their ain leid... sae like Chris Guthrie in *Sunset Song* I'll gae ower tae English... you wanted the words they'd known and used, forgotten in the far-off youngness of their lives, Scots words to tell to your heart, how they wrung it and held it, the toil of their days and unendingly their fight. And the next minute that passed from you, you were English, back to the English words so sharp and clean and true – for a while, for a while, till they slid so smooth from your throat you knew they could never say anything that was worth the saying at all.[9]

Without understanding every word many of us can say amen to that sentiment.

So if 85 per cent of people think they speak Scots, and if anthologies contain such a wealth of material, why did the census in 2011 need to link to an external website so Scots could hear samples of genuine speakers? A census question on 'good health' was also included but needed no further explanation. And yet the precise nature of 'good health' is as subjective as the definition of 'Scots'.[10]

Nor would the census administrators define what they counted as fluency – did they mean Scots lite, Braid Scots or baith thegither? Mebbes aye – mebbes naw.

Few will recall what Cathy Jamieson was talking about when she uttered that memorable Scots phrase, but it caused instant hilarity in the Holyrood Chamber and beyond. After which everyone reverted to the Parliament's usual brand of expression-free and humourless English.

And perhaps that's precisely why Scots speakers use so little Scots language in public. Perhaps a nation wary of wearing its heart on its collective sleeve (for reasons of past persecution, snobbery and social judgement) is quite happy to keep its Mither Tongue for private use.

Scots may be consciously saving their language for the private

---

9   Carl MacDougall's book *Scots: The Language of the People* followed soon afterwards with 50 writers, covering more than 800 years, including Edwin Morgan, Tom Leonard, Adam McNaughtan and Kathleen Jamie, William Dunbar, Robert Burns, James Hogg, Sir Walter Scott, Robert Louis Stevenson, Hugh MacDiarmid, John Galt, Lewis Grassic Gibbon, Robert McLellan, Allan Ramsay, Hamish Henderson, Marion Angus, Robert Fergusson, Robert Tannahill, Neil Munro, Robert Garioch and William Soutar.

10   The results of the first census question asked about the Scots language in 2011 are due to be published later in 2013.

domain – for those rare, intimate domestic moments when we *do* have something worth saying. Maybe English does just fine for the dry, impersonal transactions of public life while Scots stays private to safeguard use, connection, community, family and intimacy and avoid dilution.

All the efforts of Scots language campaigners haven't much changed that reality. So what would? In theory at least, if Scotland became independent tomorrow, Scots could be taught as a language with a formal grammar and vocabulary. After all, as the saying goes, 'a language is a dialect with an army and navy'.

The Norwegian languages are an interesting case in point.

In 1814, Norway separated from Denmark, adopted its own constitution but was immediately forced into a new union of crowns with the Swedish King. The written language, Danish, was suddenly acceptable to create distance between Norway and Sweden. What followed linguistically may sound strangely familiar to modern Scots.

The ruling class spoke Dano-Norwegian and regarded it as the cultivated language, as opposed to the common tongue of workers, craftspeople and farmers who spoke with Norwegian dialects. These were generally considered vulgar speech or a weak attempt at speaking 'standard' Norwegian – ignoring the fact that 'Norwegian' had a separate evolution from a common ancestor, Old Norse.[11]

Upon independence in 1905 not just one but two official Norwegian written languages were recognised – Bokmål (used by the majority today) and Nynorsk (based on a synthesis of regional dialects).

Confusing enough – but a century on, many Norwegians also speak local dialects which can differ from both 'official' Norwegian languages as much as they differ from Danish.

And yet despite such strong regional variation within Norway, no-one suggests the effort to establish two written Norwegian languages was worthless. Far, far from it. In 1913, Olaf Bull's crime novel *Mit navn er Knoph* (*My name is Knoph*) was the first piece of Norwegian literature to be translated into Danish – underlining the fact that the independent state of Norway now also had separate languages.

---

11 Developed by linguist Ivar Aasen from the 1840s, Nynorsk – then known as Landsmaal – was recognised on an equal footing to the adapted Danish (Riksmål) in 1885, and for use in primary schools in 1892. In 1929 Landsmaal became Nynorsk and Riksmål became Bokmål. So the two had equal status with Danish before formal independence in 1905.

Indeed, debate over the versions of Norwegian was more fiercely contested than the generally agreed path towards political independence.

Eventually, to resolve the issue, Norway's 431 municipalities were asked to decide on their main language tradition. The result was an almost even split between Bokmål (161), Nynorsk (116) and 'neutral' (156) – though smaller municipality population size means Nynorsk is spoken by just 12 per cent of the Norwegian people. Now, children are educated in the chosen main language of each locality until the age of 13 when they have to learn both – and cheerfully use local dialect in everyday life.[12]

So what Norwegians write is still different from how many Norwegians speak. And whilst a century of political independence, compulsory education and Norwegian TV have succeeded in establishing Norwegian not Danish as the *lingua franca*, even these powerful forces haven't been enough to eliminate strong local dialects from everyday speech.

This demonstrates the powerful impact of locality upon language even in a buoyant, nation building new Nordic state.[13] And maybe this has resonance in Scotland where (at least) three linguistic currents are jostling for state recognition (English, Scots and Gaelic) together with a minor host of dialects.

Effectively, all the languages of Scandinavia plus Scots and English are part of a larger Germanic language family as you can see from the (admittedly rather crafted) Scots sentence in Figure 18. There's a close proximity between many Scots words and the Norse languages (*mus hus*, *braw* and *quine*); there's also a similarity amongst all the Norse languages (apart from the Finns) while the Gaelic languages are as different to English as Finnish is to the rest of Scandinavia.

In the light of this, the fact that Scots is like English doesn't completely count against it. All Germanic languages have strong similarities. The fact there are so many dialects of Scots doesn't have to be a minus factor either. Norwegian survives with two full languages and dozens of dialects.

---

12 Despite this linguistic democracy, though, Bokmål is by far the majority written and spoken language – of 4,549 state publications in 2000 8per cent were in Nynorsk, and 92 per cent in Bokmål and the largest national newspapers (*Aftenposten*, *Dagbladet* and *VG*) are published in Bokmål or Riksmål.

13 On 13 August 1905, the Norwegians had an independence referendum. 368,211 voted in favour of separation from Sweden with just 184 against.

Languages in Northern Europe	
Scots	A quine and a moose are loose aboot the hoose on a braw bricht moonlicht nicht
Norwegian	En kvinne og en mus er løs om huset på en bra klar månelys natt
Swedish	Kvinna och en mus är lost om huset på en bra och tydig månbelysta natten
Danish	En kvinde og en mus er løst omkring huset på en god lys mane lyser nat
Dutch	Een vrouw en een muis sjin los over het huis op een goede helldere maannacht
German	Eine Frau und eine Maus sind locker über das Haus auf einem guten hellen Mondacht
Finnish	Tyttö ja hiiri ovat löysät noin talo kaunis, kirkas kuutamoyönä
Scots Gaelic	Tha boireannach agus luch ma sgaoil air feadh an taighe air oidhche bhrèagha ghealaich.

Figure 18: Languages in Northern Europe compared.

So what does that mean for the future of Scots in a different political context?

It's entirely possible citizens of an independent or highly devolved Scotland might learn Scots formally in school, continue to use their own dialect privately and use a more Scottified form of English in public. As the Norwegians have demonstrated, such a variety of 'voices' within one language is entirely possible. But would learning Scots 'properly' be worth the candle?

Might formality kill the spontaneity and privacy which has helped Scots survive, or could a single, state-taught and widely broadcast language demonstrate local accents are just that – important but hardly damaging variations on the theme.

Certainly, Radio nan Gaideal helped establish one core Gaelic tongue by letting speakers hear one another in a formal, public way on a daily basis rather than once in a blue moon. Before that it was easier for Lewis Gaels to hear minor differences with Barra Gaels and pull up the linguistic and emotional drawbridge.

One core language could emerge from regular exposure to Scots in officialdom and broadcast media. It's possible – but not very likely.

At the turn of the last century, when Norwegians made their historic linguistic break with Denmark and Sweden there were no films, broadcasters, TVs, radios or the internet encouraging the near universal penetration of English-speaking American culture. In 1905 it was relatively easy to make a linguistic change stick.

Now that may be impossible. Every language is being diluted by 'loan words' from English and according to David Crystal, the prominent American linguist, 90 per cent of the world's 7,000 current languages will have ceased to exist by the year 2100.[14]

Mind you, such dire predictions can prompt energetic defence of small languages, instead of defeatist abandonment. The Nordic Council spoke recently of the 'Scandinavian language'(singular), prompting speculation that future spelling reforms in Norway, Sweden and Denmark might result in the creation of one unified written language. But despite accountant logic, a unified 'Scandish' is a political nonstarter and each Nordic nation is stubbornly determined to keep ploughing its own linguistic furrow with just a few million native speakers apiece, despite the duplication of publishing effort, diseconomies of scale and probability of confusion.

Why? The loss of language matters in ways that go beyond mere words. It may damage the way we are able to think. According to French linguist Claude Hagege:

> Languages are not simply a collection of words. They are living, breathing organisms holding the connections and associations that define a culture. When a language becomes extinct, the culture in which it lived is lost too. What native speakers lose is essentially an enormous cultural heritage, the way of expressing the relationship with nature, with the world, between themselves in the framework of families. It's also the way they express their humour, their love, their life.

14   D. Crystal, *Language Death* (Cambridge: Cambridge University Press, 2002).

Paul Lewis, the editor of *Ethnologue* – a global database of languages – goes further. If people begin to think of their language as useless, he argues, they see their cultural identity as useless as well, leading to social disruption, depression, suicide and drug use:

> And as parents no longer transmit language to their children, the connection between children and grandparents is broken and traditional values are lost. There is a social and cultural ache that remains, where people realise they have lost something.

In short, when a language dies, a way of thinking dies with it. So what 'way of thinking' does Scots represent?

This is just my own view.

Two summers back I was cycling along one of those long inner-Highland glens that might once have been crowded but now contains only fenced-off pockets of densely packed Sitka spruce and wider hummocky stretches of heather moorland and boggy grass sweeping down to a silent, hydro dam-created loch. After three hours cycling along the rough hydro road with only a family of deer for company, I was getting used to having the place to myself.

And then, ahead, I spotted two figures – a man struggling to lift a large rucksack hampered by his over-excited dog. Realising our paths would cross in less than a minute, my mind jumped into language autopilot, sifting fast through ideas and corresponding phrases to match this reality with something appropriate.

I came within earshot.

'I see your dug's not trained for heavy lifting then...'

'Aye but you should see him bang in the tent pegs.'

Only a few seconds elapsed as I swooped past. The walker had no idea what I was going to say. Neither did I. But he was ready to devote all his mental energy to respond in the event of a worthwhile prompt. Mate and checkmate. Point and counterpoint. Serve and volley. One stranger momentarily echoing the path of another like a verbal starling murmur.

No further exchange was needed. I wouldn't recognise the walker again and he doesn't know my name. But the joy of that short spontaneous exchange stayed with me for hours, days – evidently years. Language was playfully deployed around a randomly chosen image

– not just wordplay, but mindplay. In my experience this playfulness and desire to connect is hard-wired to Scots and hard for non-Scots to reproduce even if they can use words like dreich or glaikit correctly.

Now of course, this cannot be substantiated. Not even remotely.

Even though this kind of exchange has occurred hundreds or thousands of times in my lifetime – to equal delight – it's an entirely private, intimate and perhaps imagined experience. So few column inches have ever been written about the way Scots speak or think compared to the languages of English and Gaelic, or the better-funded country cousin that is Ulster Scots. An exception is the brilliant and popular writer Des Dillon, who's discussed the place of metaphor in Scots speech many times. Des wrote *Me and Ma Gal*, *Singing I'm No a Billy He's a Tim* and countless other books and plays. He also wrote for BBC Scotland's *River City* until a dispute arose about the authenticity of the dialogue. What is Scots for Des? Scots is metaphor.

What's he like? That classic Glaswegianism is not just the prompt to heap characterising adjectives upon an unknown head. It's a credo. A way of life. What is he like? What are people like? Describe them. Put some effort into it. Colour up the world for a minute. Raise the game. Engage with me. Connect.

In my 20s I went out with an exceptionally tall, gruff-looking Glaswegian who had been in a Tongs gang during his teens. Nights out in those days began with a few 'accidental' jostles at spit and sawdust pubs like Curlers, His Nibs and the Rubaiyat. The whole point seemed to be an assertion of pecking order. Frank was at the top. Despite the slightly strained circumstances of those macho exchanges, I was always struck by the humour and metaphor.

'Good leaves up there, big man?'

'Weather changing anytime soon?'

The fact of his height was never commented on directly. That would be beyond boring. The fact was taken as read and conversation was built around it, leaning against it, pointing to it. I think that's called 'added value' in the leaden world such ways of thinking seek to escape.

I think also of a porter in BBC Scotland called Tommy – a capable, wiry, quiet man responsible for shifting scenery, props and instruments around Queen Margaret Drive. I used to work in the Victorian 'old building' – once the college that first allowed Scotswomen to take medical degrees, then a mortuary during the war and finally offices for radio programmes. The access balcony overlooked a large central atrium and a special entrance reserved for the BBC Controller and Head of Radio. It was always tempting to throw paper darts over the side.

One day Tommy was walking along the top carrying a bundle of mail. Someone opened the grand glass front door and the sudden release of air swooped in and round the letters, carrying one over the top and down the stairs. Instantly, Tommy tucked the rest under his arm, sailed down the bannisters with the skill of a man who clearly did this regularly in private moments, and caught the letter before it reached the ground.

He glanced up and smiled.

'Airmail.'

Tommy was Scots to his bootstraps. The premium placed on verbal and physical dexterity, the spontaneous confidence, the shared secret, the *mot juste*, the random moment harvested for all its performance possibilities.

This is all Scots – a language performed with metaphor, wit and physical flourish to entertain those guaranteed to understand it. Scots speakers use their language like a password or code. Native speakers don't intend Scots to be fully shared, codified, formally taught or embodied in public life. A few words on coasters and mugs for tourists and posh Scots are fine. But if Scots speakers lose the intimacy of their language they risk losing its greatest benefit. Scots currently separates the wheat from the chaff. It links and empowers those who place a very high value on local connection, physical place, family history and cultural identity and holds at a distance those who don't – and that generally means everyone in a position of formal authority.

In an elitist society, settling for linguistic control of private space makes sense. But surely, some day, we are hoping for better? What would happen if the voice of 'authority' changed to use the Scots speakers' own register? It would be a truly epic transformation.

Until then we could aim for more Scots speaking broadcasters, wider official use and some parity of esteem between Gaelic, Scots, English and the languages spoken by Scotland's ethnic minorities. Looked at differently, all these languages, their many dialects and accompanying world views, represent an incredible resource happed up in one carnaptious country. Scots could choose to celebrate that diversity instead of falling into suspicion and competition. Any chance?

In my mother's home patch of Caithness there have long been rumblings about Gaelic road signs on the grounds that the county has a Norse speaking heritage not a Gaelic one.

This grumbling resentment flared in Wick over the decision to hold the Gaelic Mód in Caithness for the first time during the summer of 2010. Councillors welcomed the income-generating potential of the festival but also argued for a local Gaelic sign ban. Such hostility and double standards prompted fears of a boycott.

A small group of Wickers opted instead to try and 'lance the boil' with a public debate about the place of Gaelic in local culture. I chaired it, a hundred people attended and the event contained a rewarding mixture of light, heat, anger and humour – exactly what one would expect during a genuine exchange about loved language traditions. The Gaels present accepted they weren't the only ones whose native tongue had all but been beaten out of their parents' generation at school in the name of 'advancement'. These days, after centuries of marginalisation, Gaels at least know their inner voice is a recognised language.

Dialects of Scots are more vulnerable to being 'corrected' as 'bad English,' even though they carry culture in the same way (if not to the same extent) as the 'full-blown' languages around them.

Just as Gaelic expresses its seaborne origins with five words for the colour blue, for example, the Caithness dialect has a small stack of words for sulking, moodiness and intransigence – *thrawn, jugend, cussed* and *pirn* being my mother's favourites.

There were, however, no *pirns* at the debate – and the Gaels were not the only learners.

Caithnessians learned Gaelic had indeed been spoken locally until the last century and many place names thought to be Norse had Gaelic origins – and sometimes both.

Trosk, for example, is a Caithness word (often used by my mother to describe the *pirning* faces of her children) which is closest to glaikit in Scots or slack-jawed and idle in English. In fact, torsk means Cod in both Gaelic and Norwegian – what the Caithnessians have done is apply a playful and expressive spin to that 'proper' word and find a new way to tease their grumpy offspring. The sudden laughter that followed 'trosk's' unravelling was overdue recognition of a precious language tradition which would have conservation status if human ecology ranked as highly as plant and animal protection in Scotland.

It reminded me also of the raucous laughter on Colin Campbell CDs – another talented man unknown or at least uncelebrated beyond the Highlands. This guitar-strumming farmer has the uncanny knack of perfectly mimicking any Highland accent and two record shops in Inverness used to have entire walls lined with his cassettes and CDs – most recorded before live, local audiences. His skill is to jump with pinpoint verbal precision between imaginary local radio stations – Radio Auchnagatt, Bettyhill, Caithness and Back on Lewis are my favourites. Some of the material is hilarious (the recipe for Curried Guga à la Back involving 100 yards of rope and running shoes is a classic) but regardless of quality the audience reaction is always the same. You can hear people almost dying with laughter in the background, gulping painfully for breath, wheezing as if a chronic asthma attack had begun at the same time as a coughing fit – shrieking as if they had been physically assaulted. Not the polite laughter of the mildly amused but the convulsive snorting of the utterly astonished.

Listening to Colin Campbell in full flow is like hearing a linguistic high priest performing an act of mass validation. Each community he mimics – often just ten or 20 miles from the next – is being recognised in the public domain for possibly the very first time.

That's powerful and empowering stuff – the sort of cultural validation that's tickled the conceit and reinforced the identity of Central Belt Scots for decades. Other parts of Scotland need it too.

Ultra-local knowledge, accent and mannerisms matter disproportionately in Scotland, because culture and language have had to do the identity building normally shared with structures of local democracy in better functioning countries. In Scotland, language does all the heavy lifting. That's why dialect and establishing connection matter so much.

Perhaps the most Scottish phrase in use throughout the country today is 'see you later' – exchanged every waking moment by people who will almost certainly never see each other later or indeed ever again. Even in a corner shop 300 miles from home, the illusion of inclusion in a never-ending conversation or relationship must be maintained. We are all kin. We are all Jock Tamson's bairns. When conversation picks up spontaneously like this between complete strangers the sense of immediate connection can feel good.

English friends however, often feel uncomfortable and excluded when the 'mission to connect' kicks in. If Glasgow taxi drivers ask where they come from, the subject is quickly changed. Wrong. Scottishness is all about connection and respect for roots. The only difficulty arises with folk who seem distant and rootless. For Scots that's like gaun oot minus yer kegs.

But 'rootless' is how evasive southerners can appear. Folk attached to something beyond place, origin or background – folk attached to 'mere' money or random happenstance and happy to let that thin pedigree speak for them.

Scots on the other hand, need to connect. It's a primal urge. Scots must know more about place, background, accent, belonging, identity and stories about home – wherever home may be. What puts the average Scot in a fankle is not different home stories but people who won't or can't trade in that verbal currency – in whatever accent or language they authentically possess. Guarded, wary or defensive folk are just a disappointment. The average Scottish taxi driver enjoys nothing better than the challenge of finding an aunty, friend or former workmate who lives in your neck of the woods. It's an extension of 'the knowledge'. But it can't happen unless both sides are willing. The desire to connect is the essence of Scottish culture and real connection is very often only made in Scots or Gaelic.

I knew so much about my last Glasgow taxi driver and his 91-year-old mother that I could identify him in a jiffy after leaving a mobile phone in his cab. For Scots that's normal – though for non-Celts who don't understand the game it probably feels more like the Spanish Inquisition. Why do Scots have to find a point of connection to relax? Perhaps that comes from the days when survival depended upon quickly establishing a common bond (or detecting ill will) amongst fellow workers or neighbours. Whatever the reason, involuntary inclusion is never far away on a night out. At a pantomime in the Dundee

Rep – the nearest thing to a global front room – I was working my way through an ice cream during the interval when I felt a tap on the shoulder. The older woman sitting behind me – at the end of a family grouping that took up the whole row – held a large poly bag in front of me and shook it. Clearly this was the designated family rubbish bag being shoogled by the family matriarch. With 12 assorted bairns along the row, one more in front hardly caused a conceptual problem. I duly finished the ice cream and chucked lid and carton in the communal poke. It felt good to be included. For just a second she was the universal mother and I was anybody's daughter. No words were even exchanged.

This constant fleeting connection with strangers is what I miss during long trips to the Nordic nations. Only the Irish have anything like the same deep-seated need to connect and entertain.

If 'having the crack'[15] with like-minded, expansive, mischievous people ever became an Olympic sport, we'd win. Scotland's linguistic tradition is a fabulous weave more complex than any tartan. Just as culturally precious, just as socially important, but far, far more neglected.

The gap between public and private language describes the mental health of a nation. The Irish have next to no gap – their formal 'front of house' register hardly differs from their informal 'round the kitchen table' patter. Indeed, I remember the BBC's Ireland correspondent raising eyebrows on Radio Scotland when he once described Charles Haughey (affectionately) as 'a foxy auld whore' (rhyming with poor). I remember too the opening concert of Celtic Connections led by the Irish pianist and composer Michael O'Sullivan whose relaxed register didn't change throughout an event in which he introduced senior fellow musicians, the audience and kids in his orchestra.

That audible 'level playing field' was the reason I used to insist on using the Christian names of all guests on radio programmes regardless of status and the same Scots words like glaikit or heid bummer whether Gordon Brown was on the line (rare) or a phone caller from Auchtermuchty.

But in general, there is no level linguistic playing field in Scottish public life. And that encourages everyone to stay at their pre-prescribed place in the pecking order.

---

15 I'm grateful to Cailean MacLean for patiently explaining the more commonly spelled *craic* is in fact Irish.

So most Scots still default to a 'posher' or grammatically correct version of themselves each time they perform in public or connect with authority. As a result there's hesitation at almost every turn – especially at formal events. Who dares to risk sounding stupid by asking a question? Who dares talk in public without a written speech or weeks of preparation? Who dares perform without a formal debating structure or a wee dram?

Moments of genuine cultural confidence are funnier, more authentic and more spontaneous than that.

I was in Belfast when Northern Ireland beat England 1–0 in 2005, ending 78 years of away wins by the 'Auld Enemy'. Expecting post-match trouble, the authorities had cancelled buses forcing everyone to walk back to the city centre. The mood was frisky (and I was the only woman I could see in that massive crowd of marching men) when they mysteriously started to sing 'Away in a Manger'. After the line, 'the stars in the bright sky looked down where he lay', the last two words were punched home over and over again. He lay. He lay. He lay. Why? Because David Healey had scored that all-important single goal. Clever. The post-match mood was transformed – thanks to smart thinking by the Northern Ireland football authorities who had given fans their own permanent Kop-style area at Windsor Park in return for some witty, non-sectarian singing. That's the kind of deal Scotland could usefully repeat – instead we have a range of chants that can't be used and a criminal sanction for anyone who crosses the line. The law can censor what's offensive. It can't create an inoffensive but funny and robust Scots register.

Fans could. Politicians could raise their game and use the Scots they have. Broadcasters could do much, much more. The BBC's mission is to reflect nation onto nation. Without reflecting the full range of authentic Scots speech in news and documentaries as well as comedy and drama, broadcasters are widening the gap between public and private language, and denting confidence as surely as RBS going pear-shaped or the national team failing to qualify for the World Cup – all over again.

In fact, beyond football, the risk of being judged by the way they speak is too high for many Scotsmen. Safer not to. So another problem with language is the unequal use of it. The Clint Eastwood approach is most favoured by powerful men (hostile stare and total silence) with women deployed as the chirpy mediators. And that's part of a bigger gender divide that harms language... and Scottish culture.

CHAPTER NINE

Women – Harpies or Quines?

PICK A PAPER – LIKE *The Scotsman.*

Pick a day – like today.

24 April 2013.

'UK jobs market is female unfriendly.'

Peter Dawson on the men only policy at Muirfield.'

'Glasgow – most violent city in UK.'

Is there a gender dimension to these and other headlines? Yip.

Is there a gender dimension to Scottish public life? Apparently not.

Strange, isn't it?

News testifies every day to the gendered and unequal nature of Scottish society – and yet try to raise issues of women's representation, men's health, women's pay, men's violent behaviour or gender divisions in modern Scotland and you find yourself talking to the collective hand. We live, it seems, in a 'post-feminist' society.

The first Scottish Parliament had (almost) gender parity and half the main party leaders are currently female. Very few women must endure the difficulties faced by their mothers or grandmothers. Contraception has changed women's lives. Equal numbers at university will work through to general equality in the next generation. Men will get overtaken in a world of soft skills (though evidently not quite yet). Society is gradually equalising and women demanding quotas and reserved places on boards are greedy, slightly embarrassing and just plain wrong.

We know how the script goes. Women in a man's world do 'see ourselves as others see us'. Constantly. We detect the whining offence caused by 'special pleading'. We feel the wince, hear the sigh and watch the eyes glaze over. All women do. It's why so many shut up and learn to channel the creativity that could energise society, policy, community building, politics, business and job creation into the considerable effort of raising a family and holding down a part-time job instead.

Politics are always about bigger things, more universal things or more distant things. Not the age-old division of labour and the share-out of power, wealth and control between the sexes.

And yet, gender is still the easiest predictor of who commits violent crime, runs a business, goes fishing or dies prematurely. Whether it's setting new records – or settling old scores – men are still the actors in Scottish society and their actions create, destroy and shape our world. Women generally have a different role. We facilitate, research, nurture, support and complain but never threaten to usurp men as leading actors. And it's gone on for so long, that divvy-up feels quite natural.

In journalism men tend to make news, decide how and whether it should be reported and analyse the most important happenings as correspondents and editors. Women tend to 'present' and front news programmes – delivering decisions made by men the same way a midwife delivers someone else's baby. One sex is the arbiter of almost everything that matters in Scotland's public world – and the presence of a few exceptional women only validates that underlying reality.

That wouldn't matter one iota if gender distinctions were trivial. After all, as a blue-eyed person I'm perfectly happy to be represented by brown, hazel or green-eyed folk. But gender is not a trivial distinction.

Not in Scotland. Not anywhere. And certainly not in the press.

Everyday male values, preoccupations and outlooks shape front pages and determine the spending patterns and political priorities of the nation. Every day, women readers peel away from newspapers prompting editors to try a different offer, feature or supplement to coax them back in. What would happen if the values of the main stories on the front page and the hands on the editorial tiller were female? One day in 1995, that's precisely what happened.

I first set up a feminist magazine at Oxford University in 1978. It was called *Lilith* after Adam's mythical first wife who refused to lie beneath him and was banished from Eden for her cheek. Much of the content was desperately worthy – I remember trying to make a story out of the Boilermakers Union donating £40 to the local Women's Aid hostel. And having to argue strenuously that *Lilith* would not be avoided by women embarrassed that the name reminded them of – whisper it – tampons. We thought we were ground-breaking but were more like primary kids painting with colours for the first time. Opinions were easy things to have and hold. To chant during marches, to push doggedly over too many pints late at night. But to develop, adapt, refresh, relate – to write about? Even at lofty Oxford University, gals learned and regurgitated facts but tended not to develop personal agendas, never mind world views. We acquired knowledge but were not encouraged to apply or develop insight. Got our brains working to analyse massive problems but weren't expected to persevere or suggest solutions. Clever girls. Boring newspaper. But we were young.

Feminist magazine number two was born in 1991 in Glasgow, named *Harpies and Quines* after the two caricatures of womanhood – evil mythic Greek demons dragging innocent men to the afterlife on the one hand and innocent, biddable lasses on the other. Our contention was that most women live somewhere between these two extremes. Anyway, mothers and baby were slightly surprised to be sued immediately by the mighty *Harpers and Queen* – owned by National Magazines – for 'passing off'. Apparently they thought our scurrilous rag with regular features like Wanker of the Month could be mistaken for a glossy homes, frocks and gardens magazine. Our tiny feminist collective with rented offices and an almighty £3,000 of investment stood poised on the verge of legal defeat and the payment of a five-figure sum in damages. Our own lawyers were so convinced we would lose, an anagram was created for a defiant relaunch on the steps of the court. As it turned out, thanks to the free publicity, *Harpers* backed down, accepted that 'Quines' had a distinctive meaning to Scots readers, and Sequinned Pariahs – the product of in-depth piloting on the back of a fag packet – became my company name instead. We kept calm, used the press, got supportive UK-wide publicity and published for three years before the nightmare of distribution costs closed us down, a month after our biggest ever sale. By 1994, *Harpies and Quines* was toast.

In 1995 I became assistant editor of *The Scotsman*, appointed by Andrew Jaspan to help modernise the paper. Female readers were drifting away from almost all broadsheet papers and *The Scotsman* was no exception. Was the content unreflectively male-oriented?

Well, obviously it was. A well run paper is rarely a deeply reflective one. The men who ran *The Scotsman* did not – maybe could not –

Harpies and Quines.

challenge their decision making on a daily basis. The relentless pressure of newspaper production required fast and unselfconscious decision-making about who should cover stories and how they should be written. The suggestion that a male news agenda was at work provoked a very frosty, hostile reaction. And yet the evidence was in front of their noses. Across all the media, there were a few female reporters but hardly any female correspondents, leader writers, political columnists, news editors, programme editors, newspaper editors or owners. Jobs that required comment, judgement and well cultivated contacts – jobs for opinion formers and agenda setters – these were almost always the sole preserve of men. Women described, men analysed. Women presented, men opined.

I realised there was only one way to show how male values underpinned every word, picture, opinion and promotion chosen. So I took a deep breath and suggested an edition of the paper should be written, produced and edited by the women on the paper, that the men could go home or perform 'down-table' tasks and that *The Scotsman* should publish as *The Scotswoman* on International Women's Day, 1995.

As the only female member of the paper's 13-person editorial board I was amazed (and mightily relieved) to discover I didn't have to argue the case. Some men reacted so strongly and so angrily to the very idea of change, they converted more moderate men into instant allies.

So we had ten weeks to achieve a world first – the first *Scotswoman* paper. Some women maintained the idea was patronising, others objected that there wasn't a single 'women's view' on any issue and that the whole project was a tokenistic waste of time. I let the staff argue out these important questions and come to a majority decision. Thankfully, all meetings decided to go ahead with at least 70 per cent of women in favour.

So a month before D-Day, 30 female journalists sat in a room for two hours and discussed news coverage. At first it was hard. When no-one has asked your opinion on really big stories, it's tempting to revert to passive silence. But soon the opinions were flowing.

What is foreign news anyway? Largely pictures of men in flak jackets and men you don't recognise in suits. Much war and conflict, a lot about how people die and fight but little about how people live across the world. No-one suggested we ignore wars but we made space for 'lifestyle' stories too. On the day though, if Miss India had not become Miss World and met Mother Teresa, there would not have

The Scotswoman.

been a single foreign story about women on the news wires. Women don't own or scare enough to make headlines. Problem number one.

Another pet hate proved to be speculative stories. We felt head-lines predicting 'Brown to make a quarter per cent interest rate cut' could be more honestly rewritten as 'Brown is the Chancellor and he's a powerful chap' or more succinctly still, 'Gordon Brown'. But specu-lation about the likely actions of important men sells papers. Problem number two.

Sports coverage was another headache. Scotswomen don't yearn for match commentary on badminton matches or women's rugby. Statistically, women prefer the solitary pursuits of jogging, aerobics, walking and yoga to any team sport. Perhaps that's no surprise. Despite the stunning success of women in the 2012 London Olympics, women's sport receives only a tenth of the TV airtime devoted to men's sport.

We wanted women as actors in the news not passive objects. But the truth was then and still is now, that women just don't make the 'news' as it's conventionally defined. Women's opinions don't shake stock markets, their actions don't provoke wars or strikes or disputes, their single casual purchases don't destroy or create thousands of jobs, their work doesn't often attract Nobel prizes or vast research awards and their hopes don't shape new political parties or movements. We wanted to produce a real newspaper not a fantasy one. So we had to find ways to make women's views newsworthy.

I commissioned a prominent transport expert to look at the (then) newly proposed M77 motorway south of Glasgow. Dr Carmen Hass-Klau travelled from Brighton to Glasgow but was doubtful she would have time to sift through all the evidence before our deadline. Then she accidentally wandered onto the M8 beside her Glasgow hotel and rapidly became a woman with a mission. She measured the width of American freeway-style streets like one way St Vincent Street and took pictures of the male-dominated space for individual cars over-whelming the female-dominated pavements. Within a mere three days Carmen concluded that the authorities were indirectly discriminating against women by spending millions on motorways not public trans-port, which women were twice as likely to use. Likewise, we found the most inaccessible train platform in Scotland (Stirling, Platform Three) and encouraged the late Campbell Christie, then Scottish Trade Union

Congress leader, to cross it with one pram, two children and four bags of shopping. The resulting hilarious pictures helped persuade Railtrack to install lifts.

We had a men's page with a self-examination graphic for testicular cancer – a subject none of the male production team had previously covered. There was a rather provocative fashion spread on men matching shoes with briefcases using a scantily-clad male model. This went down surprisingly well – with both sexes. Humour was important amongst all the 'earnest' stuff male staff feared and readers clearly expected. On the night – after a few terrifying hiccups – the presses went into action and vans and trains shot off round Britain to deliver this very special edition.

The Scotswoman sold out in around half an hour in most parts of Edinburgh. Despite promises to double the print run, the circulation department printed the usual number. There was publicity in 22 countries around the world and letters and faxes came pouring in for weeks afterwards. The vast majority were supportive, a very few appalled.

But the next day it was business as usual at *The Scotsman* without much analysis of what had been achieved. The next year *The Scotswoman* was 'downgraded' to a tabloid pullout section. One piece focused on the pressure facing the late Donald Dewar after his wife unaccountably went off with Lord Derry (Wallpaper) Irvine. It seemed that 'society' wanted the Scottish Labour leader to find a new partner fast. The *Scotswoman* team objected to this undue pressure, but we all felt a finger-wagging piece would be counter-productive. Graphics staff came to the rescue and airbrushed the soon-to-be First Minister's heid onto a variety of celebrity couple pictures, suggesting Donald was actually out on the razzle every night.

As the paper was about to go to print, I had a moment's hesitation. Suppose Donald didn't get the joke? It wasn't worth souring relations forever over one day's amusement. So I faxed the page over to his office (yip, it was that long ago) and waited. And waited. Production staff came through to see what the hold-up was. We all sat staring at the fax machine. Suddenly it shuddered into life and a message chuntered out from Donald Dewar.

'Great – I can't remember which date I enjoyed the most.' Once again, *The Scotswoman* sold out fast.

The following year there were big changes at the top. Andrew Neil became Managing Editor and *The Scotswoman* was scrapped. After months of having my work 'spiked', I left the paper and sued successfully for constructive dismissal. A troublemaker without a job in Scotland, I headed to London and co-presented the consumer programme *You and Yours* on BBC Radio Four and BBC2's *Midnight Hour* political programme along with none other than Andrew Neil. He was charming when we met on the grounds that he liked a fighter and respected anyone who worked on network TV.

Weird.

In 1999, the Secretary General of UNESCO encouraged female journalists to 'do a *Scotswoman*' and nominated International Women's Day 1999 as 'Takeover Day'. With UNESCO's backing, 600 news outlets across the world made a *Scotswoman*-like switch. But by that time the 'mother' paper had dumped the whole idea.

African women however took so much interest that I set up a charity called *Africawoman* to train a hundred young women journalists in Kenya, Uganda, Ghana, Malawi, South Africa, Zambia, Tanzania and Zimbabwe, backed by the British Council. A small group of Scottish volunteers acted as mentors via the internet and we published monthly 'papers' online including special editions at the 2005 Earth Summit in Johannesburg and the G8 summit at Gleneagles. Indeed, we held a w8 conference in Edinburgh featuring eight women who could transform Africa with the champagne budget of Gleneagles – but although the women made a big impact on MSPs and 100,000 newspapers were distributed on Scottish buses and trains, funding dried up. *Africawoman* went bust and none of the w8 women was deemed sufficiently interesting to merit a column inch in a Scottish newspaper.

Astonishing really.

Graça Machel, Nelson Mandela's wife, was Minister of Education in Mozambique where she spent 12 per cent of the national budget on schools, cut illiteracy by 22 per cent in five years and quadrupled the school-going population.

Lornah Kiplagat from Kenya is a superb long distance runner who became a world record holder without any state support and now ploughs part of her winnings into a High Altitude Training Centre for young Kenyan women.

Africawoman front cover, and a risqué but well-received article from *The Scotswoman*.

Hauwa Ibrahim, the first female lawyer in her part of Northern Nigeria, secured the release of Amina Lawal at a Sharia court in 2003 after Lawal had been sentenced to death by stoning for adultery.

Alivera Kiiza, a coffee grower in Tanzania, protested that women could not own trees and were therefore effectively excluded from Fair Trade co-operatives. The rules were changed and now women (80 per cent of farmers) are co-op members in their own right.

Winnie Byanyima was an MP who encouraged Uganda's policy of openness about HIV/AIDS, leading to lower transmission rates.

Anna Tibaijuka was head of the UN Habitat Agency who highlighted the catastrophic flight to cities created by starvation, crop failure and land shortages in the African countryside.

Africawoman writer Grace Githaiga helped set up 100 community radio stations with 250 million listeners – an important resource in a continent where 70 per cent of women are illiterate.

And the late Professor and Nobel Peace Prize winner Wangari Maathai from Kenya was responsible for starting the reforestation of Africa. The Greenbelt Movement she founded paid two pence per tree planted. Seven hundred planted trees finance a beehive, pottery or oven. So by 2005, 30 million trees in 30 countries across Africa had been planted – reclaiming disputed land, establishing local access rights and creating 43,000 small businesses. Ingenious.

All these leaders could have transformed their countries and their continent given half the chance. And that's the most important point. They had a vision of sustainable growth, shared prosperity and grass-roots development which contrasted starkly with the 'winner takes all' vision of the continent's male leaders. They didn't have a narrow 'women's view' – they had a different world view. And yet, though measurably successful, the world simply ignored them. In 2010 more than 12 billion trees had been planted by the Green Belt Movement. This could have been the template for a real 'African Spring'. Instead, governments like our own backed dictators, multinationals grabbed land and local people were displaced to grow biofuels and cash crops. Oxfam has just published evidence showing an area the size of north-west Europe has been sold, leased or licensed to international inves-tors in secretive deals since 2001.

So what has any of this got to do with Scotland? Well, sometimes it's easier to see familiar truths in unfamiliar places. The exclusion of women doesn't just narrow the pool of talent available to play the existing game – it excludes the most likely game-changers. And Scot-land needs to transform, not just raise its game if it wants to emulate our more equal, affluent Nordic neighbours.[1]

Don't believe me. Believe a Dutchman.

Macho Caledonia

Geert Hofstede wrote a seminal book called *Cultures and Organi-sations* in 1980 which is still being used to compare societies today. From 1967 to 1973, while working at IBM as a psychologist, Hofstede collected and analysed data from over 100,000 employees in 40 countries. From those results and later work, he developed a model for comparing cultures. The entire book makes fascinating reading. But let's cut to the chase.

By Hofstede's calculations, the UK is a masculine culture while our

---

1   Richard Wilkinson & Kate Pickett in *The Spirit Level* (London: Penguin, 2010) make similar correlations.

small northern neighbours are feminine – with Sweden the most feminine of the lot. If Scotland was to become an independent country right now, it would probably also sit on the masculine end of the graph. How come?

Because of the way different IBM cohorts answered the same questions.

Britain sits in 62nd place on Hofstede's index and typifies a masculine society driven by competition, achievement and success, with success defined as having winners (with less importance attached to overall or average performance).[2]

Sweden sits in first place and typifies a society in which the dominant values are feminine – caring for others, achieving a high quality of life for all and not necessarily wanting to stand out from the rest. Hofstede's model also divides societies by what motivates people – wanting to be the best (masculine) or liking what you do (feminine). The masculine society prefers achievement, heroism, assertiveness and material reward for success – and those values are espoused by male and female members of that society – not just men. And it tends to be competitive. A feminine society prefers co-operation, modesty, caring for the weak and quality of life – and both men and women subscribe to those goals. It tends to be consensual.

In Sweden it's important to maintain a life/work balance and make sure all are included. An effective Swedish manager is supportive to his/her people and ensures decision making is achieved through involvement. Managers strive for consensus and people value equality, solidarity and quality in their working lives. Conflicts are resolved by compromise and negotiation and Swedes are known for their long discussions until consensus has been reached. Incentives such as free time and flexibility over working hours and place are favoured. And it's worth repeating that this outlook in 'feminine' societies is espoused by men and women, as fans of the Swedish *Wallander* crime series can testify. Consensual team meetings, respectful professional relationships and resolutions where someone other than Wallander finds the vital clue are genuine features of Swedish life and contrast starkly

---

2   In editions of Hofstede's work since 2001, scores are listed for 76 countries and regions, partly based on replications and extensions of the IBM study on different international populations.

Country	Country Feminine rankings (Hofstede 1980)	Child Wellbeing rankings 2003 (Unicef)	Child Wellbeing rankings 2013 (Unicef)	GDP per capita Ranking 2010 (OECD)
Sweden	1	1	4	11
Norway	2	5	2	2
Netherlands	3	3	1	5
Denmark	4	4	6	9
Finland	7	2	3	15
France	27	6	8	18
USA	56	20	21	4
UK	62	20	16	16
Germany	63	7	5	14
Ireland	66	12	8	8

Figure 19: Masculinity/Femininity, Child Wellbeing and GDP Compared

with the British Kenneth Branagh version where shouting, table bashing and 'leading man' ego make the series inauthentic and totally unwatchable (for me anyway).

Having made a couple of trips to Sweden I can absolutely vouch for the very different way they do business. During a radio interview with the manager of Europe's largest recycling plant at Helsingborg in Sweden, an unknown woman selflessly held her umbrella over us as it started to rain – getting fairly wet herself in the process. After the interview I turned to thank her and discovered she was the local Mayor. Such modest, low-key helpfulness in a leading politican would be unthinkable in Scotland. On another occasion, turning up on time (very important for Swedes) to meet a local radio station manager in Visby on the Swedish island of Gotland, I was asked to wait for half an hour (normally unthinkable amongst punctual Swedes), because the most important meeting of the week was under way – between union and management representatives. In Scotland, union 'consultations' are sporadic. In Sweden they help run every business as part of the social contract that means strikes, industrial disputes and a grumbling 'us versus them' atmosphere in the workplace are virtually unknown.

Sweden gives a whole new dimension to co-operation and 'flat' management styles – professors clear their lunch trays along with everyone else in university canteens, dads push prams and equality is the name of the game. Above all, people work to live – not the other way round. On a visit to Kirkenes in Arctic Norway, just 13 kilometres from the border with Russia, I visited the world's north-ernmost iron mine run by new Australian owners. They were finding it hard to adjust to the climatic extremes of near permanent darkness and light – but even harder to get local Norwegians to work shifts. Almost no monetary reward was enough to tempt locals away from their sacrosanct leisure and family time. This gave an additional spur to the campaign for a visa-free zone around the border which would let the mine recruit hard-working Russians.

Swedish culture is based around the concept of *lagom*, which is hard to translate but means 'not too much, not too little or too notice-able'. Everything in moderation. *Lagom* ensures everyone has enough and nobody goes without. Some feel this discourages individual effort and creativity – and they could be right (though try arguing that with the founder of IKEA).

There are swings and roundabouts. Sweden has a tendency to con-formity – Britain to creativity. Feminine societies have a tendency to rate friendliness over brilliance, to make the average the norm not the best student, to praise the weak not the excellent, and to regard failure in school as a minor problem. Every system has downsides. The down-side of being British is inequality of a kind that cannot easily be eradi-cated within the existing competitive system and 'masculine' mind-set. It would be hard for market-driven England to change – it might be easier for a social-democratic-leaning nation like Scotland. But only if political and civic leaders consciously construct a new 'feminine' path.

And yet, with every male-only panel and 'shovel-ready' invest-ment plan, it's becoming more and more obvious that Scotland isn't currently on the High Road to becoming a 'feminine' Nordic society. Instead, Scotland looks set to become a pale version of Britain's mas-culine society – oriented towards individual success with advantages for the few, downsides for the many and a belief (subconscious these days rather than overtly stated) that money won by male breadwinners will trickle down to help women and families. It's a very old-fashioned notion. Hofstede noted that:

> In comparison to feminine cultures such as the Scandinavian countries, people in the UK live in order to work.

Is Scotland really so different? Now you could say Hofstede's national differences have nothing to do with gender. Indeed Hofstede has four other measurements of national culture: the Power Distance Index (PDI), which measures attitudes towards authority; the Uncertainty Avoidance Index, which rates national tolerance of ambiguity; the Individualism Collectivism Index or IDV, which compares the importance attached to the collective versus the individual in each society and the LTO, which measures long-term and short-term perspectives.

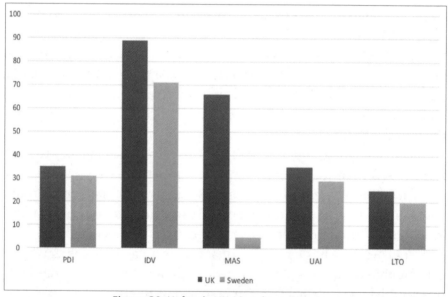

Figure 20: Hofstede UK / Sweden comparison

Figure 20 above shows Hofstede's comparison of the UK and Sweden in all five dimensions. Whilst Britain scores higher than Sweden in every dimension (more authoritarian, more rule-bound and keen to avoid uncertainty and more individualist) the dramatic difference is in the Masculinity/Femininity index (MAS) where the two countries occupy opposite ends of the cultural spectrum.[3] But of course there are caveats.

---

3 The Hofstede Centre has an online tool: http://geert-hofstede.com/countries.html which allows comparison

Hofstede defined culture as the collective mental programming which distinguishes one group of people from another, creating patterns of thought reflected in the value people attach to different aspects of life and institutions of society. Of course, this doesn't mean everyone in Scotland or the UK thinks the same way: there are considerable differences between individuals and classes. This is one of the biggest criticisms of Hofstede – how on earth can the responses of IBM employees be representative of a whole country (especially with such profound income inequality as Scotland) and how can data gathered in the 1970s still be relevant today?

It's a fair question, but Hofstede's many advocates think his usefulness lies not in individual scores but in international comparisons of like-minded middle-class, white-collar cohorts.

There are also exceptions which appear to buck Hofstede's trends. Germany and Ireland are both strongly masculine in Hofstede's table, yet did better than Britain in the last UNICEF child wellbeing index. 'Masculine' countries usually have the fewest women in democratically elected governments, yet Holyrood in 1999 was the most gender-balanced legislature in the world bar Rwanda (Figure 21 below).

But despite these caveats, two aspects of Scotland's persistent underperformance are well explained by Hofstede's analysis.

Firstly, although Scotland manages to outperform England in health, happiness and wellbeing, all parts of the 'masculine' UK are half a league table below the outcomes of our 'feminine' Nordic neighbours. So progressive Scots should be aiming higher than merely outperforming England.

Secondly, a 'feminine' society is defined by its outlook and core values – not by random policies grafted onto a 'masculine' model. So which kind of society do we want? Or rather, what kind of society do Scotland's opinion formers, politicians, party leaders, decision makers and media want, because it is they – not the people – who shape choices, explore possibilities and bestow credibility on certain options. Indeed that's why it matters so much that some of those decision makers are 'unusual suspects'. The great and good are not without the capacity to change or the intelligence to support new directions. But

between almost all the countries of the world... though of course not Scotland. This might be a small mercy. Our higher rates of teenage pregnancy and children living in poverty would probably pull Scotland below the UK ranking in the UNICEF wellbeing index.

logic and historical precedent suggest transformational change rarely comes from the A-list who benefit from current arrangements. More diversity in the corridors of power is not an end in itself, but a means to that end. It's also a sign that society means business. So which kind of country do most Scots want to see?

If you are 'old school', you will not favour any restrictions on your freedom to act, believe (however discreetly) in the survival of the fittest, enjoy the 'cut and thrust' that comes with a 'masculine' society and regard all the above as wafty bunkum.

If you despair of 'old school' thinking you'll want a feminine society which promotes and rewards capable women, and delivers affordable childcare, high levels of child wellbeing, more equally shared wealth and more local organisation instead of just talking about these as desirable 'long term' goals.

Leading (female) Scottish politicians seem to aspire to the latter, consensual *Borgen* style democracy, whilst more leading (male) politicians are animated by the venal, aggressive and competitive world of the *Thick of It* (and yes, it's perfectly possible to enjoy watching both programmes but impossible to inhabit both worlds).[4]

So which is to be?

On the face of it, Scotland's looks to be headed for a *Borgen* future – the leaders of Scottish Labour and the Conservatives, the Green co-convenor and Alex Salmond's anointed heir are all female. The female 'look' of politics and our northerly latitude, population size and (till 2011) wheeler-dealing coalitions would make Scotland feel very familiar to Denmark's fictional *Statsminister*.

But there the resemblance ends.

Compare how the two nations spend money and on what. Compare who decides and at which level of society. Compare how highly equality is rated, how much voters trust government and how much government trusts genuine local communities to run themselves and deliver services. The conclusion is inescapable.

Scotland is masculine to its bootstraps.

---

4 *Borgen* is the unexpectedly popular political drama shown on BBC4 about Denmark's first female Prime Minister and her impact on Danish society.

Feminine	Masculine
Welfare society ideal; help for needy	Performance society ideal; support for strong
Permissive society	Corrective society
Environment should be preserved	Economy should continue growing
Small is beautiful	Big is beautiful
Voters view themselves left of centre	Voters view themselves in political centre
Politics based on coalition	Political game adversarial
Polite political manners	Frequent mudslinging
Many women in elected politics	Few women in elected political positions
International conflicts should be resolved by negotiation and compromise	International conflicts should be resolved by a show of strength or by fighting
Being responsible, decisive, ambitious, caring & gentle is for men and women	Responsible, decisive, ambitious is for men but being caring & gentle is for women
Girls don't cheer for boys	Women's ambition is channelled towards men's success
People work in order to live	People work in order to work
Careers are optional for both genders	Careers are compulsory for men optional for women
Women's liberation means men and women take equal shares at home and work	Women's liberation means women are admitted to 'male' areas of society and work
Single standard; both sexes subjects	Double standard; men are subjects, women objects

Figure 21: Key differences between feminine and masculine societies.[5]

5   A graph compiled from three Hofstede tables – Key Differences between Feminine and Masculine Societies; The Workplace, Gender and Sex, The State and Religion – Hofstede G & Hofstede G, Cultures and Organizations, McGraw Hill 2005.

You could make many relevant comparisons between Denmark and Scotland – here are two.

Firstly, childcare costs around £1,400 for two toddlers full-time in Edinburgh and £500 in Copenhagen (despite the fact the Danish Krone is twice as strong as Sterling.) Thus more women in Denmark work – 74.4 per cent in 2010 against 65 per cent in Britain (figures for men are closer with 79 per cent and 76 per cent respectively). In large part that's because the British welfare model puts family support into complex, behaviour modifying tax credits (nudging and coaxing), while the Danes put only slightly more directly into services and child-care subsidies, to much greater social and economic effect. A British think-tank, the Resolution Foundation, has calculated that the crip-pling cost of childcare here means a million women are 'missing' from the UK workforce. And yet despite sympathy, hopeful words for the future and support for some of the poorest mothers, Scotland has done little to tackle this systemic imbalance.

Secondly, Denmark regards the welfare system as a way of redis-tributing income across the lifetime of each individual (making depos-its during working years, and withdrawals during child-rearing, illness, retraining and old age) as well as redistributing income between people. So the Danes provide high quality services for all to keep welfare attrac-tive for the affluent and affordable for everyone else.

Even though Social Democrats in each Nordic state have lost their monopoly on power – and even though free schools and private pro-viders are more common, no new governing parties have dismantled this basic model. There is no political 'ping pong' or pendulum swing-ing with the election of a new government every five years.

There is general political and social consensus.

Danish Professor Jon Kvist has put it succinctly:

> Without high levels of female employment there's not enough tax income to fund the Danish welfairytale. The social investment pol-icies of the Nordic countries not only mitigate social ills but also prevent deep social cleavages.

No-one in Denmark or indeed any of the Nordic countries seriously disagrees.[6]

---

6   www.nordichorizons.org.

Scotland, hand on heart, cannot say the same. Yet.

So as things stand, Holyrood could no more replicate the back-drop to *Borgen* than BBC Scotland could produce it. Danish State TV's surprise international hit revolves around real, believable, inde-pendent-minded women – because Danish life does the same. Liter-ally. A year after Borgen was first broadcast in Denmark, the young, engaging mother of two and leader of the Social Democrats, Helle Thorning-Schmidt, actually did become the country's first female prime minister. And the strongest Nordic fictional characters – Birgitte Nyborg and the fearless, damaged heroine of the *Millenium Trilogy*, Lisbeth Salander – were created by men: Adam Price and the late Stieg Larsson. Who says feminist fiction is boring?

To be absolutely clear, neither Denmark nor Sweden is a feminist nirvana. Even in a world where powerful, attractive and capable men take responsibility for childcare, share power and occasionally play second fiddle, things go wrong. Egos appear. Marital stress remains. Promises aren't kept. Good intentions aren't realised. And women in positions of power occasionally make mistakes, act nasty and still can't have it all. That perhaps is the real fascination of *Borgen* for Scotland's female politicians. It doesn't create female characters as sidekicks, victims or female versions of Alan Sugar. It suggests women are per-fectly capable leaders but observes no-one is (or needs to be) perfect and there is often a high personal price to pay, for professional success.

All of which is patently true.

So might independence be a gender game-changer? Obviously, it might – but just as easily might not. Without conscious change and active intervention by government, presumption, entitlement and exclu-sion will keep gender segregation in Scottish public life eye-wateringly extreme.

Shovel-ready Scotland

Scottish Enterprise figures show women constituted 0.9 per cent of Modern Apprenticeships in construction and 97.8 per cent in childcare in 2008, making up just 22 per cent of the total. This is perhaps the most polarised take-up of apprenticeships in Northern Europe and means the number of Scottish women able to gain employment in construction, building or engineering projects is practically zilch. That matters, because Scottish politicians and civil servants have backed construction projects as the best way to kick-start the economy, restore optimism and provide jobs. There will be new jobs – just next to none for women. Even though female employment is the perfect strategic tool for a Government that wants to increase equality and stimulate demand – women have been hit hardest by job cuts and service reductions and more of a woman's wage is spent immediately (and especially on children). It's all been said many times. And totally ignored.

Early in 2013, Scotland's Finance Secretary, John Swinney, published a list of preferred 'shovel-ready' projects including £34 million worth of trunk road schemes, a £5.7 million revamp of ferry ports, £308 million for NHS buildings and £65 million on college upgrades. Of course, building projects are important and of course the SNP will try to appease powerful sectors in Scottish business before 2014. But what about the powerful sector called women – currently rather underwhelmed by the independence message?

2013 could just as easily have been the Year of the Soft Hat – with £394 million invested in human capital, not road junctions. Why not? Our better performing Norwegian neighbours have shabby community centres, un-painted doctor's surgeries and ice-splintered roads – but they never neglect basic investment in people and children the way we do.

In Norway every child has a statutory right to a kindergarten place from the age of one till six/seven with a maximum means-tested parental contribution of £200 per month (and once again their currency has twice the purchasing power of sterling). Norwegian children spend the bulk of the day outdoors – often in snow and sub-zero temperatures – fully equipped in snazzy, thermal, waterproof gear. Some kindergartens are even co-located with farms so the kids can feed and play with animals. I visited the Medas nursery near Bodo where children collect eggs, grow tomatoes, make hay and even watch slaughtered cows being dissected to learn more about animal biology. The Norwegian belief is that children divorced from the cycle of life and death become estranged from nature and are less independent, confident, co-operative and happy as young adults.

An activity centre in Arctic Bodo is part of every local pupil's week

– especially children with autism, learning difficulties, hyperactivity or truant tendencies. They drive on quad bikes, abseil on cliffs, climb trees, drive go-karts and eat and learn outside around sheltered camp fires – even in winter. As educational pioneer Henny Aune puts it, 'children have more physical energy than adults and children with attention issues have more energy still. They just need to run it off. Then they can focus'.

I can hear the objections already. Too expensive. Alright for the Nordics. A luxurious irrelevance when essential school services are being cut here. Destruction of the 'mother-at-home' parenting model that has worked here for generations. These are the kneejerk responses of a masculine society. The Nordic approach is not only humane and sensible – it gets better results. The sort employers actually want. Scottish employers placed the following skills top in a 2004 Future Skills survey: planning and organisation, customer handling, problem solving, team working and oral communication. When are these missing 'soft' skills learned – between birth and three years old. Which age-group gets least education spending in Scotland? Birth to three. And which age-group gives the maximum 'bang for educational bucks' according to Nobel prize-winning economist James Heckman? Three year-olds (Heckman didn't include younger children in his surveys.)

How are soft skills most easily acquired at the age of three? Through engaged play in traditional, extended families or in highly social kindergarten.

What are we doing?

Keeping kids in splendid isolation at home or sending a few to under-funded nurseries until the school gates swing open and working mothers can finally get affordable day care for their children at primary school. Is four (in Scotland) or six/seven (in the Nordic nations) the best age for children to begin school? We can't even have that discussion. The Scottish Government won't open up the dizzying and currently undeliverable prospect of Nordic style affordable child-care provision for all between the age of one and seven. And Scottish mothers can't afford to postpone their return to work or take the 'hit' of sky-high childcare costs for longer than four gruelling years. So it's stalemate.

Scotland will keep spending millions trying to 'retrofit' skills onto the teenage and adult casualties of substandard childhoods in the belief that happy, healthy kids are a luxury we cannot afford.

Of course our Nordic neighbours are independent countries, able to fund big changes of policy by rebalancing entire budgets. But thanks to the larger slice of tax raised and spent by local municipalities even independent Nordic governments don't have complete, central control over purse strings or practical, political priorities. Which makes Nordic achievements all the more impressive. Central governments do have the political and social power to bestow rights upon children and provide subsidies. But it's men and women in relatively tiny local councils who have decided to transform the life chances of their women and children by spending taxes on the best childcare in the world.

If Scotland was consciously aiming to move from the masculine to the feminine side of Hofstede's graph, Nordic style childcare would be as important to deliver as free university tuition. Instead we have a remedial society – which spends relatively little cash on the formative early years, stores up social difficulty as neglected children become unemployable adults, and then makes harsh judgements upon those who fail.

This unchanging, grimly predictable pattern of public spending means most single parents will continue to live in poverty and their children will go on paying the price – no matter how well stoic mums and dads shield the adults of tomorrow from the stresses of today. These are the downsides of a masculine society. No matter how many times a few prominent women speak, the priorities of successive Scottish governments speak silent volumes.

Scotland urgently needs a wider economic strategy to put lost value back into the domestic sphere. We won't get that until economists recognise the household as a source of value and creator of wealth and we won't get that as long as male economists dominate the political sphere.

'The purpose of studying economics is... to learn how to avoid being deceived by economists' said British post-Keynesian economist, Joan Robinson.

She was right. If the home was recognised as a source of value in the economic system, the Scottish Government could more easily justify plugging 'leakages' which lower productivity through absenteeism and under-performance. In a world dominated by the narrow values of business 'giants' like bickering tycoons Donald Trump and Alan Sugar, that may sound like cod economics. But since women have been working outside the home in almost equal numbers to men for decades, the household has been losing labour and energy and that loss must be stemmed. One answer is universal, state-subsidised childcare as the building block of free education for all.

And yet, when capital investment is under discussion, childcare is still never mentioned.

That should matter more to economists than feminists and childcare activists. It doesn't.

Women and depopulation

Community building strategies could also usefully recognise a gender dimension. According to the Outer Hebrides Migration Study, in 2007 twice as many young women as young men have been leaving the traditional crofting areas on the Western Isles and 71 per cent of incomers are men. Traditionally Hebridean men have left for work and women have stayed. But now that bedrock is shifting, and with it the whole infrastructure of island life. Fewer children are being born, the population is ageing and old people need care – traditionally supplied by women – who have left. Why are they leaving?

If anyone could categorically answer that question, rural societies across the world wouldn't be sharing the Western Isles' dilemma. At least on the Outer Hebrides, the creation of a 'Spinal Route' has helped. Causeways now connect outlying islands to larger ones and that means people can come and go when they want – lifting car keys, not outboard motor, to cross a treacherous sea.

But in a society that still calls girls Hughina and Williamina (sometimes to curry favour with a croft-owning relative who might assign it to a namesake after death, sometimes to remember a relative lost in the wars, and sometimes to continue the fathers' own name) few seem to understand women might resent second class status. And that's in part because women have accepted it for decades and left quietly rather than risk family wrath by questioning the 'Island Terms of Trade'.

Women don't argue back in public. I don't know what happens in private. But that absence of public dissent may be mistaken for widespread female satisfaction with local life. Wrong. Women accept the deal and moan in private, or leave without warning when the brick wall is finally revealed in its full impenetrable glory. Excuses will be given, punches will be pulled, but no-one close to the decision will be in any doubt. Intelligent women leave the Isles just as intelligent women leave Africa as nurses or Belfast as students. Societies that offer no opportunities to capable women lose them. And since the Western Isles Council has closed almost a dozen schools over recent years, the number of decent jobs for women has plummeted.

In 2003, ten per cent of Western Isles councillors were female – the lowest percentage of women councillors in Scotland and half the Scottish average. Of course, gender parity in island governance would not stop depopulation, but the fact it's currently unthinkable speaks volumes. Doubtless some Gaels think they're better off without demanding, 'modern' women. But ironically, the language leaves with all young women – whatever their outlook on life. One of the biggest and least discussed problems for Gaelic is the loss of fluent would-be mums. Some incoming women will learn Gaelic, many have tried, but most know only a few words. And an uncertain mum can be enough to stop Gaelic's informal use by her children – even though dads are native speakers. Ironically again, the more 'traditional' the household, the more it falls to women to inculcate language skills and prompt basic, intimate communication with children. So Gaelic is losing sassy, young would-be mums at its peril – and not just for their linguistic abilities but for their economic skills too.

On Orkney, women have helped build up the largest jewellery industry in Britain outside Birmingham, as well as thriving knitwear companies. They're also behind brands like Orkney Ice Cream and Orkney Cheddar, which add value to the basic foodstuffs island men produce. By contrast, on the Outer Hebrides everything from seaweed and lobsters to tweed and wool has been exported as a raw material for centuries. And the value-added skills of design, clothing manufacture, marketing and processing have gone to the mainland.

Women's involvement has also been critical in managing successful community buyouts. The role of women on Eigg was pivotal. Women like Maggie Fyffe, Camille Dressler, Sue Kirk, Marie Carr, Fiona Cherry, Sheena Kean, Amber Robertson made it their business to keep sceptical, meeting-averse islanders informed of progress. Their ability to build bridges with outsiders and local doubters and determination to restore island culture as well as bricks and mortar paid massive dividends. Strangely, this echoes the mythical past where Eigg was run by a pagan race of 'Big Women' who killed the Christian St Donan and were in turn 'charmed' to walk off high cliffs to their own deaths. I'm not saying the current generation of powerful women on Eigg developed because of the 'Big Women'. But the locally popular myth did question the 'natural' order of things, and may have helped release Eigg women from the prevailing Hebridean belief that women should still be 'seen and not heard'.

Many Scottish 'traditions' do exactly the opposite – for no good reason.

The Lerwick Up Helly Aa, for example, is described as Europe's greatest fire festival which includes the burning of a Viking galley by 800 winged warriors or Jarls. Visit Shetland says only men are involved, 'no women, thank you, we're vikings!' Most folk assume this exclusion is based on centuries-old Norse practice. In fact women did travel on Viking raids – and the Shetland 'tradition' was invented as recently as the 1880s. Six hundred miles south, it's the same story. In the Borders, Common Ridings arose from the need to patrol boundaries. The Hawick Riding is one of the most important and no women are allowed as riders or entrants to 'the Hut.' This tradition is not a piece of ancient history either but a ceremony invented in the days of Sir Walter Scott. Meanwhile in St Andrews, the annual all-male Kate Kennedy procession which started in 1926 finally voted to admit female members in 2012 – after pressure from the University's first female Principal, which suggested university funding might be cut.

Public pressure – recently exerted by Alex Salmond – could yet bring change to men-only golf clubs like the R&A and Muirfield. As *Herald* sports writer Doug Gillon observed in 2012:

> Even Saudi Arabia and Qatar sent women to the Olympics this year, but the male fundamentalists at the governing body of golf, the Royal and Ancient, remain resolute in their female fatwah. They do not permit women members. Nor does Royal Troon. Even Augusta

National, a notorious former bastion of racial and gender discrimination, has fallen.[7]

Here in the home of golf it's men first and business as usual – ironic, since golf is one of the fairest games in the world, thanks to the handicap system. Sex discrimination has also been common in bowling – few clubs are men-only these days but many allow women associate membership only and confine their play to a few hours on the least popular day. Some folk will think the trials and tribulations of access to a few (often rather stuffy) private sports clubs hardly matters. But it does. According to researcher Jane Ann Liston:

> Keeping women out of prestigious roles in public festivals makes it difficult for them to be fully involved in local networks... the female characters are portrayed by men, reduced to clowns and confined to men's ideas of them. Also some women have fallen victim to the insidious message that their participation would 'spoil' the occasion; they feel in their hearts that a bogus female *is* a legitimate harbinger of spring or an all-male case of romanticised Vikings *is* better than one involving women.[8]

Above all though, these 'traditions' reinforce the pattern of active male actors and passive female onlookers. Look again at the Hofstede graph – one characteristic of a masculine society is that women's ambition is channelled towards men's success.

Independence game-changer?

Ironically, since women are the most doubtful supporters of Scottish independence they suddenly (and temporarily) carry considerable clout.

A Panelbase survey in March 2013 found men are almost twice as likely to support independence as women – 47 per cent against 25 per cent – and the 22 per cent gender gap is part of a trend. It was 15 per cent in 2012 (according to Ipsos Mori).

Small wonder then that Alex Salmond used his leader's address at the 2013 SNP Spring conference to reach out to women voters, saying a 'transformational shift towards childcare should be one of the first

---

7   http://www.heraldscotland.com/sport/opinion/what-chance-the-r-a-buckling-under-assault-from-a-new-front-and-another-thing.19410210.

8   *Harpies and Quines*, Edition 3, November 1992.

tasks of an independent Scotland'. That single prominent plug meant childcare finally made it onto newspaper front pages – for a day. But the pledge came with very little detail and therefore a small stack of questions.

Can European style public services be delivered without raising taxes to Scandinavian levels – probably not. A Scottish welfare system could scrap tax transfers and switch the cash to subsidised services (a la Denmark.) But that would require massive reserves of political will and complete control of economic policy. So do women believe that a Yes vote in 2014 will result in better childcare? Strange that other policies best achieved after rebalancing in a post-independence scenario somehow get delivered – free prescriptions, free higher education, free personal care and 'shovel-ready' construction projects. How come childcare is always too hard to fund right here and now?

To the victor go the spoils. Unless the SNP sound like wholehearted drivers of transformational childcare and greater social equality, the party will not be rewarded by grateful women at the polls.

Social reforms that are too timid and conservative waste time and please no-one. Weak AV voting reform offered such limited change that PR supporters campaigned against it. Likewise the limp Scottish Assembly proposed in 1979 and John Prescott's toothless North-East assembly in 2004. Indeed, the Scotland Act is currently being 'improved' by all its Unionist supporters. That's what happens when you heed the great and good… and miss the boat of popular opinion.

Progressive Scots understand a whole new type of society is possible – if economic levers are deployed by a diverse range of capable people in pursuit of well-articulated progressive policy goals. Indeed that well-known revolutionary feminist organ *The Economist* compiled its own 'glass ceiling index' in March 2013 to show which countries give women the best chance of equal treatment at work. Based on OECD data for 26 developed countries it compared the number of men and women in tertiary education; female labour-force participation; the male-female wage gap; the proportion of women in senior jobs; and net child-care costs relative to the average wage. The top ten (in order) were New Zealand, Norway, Sweden, Canada, Australia, Spain, Finland and Portugal, Poland and Denmark. The UK came 18th – after Israel.

Six of the top ten have populations of ten million or less and all but one is a 'feminine' society by Hofstede's classification. So the good news for the SNP is that small countries do better for women – perhaps Alex Salmond could talk about an Arc of Equality. The less good news is that the Arc only seems to work in countries which have jettisoned the 'winner takes all' masculinity of the UK and present-day Scotland.

Will a desperate urge to woo women voters offer the chance for long-term social change in Scotland? Perhaps. Swedish women had to be opportunistic to force quotas on reluctant parties in the 1990s and Norwegian women extracted subsidised kindergarten as the price of their re-entry to paid work during labour shortages around the same time. Are Scottish women ready to flex their collective political muscle? Or are Scotswomen hesitant and downright hostile to constitutional change? In 2013 Strathclyde University's John Curtice wrote:

> Perhaps in inviting us to step boldly into a bright, but as yet unfamiliar future, the rhetoric of the Yes camp is one that resonates more with the hunter-gatherer, assertive side of our natures rather than our desire for calm and security. And stereotypical though the observation might be, maybe this appeals to fewer women than to their male, more macho counterparts.

But David McCrone's research has shown that women are no less likely to feel Scottish than men and express high levels of interest in health, education and equality.[9] If women don't associate these key issues with politics or the constitution, that surely says more about the alienating, exclusive nature of current debate than female fear of change.

According to Edinburgh Professor of Politics Fiona Mackay, the current independence gender gap may be a rational response to the lack of authoritative, non-partisan information and analysis.

> Women may also be more willing to admit they don't know and men more likely to overestimate their own competence.

I'd go one further. Female hesitation over independence is probably a rational response to warm words that never quite translate into action, great frameworks that are rarely matched by competent delivery, and the prospect of a new boss just like the old boss – male, stale and pale.

---

9   D. McCrone, *Understanding Scotland: The Sociology of a Nation* (London: Routledge, 2001 2nd ed.).

Women aren't buying the rhetoric – they want concrete evidence that independence will change all lives – not just some lives – for the better.

A study of the 2011 Social Attitudes Survey (SSA) categorised 23 per cent of men but only ten per cent of women as 'heart' supporters of independence, backing change even if standards of living might fall. Senior Research Director at ScotCen Social Research Rachel Ormston observed that more men are 'emotional' nationalists – supporting Scottish independence as a matter of conviction.

The SNP is unlikely to convince women through appeals to national pride, freedom or other 'emotional' concepts. It will have to convince them through rational arguments about practical consequences.

In a debate full of rhetoric and technical preoccupation with currency, army and the nature of EU membership, such a practical focus has been missing.

Despite Nicola Sturgeon's high profile and very positive public rating – +17 compared to David Cameron (-40), Alistair Darling (+1) and even Alex Salmond (+7) – every key appointment, event or policy launched by the SNP or Yes campaign has left women and their primary concerns as an afterthought, or forced 51 per cent of the population into special pleading for even a small share of the action.

Perhaps the Scottish Government has become a tad smug about female representation at Holyrood. Thanks to Labour's decision to twin seats and 'zip' the list back in 1999, women constitute 35 per cent of MSPs, compared to 21 per cent of MPs at Westminster. But that's down from 40 per cent and female involvement in local government, quangos, public boards , independence-related commissions and the cohort of special advisors is far lower.

Even the socially conservative Irish are heading in the opposite direction. Currently there are just 25 women TDs in the Dail – at 15 per cent of the total that's a record high. But change is coming. Thirty per cent of candidates in all parties must be female in the next general election, rising to 40 per cent by 2019, or political funding will be withheld.

So Holyrood is about to lag behind the Dail just as the SNP already lags 20 per cent behind Labour in the number of women it gets elected as MSPs. A recent proposal by Labour to adopt European Commission plans for female quotas on public boards in Scotland got no official support from the SNP. Alex Salmond's backing for a written constitution also missed a trick when he suggested it might be drafted by 'an all-party panel with contributions from the public and civic Scotland'. On present performance and without gender quotas that writing team will be 99 per cent male and professional in composition. Instead, the First Minister could have emulated more socially adventurous colleagues in the 'Arc of Prosperity'. Ten years ago, the male Norwegian Trade Minister extended the country's existing 40 per cent quota of women on public boards to the private sector. It took just two years for Norway's boardrooms to comply. Their economy has not noticeably collapsed.

The Irish Deliberative Assembly, currently examining the constitution, has a hundred members – 66 citizens and 33 politicians: 60 men and 40 women.

The Icelandic Assembly was composed of 475 men and 475 women. It suggested a Commission elected by popular vote to draft a People's Constitution and the 15 men and 10 women chosen in a nationwide online vote devised this opening line: 'We the people of Iceland wish to create a just society with equal opportunities for everyone.' Amen. Across the world confident societies have used process and structure to devise more thoughtful, gender equal, adventurous and people-based constitutional processes than anything being suggested for Scotland.

It's not too late to make the independence debate more practical and legislate to put women at the heart of Scottish public life – for 2014 and beyond.

CHAPTER TEN

Whose Culture is it Anyway?

SCOTLAND IS AWASH with culture.

When the independent Scottish state was formally dissolved in the Treaty of Union, our culture became the chief standard bearer of Scottish identity just as a large injection of British thinking was added to Scottish life – especially to the lives of the elite. Crackdowns, clearance and emigration after Culloden removed Gaelic and Scots speakers along with their songs, outlooks, traditional instruments and folk customs. British cultural values became the safest to espouse and highbrow English traditions the most profitable to learn. And yet, Scotland's native traditions somehow survived to be revered, adapted, neglected, forgotten, misrepresented and rediscovered all over again. But in this bubbling mix one thing has been constant – the power wielded by funders, civil servants and arts administrators over what to show and what to store, what to expose to a Scotland-wide audience, what to confine to 'experimental spaces' and what to simply ignore.

There are too many artefacts, too many traditions and too many distinct cultures to fit into the pint pots of funding streams, exhibition space, official events or time in the school curriculum. There is no way to avoid choice. And choice is a political act.

I began choosing early, 'correcting' school books which seemed to confuse Britain, England and the UK. Despite the neatness of my work I was suspended. My first post-school boyfriend was a Glasgow painter who shared a flat with 'New Glasgow Boy' Adrian Wiszniewsk. Later I married a poet which allowed me to bump into Iain Crichton Smith making toast in an Oban hotel at three in the morning, Hamish Henderson in Sandy Bell's bar, Angus Peter Campbell, the uncompromising Gael, and the effervescent Meg Bateman, whose love poetry was often a gentle antidote to all the men. I once interviewed Norman MacCaig for a radio celebration of Hugh MacDiarmid's life, argued about feminism with the 'young' David Harrower, stayed with the editor of *Chapman,* Joy Hendry, watched the late Michael Marra nervously prepare to sing at Glenuig, first-footed Capercaillie's Donald Shaw and Karen Matheson when they lived in Partick and shared choppy boat crossings to Eigg with loyal buyout supporters, Shooglenifty. Scottish artists and Scottish culture have always been accessible.

Lucky to sample the incredible wealth of Scottish song, poetry, writing, painting, sculpture and architecture early in life, I was baffled then infuriated to see how few artists could make a living, let alone a mark, on mainstream Scottish consciousness – no matter how sought after outside Scotland. Opportunities to reach beyond 'specialist' audiences, or receive more than travel expenses here were extremely limited – even for giants in their own fields. When the renowned Shetland fiddler Tom Anderson died in 1991 I was in Ireland and watched a one-hour tribute programme on RTE. Back home on BBC Scotland, I found nothing. Mercifully, thanks to the explosion of book festivals, traditional music events like Celtic Connections, volunteer learning projects like the Gaelic *Feisean* and the internationally acclaimed National Theatre of Scotland – all established after years of lobbying by artists – the situation is now better. Scotland still isn't Ireland, where artists effectively live tax-free. But Scottish artists are taken more seriously – especially by dislodged directors of Creative Scotland.

And yet the dilemma remains. Which artist to choose? What performance to fund? And who should decide?

In 2012 Alasdair Gray hit the headlines after protesting about the high number of non-Scots in top arts jobs making these important judgement calls. He was particularly critical of folk who come and go without getting Scotland under their fingernails. All hell was let loose online and one of Alasdair's 'colonists', Vicky Featherstone, wrote about feeling bullied because of her English origins when she became the first Director of the National Theatre of Scotland. It all got very personal, very fast. The terms employed in the book chapter from which the controversial newspaper article was taken were definitely loaded. 'Settler' has the ugly connection of 'white settler' – 'colonist' has the unattractive overtone of colonialism. But there was a choice. Readers could react to Alasdair's terminology – or focus on the crucial subject he raised – rather lost in all the furore.

Is there a disproportionate number of non-Scots in top jobs, particularly in culture and the environment?

It seems strange that merely asking the question prompted immediate cries of anti-English racism. Most nations monitor the distribution of benefit – it's the only way to counter elitism and understand the impact of public policy. Only the very perverse would ascribe sexist motives to those who thought most speakers at the Yes Campaign launch were male. It was patently true.

But cultural outlook is far harder to define. Perhaps – to re-apply Bourdieu – it's easier to say that high-profile managers have a certain habitus. And 'British' values are probably a good measure of suitability. Now I say that and know there's absolutely no easy way the observation can be measured. But that doesn't mean the issue is any less real or important.

This is where *Gary Tank Commander* comes in – a 2012 BBC Scotland sitcom in which a bunch of soldiers find ways to pass time in the unglamorous surroundings of a Glasgow barracks, waiting to do combat in defence of Queen and Country. In one episode, the eponymous hero holds up a small orange and asks if it's a clementine, tangerine or satsuma.

'Naw,' he concludes. 'It's jist a wee orange – they're all wee oranges.'

Now this either prompts a laugh or you don't get it. Scots don't see much value in learning the tiny differences between exotic objects. Instead they save their energies for the vigorous use of metaphor. Thus, you might be thinking, see this argument – see mince.

But can a leader, top person or manager really be someone who (defiantly) calls mandarins 'wee oranges' in the upper echelons of society? Can you say 'aye' in a Scottish court without being done for contempt? Can Scots confidently bring their 'whole selves' into the limelight – and particularly into the highly contested domains of arts and the environment where 'proper sounding' people abound? Of course issues of entitlement affect every part of the class-ridden UK. Perhaps that's why Bradley Wiggins was a shoe-in to win Sports Personality of the Year 2012. He is that very rare thing, a working-class lad made good without corners visibly knocked off in a sporting world dominated by those with time and parental cash.

And this is where *Dirty Dancing* comes in. I'm not ashamed to admit (well I am a bit) this is my favourite film and not just because of the late Patrick Swayze. The best line in the film was the exchange between the cringingly named 'Baby' and her dad after she confessed to having a fling with Pat. 'You lied too,' she says. 'You told me everyone has the same chance in life, everyone deserves to be treated equally. But you didn't mean everyone. You just meant people like you.'

And that of course, is the moment kids really grow up. When they realise adults say a lot of things they don't actually mean. Life should be fair – but in practice it isn't. Boundaries and limits are quickly established, learned behaviour helps to firm up that 'place in life' and peer-group policing takes over. Thus girls can do whatever they want at school – as long as they all wear pink anoraks. Kids from backstreets can make it to the top if they lose unsuitable friends and accents. And Scots can mumble away about the obscure-sounding people and places that have inspired them and still get top jobs. Except they don't. If this was easy to measure or remedy, Scots would have cracked inferiorism, a problem observed across the world where less dominant communities hesitate before asserting or developing their own values. So of course it's impossible to say what proportion of top appointees 'should' be Scots, impossible to say which individual non-Scots have sufficiently understood the Scottish zeitgeist to become 'honorary Scots' and which are stubbornly 'rolling out the barrel' in defiance of all local tradition. Impossible to prescribe – and undesirable. Change takes time, patience, encouragement, small step promotion, risk and – above all – balance. The last thing that would be natural for a trading nation like Scotland, is an unwelcoming reception for anyone who wants to come, visit, live or leave. The last thing that would ever be appropriate in this 'mongrel nation' would be a state-prescribed monoculture of (inevitably) synthetic Scottishness to replace the current and decidedly synthetic model of 'Britishness'.

But the question still remains. Is Scottish culture in the hands of Scots?

It's a subjective argument – but that doesn't make it any less important. Just much, much more sensitive.

Before devolution, the average Scot stood on the sidelines and watched for decades – maybe centuries – as people with different habits, accents, vocabulary, cultural preferences, reading material, university backgrounds and presumptions about life got almost all

Scotland's top jobs. Of course some of those 'leadership voices' were 'educated Scots'. But educated in what? Scottishness? Indeed, what is that anyway?

Strangely, I've never heard Scottish culture better described than by a Yorkshireman I once interviewed for a Radio 4 programme. Church of Scotland Minister Robert Pickles headed to Fife more than two decades earlier and still admires what he calls the 'Scottish mentality':

> Celts live for the day. Not money. It's not what you've got but who is related to who and who you know. Scots are very family-oriented and they are people with many layers. Scots are like oil – there's a lot more going on underground. There's a spirituality here I love. And less of a fuss about material things because there's an understanding of a more fundamental connectedness – music and art evoke very deep feelings. Celtic knotwork is intricate – so are the Scots. There are fewer layers in England. Scotland has been preserved from that blandness. Life here is far richer… and in that respect Scotland is 30 years behind. But not in a bad way.

I interviewed many people for that programme and yet Robert's wistful description of the Scots' intense experience of music is the image that remains. Because it rings true.

A few years ago I sat at the back of a packed function room in the Dark Island Hotel on Benbecula for a piping concert. A large crofter sat in front of me, a freshly washed and starched-looking white shirt drawn tight as a barrel across his massive back and damp hair, fresh from the shower – further evidence of the importance he attached to this event. As the lone piper started to play pacing slowly up and down the room, the great back of the crofter swayed and heaved. At some moments he was softly singing along, at another moment quietly wiping away a tear – and he was not alone.

Surely this easy and emotional response to traditional music is one of Scotland's most authentic cultural legacies – and yet despite several lifetimes' effort by traditional musicians, it's still the poor relation for funding compared to the 'Victorian art-forms'. That has some upsides – the voluntary effort needed to sustain the Gaelic Feisean movement has become part of its spontaneous, un-stuffy charm. A group of Sami writers from Arctic Norway I guided round Skye was astonished by an un-rehearsed, impromptu performance by Talitha MacKenzie,

Christine Primrose and Margaret Bennett at a ceilidh in the Gaelic College on Skye. And even more impressed the event was not organised by a full time music co-ordinator financed by the local municipality. Stalwart promoter Duncan MacInnes snorted wryly at the very notion. 'Not a chance.' The selfless voluntarism that underpinned the ceilidh was commented on for days – until it was overshadowed by a crofter who came to the rescue after the tour bus unaccountably burst into flames in a car park above the Talisker distillery. Murdo arrived quickly in a vintage bus kept for emergency school runs, drove us to lunch in Dunvegan without asking for payment, and afterwards persuaded a Skyeways colleague to ferry us back south again. The entire trip was regarded as a precious gift, a possible demonstration of shamanic powers (still very valued by Sami people) and a minor miracle.

There's no doubt the voluntary effort required to keep traditional culture alive has become a vital part of its character. It's also become an excuse for putting Scottish culture second. So it wouldn't matter who was in charge of Scottish culture if we were all singing from something like the same hymn-sheet. We aren't.

When there are two competing realities, but space for only one narrative, it's the official British version that tends to prevail – and since 1707 that has only sometimes coincided with Scottish reality. Nowhere have the two diverged more strongly than in the portrayal of the Scottish 'wilderness'. The London-based Scot James Boswell once said Voltaire looked amazed when he announced his intention to visit the Scottish Highlands: 'He looked at me as if I had talked of going to the North Pole.' The fearsome nature of Scottish weather and landscape had long kept visitors away until Queen Victoria braved the elements to set up a second home at Balmoral. Deer stalker-clad southerners and wealthy lowland Scots followed her north to shoot deer and grouse in deer 'forests' newly emptied of local people. Aided by the romantic novels of Sir Walter Scott, Scotland was soon transformed from a place with nothing to see before 1760 into the most fashionable holiday location for the wealthy in Europe. Landowners often cleared labourers cottages and sometimes whole communities to improve the view from their country seats, a practice attacked by English reformer William Cobbett, who made a tour of Scotland in 1832. He was outraged that Edinburgh – which he regarded as the finest city in the world – was not surrounded by thriving agricultural villages because aristocrats kept their estates empty, rural and 'unspoiled'.

He also raged against the Clearances, arguing that:

> It may be quite proper to inquire into the means that were used to effect the clearing, for all that we have been told about [Scotland's] sterility has been either sheer falsehood or monstrous exaggeration.[1]

An outraged visitor could say what local Scots could not. And yet the British narrative could not contain such a critique so Cobbett was roundly ignored.

Sir Walter Scott and Queen Victoria decided to reinvent the kilt. Less than a century earlier, in the aftermath of Culloden, wearing it was enough to get you killed.[2] One object, two stories. Indeed, thanks to the Scottish habit of deferring to the tired, toothy old war horse of Britishness at every turn, there are two stories about nearly everything.

Take piping, place-names and Scottish country dancing. The 1746 clampdown and associated loss of Clan Chief power, along with clearances and emigration led to a near collapse in the old piping traditions. The MacCrimmons' piping school for example, closed down in the 1770s in a dispute over rent with the Chief of the Macleod's, not helped by falling numbers of would-be pipers as Chiefs struggled to spare pipers for the years it took them to train.[3] But while traditional clan piping was in decline, piping in Scottish regiments of the British army was on the rise. As Calum MacLean puts it in *The Highlands*:

> The Hanoverian regime recognised the fact that every Gaelic speaking Highlander was a potential nationalist, Jacobite and rebel. Towards the end of the century, there was formulated the brilliant policy of enlisting the 'secret enemy' to destroy him as cannon fodder. Highlanders were again dressed up in kilts and, by the ingenious use of names such as Cameron, Seaforth and Gordon, old loyalties were diverted into new channels. The end of the Napoleonic wars necessi-

---

1   D. Green, ed. *Cobbett's Tour in Scotland* (Aberdeen: Aberdeen University Press, 1984).

2   The Act of Proscription 1747 says: 'No man or boy, within that part of Great Briton called Scotland, other than shall be employed as officers and soldiers in his Majesty's forces, shall on any pretence whatsoever, wear or put on the clothes commonly called Highland Clothes (that is to say) the plaid, philibeg, or little kilt, trowse, shoulder belts, or any part whatsoever of what peculiarly belongs to the highland garb; and that no tartan.' Carrying weapons had already been banned in the Disarming Act of 1716.

3   J.G. Gibson, *Traditional Gaelic Bagpiping 1745–1845* (Montreal: McGill Queen's Press, 2000).

tated another fresh policy... the horror of the Clearances was now to
be let loose on the luckless Gaels.[4]

Meanwhile there were (at least) two versions of place-names as English-speaking map makers and 'civilisers' found their way to the most
distant places of Scotland and inevitably changed what they found.
They didn't speak Gaelic and locals didn't speak English. The resulting
misunderstandings, misnamings and resentment was documented in
Ireland by the playwright Brian Friel in his play *Translations*. The
same thing happened in Gaelic speaking Scotland and in the 1881
Census (the first to count Gaelic speakers) that accounted for 60 per
cent of Highland Perthshire alone.

Likewise with dance, many of the most popular 'Highland Dances'
sprang from the English military barracks, not ancient Scottish tradition. The origins of dances like the Gay Gordons and Dashing White
Sergeant are pretty obvious when you pause for a second to consider
the names. But what of it? 'Scottish' country dancing is part of Scotland's story now, isn't it? Quite so. It's just that the Balmoralised, pac-
ified face is accepted, packaged and exported as Scotland's genuine
article – whilst the old Gaelic clan 'warrior' face has long been marginalised and feared as backward, slow or vaguely threatening. Unless
of course it's worn by Mel Gibson.

This fabulous complexity – all of it – is unquestionably Scotland's
story. A massive, rich, chewy cultural heritage with a central issue
grinding away at its core: whose story to choose?

As the Englishman Edwin Landseer was painting the classic image
of the Scottish Highlands, *The Monarch of the Glen*, in 1851 thousands of real Scots were being cleared from real hillsides to make way
for deer. This idealised hunter's image of the noble beast became the
classic portrait of deer in the Highlands – for some. But for native
Gaels, that place would always be occupied by a different man –
Duncan Ban MacIntyre a century earlier reciting a poem from memory
to a pibroch pipe tune which described deer and mountain life in a
very different way. 'In Praise of Ben Dorain' was transcribed by the
son of a neighbouring minister, and much later translated into English
by Hugh MacDiarmid and Iain Crichton Smith who said of it:

---

4   MacLean C. *The Highlands*, Mainstream Edinburgh 2006.

Nowhere else in Scottish poetry do we have a poem of such sunniness and grace and exactitude maintained for such a length, with such a wealth of varied music and teaming richness and language. The devoted obsession, the richly concentrated gaze, the loving scrutiny, undiverted by philosophical analysis, has created a particular world, joyously exhausting area after area as the Celtic monks exhausted page after page in the Book of Kells.[5]

And yet, despite such fulsome praise from the venerated Crichton Smith, educated Scots probably don't recognise the name of Duncan Ban MacIntyre but have seen Landseer's *Monarch*. Whose reality gets pride of place? The official or the unofficial, the British or the Scottish? Indeed, the Scots or the Gaels?

Perhaps, you might think, a cheerful amalgam of all outlooks and artefacts is possible. Why not let a thousand flowers blossom? After all, in the modern world many cultures co-exist, enriching and enlivening one another.

That's true.

But choices still have had to be made. For our national galleries there's just too much to fit in. With limited funds and only so many square metres of gallery wall or museum floor, one artefact taking pride of place means several others must go into storage. What goes and what stays? Indeed, is an institution like the Scottish Portrait Gallery meant to capture the zeitgeist of modern Scotland at all? Reaction to the gallery's renovation has been overwhelmingly positive since it re-opened but I found myself mightily disappointed by the relative absence of modern Scots on display and slightly bored by 'imperial history.' Hey ho, I thought. That's just me.

But then six months later, the genial giant and subversive sculptor George Wylie died and I found myself mourning his absence from life... and from our National Portrait Gallery. George was so universally popular he managed the near-impossible on the day he died – a smiling portrait on the front pages of both the *Herald* and *Scotsman* newspapers uniting east and west.

George also fused together everyday life, industrial heritage and Glasgow humour like the master welder he was, with installations

---

5   T. Pattison, Selection from the Gaelic Bards, Edinburgh 1866.

like the *Straw Locomotive*, the 80-foot *Paper Boat*, the giant nappy pin outside the Glasgow Maternity Hospital and the *Walking Clock* outside the Bus Station. When artwork for the M8 was first proposed, George suggested an empty candelabra at the Edinburgh end and lit candles at Bailieston. Cheeky monkey.

In a world where 'high culture' has long been the preserve of the few, George was a feisty, thrawn, characteristically Scottish and democratising force. Everyone who saw his sculptures could hold an opinion about art. *The Straw Locomotive* hoisted up on Glasgow's Finnieston crane was fun, daft, spectacular and – swaying gently over the largely shipbuilding-free landscape of the Clyde – profoundly sad. I think it's no overstatement to say the man was loved. And yet, at the time of writing, there is no image of George Wylie on display in Scotland's Portrait Gallery. Indeed, as far as I can see, other important artistic contributors to 20th century Scotland are missing too. Poets like Norman MacCaig, Sorely MacLean, Iain Crichton Smith and Hamish Henderson. People like the current super-league of artistic talent from Makar Liz Lochhead to Poet Laureate Carol Ann Duffy and Booker prize winner Jim Kelman. In fact, when you start to think about it, the list of well-loved, internationally respected, larger than life, modern Scots missing from the walls and plinths of the Portrait Gallery is huge. Of course there are reasons for that.

The Gallery was banned from commissioning portraits of living Scots until the early 1980s, so the collection is inevitably skewed towards high quality older pieces. But once again, there's no getting away from the tyranny of choice. The Gallery owns 3,000 paintings and sculptures, 25,000 prints and drawings and 38,000 historic and modern photographs. So even with extra space, tough choices have to be made. The hopelessly inadequate ground floor space means sculptures and portraits of modern Scots are kept in storage and shown on rotation. I'm left with the feeling 'my' Scotland isn't in there. More importantly, I didn't expect it to be. Perhaps I'm not alone.

A *Telegraph* critic praised the Gallery's renovation but asked, 'where is the former Lord Chancellor Derry Irving or, for that matter, Scotland's First Minister, Alex Salmond? Most surprising of all is the absence of both Tony Blair and Gordon Brown.'

Well, quite.

Why are larger than life modern Scots missing from the Scottish Portrait Gallery? Perhaps the answer lies in the streets all around.

Edinburgh's New Town is the crowning achievement and physical embodiment of Britain's 'finest hour'. After Culloden, the need to expand beyond the overcrowded Old Town combined with a desire to appeal to the triumphant Hanoverians and reassert the primacy of the newly created and almost toppled British state. So in 1767 James Craig devised a New Town plan which reflected the ruling elite's love of classical antiquity – and street names that reflected their naked power.

George Street – the largest and most prestigious thoroughfare – was named after King George III. Queen Street was named after his wife. Princes Street, originally planned as 'St Giles Street', was named after his sons, Hanover Street after his family and Frederick Street after his dad. St Andrew's and St George's Square (later Charlotte Square) were named after the patron saints of the two recently unified nations, while Thistle Street and Rose Street represented their national emblems.

Welcome to Edinburgh, where Britishness is still working its way through Scottish culture like a kidney stone.

Take Holyrood.

Edinburgh's controversial parliament building incorporates Queensberry House, whose most famous resident was James Douglas, 2nd Duke of Queensberry. In 1707, when the Duke signed away Scotland's independence in the Treaty of Union, riots allowed his violently insane son to escape the room in which he was normally locked and roast a servant boy alive on a spit in the kitchen. The Earl of Drumlanrig had started to eat the boy before he was discovered and caught. No charges were brought, and 'The Cannibalistic Idiot' was whisked across the border to England. Astonishingly, the oven can still be seen in the Parliamentary Allowances Office.

Why did architects decide an 18th century murder scene was worth saving at such great expense? Later in its career, Queensberry House was deployed as a hospital, barracks and refuge for 'female inebriates' until S&N Breweries and then the Parliament bought the entire site. A contractor told me that behind the plaster, Queensberry House was a surprisingly poor building – assorted rubble rather than dressed stone. I know arguments about building quality are subjective, but one thing's for sure. The decision to retain this List A 'historic' building within Miralles' new Parliament contributed to the complexity, delay and massive bill which in turn nearly destroyed the early authority of Scotland's new Parliament. The Duke of Queensberry might have been rather amused. All that effort to preserve a building made special only by the appalling barbarity of his murderous son. In the old days, nobles and barons had the power to stifle dissent. Nowadays an 'A' listing does the same job quite nicely. In Edinburgh, 'heritage' is King. And its subjects dare not ask whose heritage we are preserving.

Edinburgh contains contrast – as any good capital city should. It also contains a contest. Holyrood sits astride a cultural fault-line as real as the geological rift that produced Arthur's Seat and the Castle Rock. Just as the gathering place of the world's oldest parliament sits astride the clash of tectonic plates at Thingvellir on Iceland, so 900 miles further south, the world's newest parliament straddles the place where imperial Britain and modern Scotland meet, sometimes mingle and sometimes hardly touch.

The result is a physically awe-inspiring city that sometimes feels like it belongs to someone else.

Old Town and New Town, medieval and Georgian, formal and informal, *Kidnapped* and *Trainspotting*, Opera and step-dancing, the Usher Hall and Sandy Bell's, Morningside and Leith, Royalists and Republicans, Burke and Hare and Jekyll and Hyde – every conceivable contradiction in Scottish society grumbles away in Edinburgh. Quietly.

I suspect Labour's First Minister, the late Donald Dewar, had a profound fear of stirring this hornet's nest by building a Scottish Parliament that might rival the Britishness of the New Town. The (very) well-rehearsed argument about the location of the Scottish Parliament suggests he rejected Calton Hill as a possible site because it was a 'nationalist shibboleth'.

If that's true, what did it mean? Almost every building on Edinburgh's elegant Calton Hill dates from the Enlightenment – when Scottish luminaries rejoiced in the description 'North British'. Greek architectural references abound; the National Monument is based on the Acropolis and the Royal High School has Doric columns based on the Temple of Theseus. Why would the choice of such a location tilt a nation inevitably towards introversion and petty nationalism? Water-loo Place, Royal Terrace and Regent Road – the unrevolutionary character of the wide, elegant streets flanking Calton Hill is self-evident.

The Royal High School itself was converted by Jim Callaghan's Labour Government at the cost of several millions to accommodate a Scottish Assembly Debating Chamber after Scotland's first devolution referendum in 1979. A nationalist shibboleth? Hardly.

Perhaps it was actually Calton Hill's suitability as a parliament location that bothered Donald Dewar. According to the civil servants, a parliament there would have created:

> A magnificent historic setting in an accessible city centre location: highly visible, adjacent to the Scottish Office, approachable through a civic space comparable with other European capitals, and without causing any major traffic problems.

'Comparable with other European capitals'. Without realising it, this advocate probably sealed Calton Hill's fate. Labour's devolved assembly was not to be compared with other European capitals. It was to be a workaday place – a big council, not a small parliament. Devolution could have created a fabulous British building on a hill studded with British architectural gems. But instead a parliament was built in a low-lying shoebox of a space (or rather, the constrained footprint of a disused brewery) in case it offered a new centrepiece of Scottish culture and an emotional rallying point for Scots.

It all speaks volumes about Labour's early lack of confidence in devolution. It speaks volumes too about the territorial minefield that is Edinburgh – a profoundly divided city which could be a cold, unloveable place, trapped in the empty fabrication of 'Britishness' but for the humble tenements which have been Edinburgh's salvation binding the city's inhabitants together.

Coveted and slightly invaded during the summer, Edinburgh is Scottish all winter long, in the snell wind, in each quick stolen glance down the wynds towards the radiant blue or scudding grey Firth, at bus stops beneath polished outcrops of volcanic rock or on the sharp, whin-covered ridges of Arthur's Seat and the Crags.

Edinburgh is not just the British Athens of the North. It is also our spiritual mountain home.

Meanwhile, Glasgow expends its energy mediating another relic of Britishness – an endless reworking of the Battle of the Boyne in which Protestant King Billy gubbed Catholic King James.

If Edinburgh revisits the failure of the Jacobite challenge at every New Town street corner then Glasgow re-enacts the struggle for Irish Independence at every Old Firm match.

Four times a season, for more than a century (until Rangers' recent relegation) two sets of Scottish football fans have gathered to hurl insults and sing the Famine Song and IRA songs across the terracing. Chants of 'orange bastard' and 'fenian scum' flew backwards and forwards and large numbers of police were employed to enforce a strict segregation of fans, reinforcing the idea that nuclear meltdown would occur if the two sides should ever meet. Not long ago, a Catholic player was cautioned for crossing himself on the pitch. An alien beamed down from another planet might conclude that Scotland is emerging from some kind of civil war.

He would be right. But it has nothing to do with religion or Scotland – at least not directly – and everything to do with the Irish Independence struggle. Listen to the songs and read the slogans. Whether it's the Billy Boys, Fenian B******s, No Surrender, Tricolours, 1690, Union Jacks or Red Hand Salutes – Irish history is being re-enacted in Glasgow every weekend. Why can't Glasgow leave Irish history alone? Or find symbols of Scottish history to fight over? Simply put – because the Irish won. This is the love that dare not speak its name.

Celtic supporters identify with cousins who sent the British packing (though ironically, Catholics have traditionally voted Labour). Rangers fans identify with the Britishness that built an Empire and transformed the Clyde's Protestant craft and design tradition into a world-beater (though statistically many of them voted SNP at the 2011 Holyrood elections).

Of course the whole of Scotland does not revolve around Glasgow, the whole of Glasgow does not revolve around football and the whole of the Old Firm's loyal support is not preoccupied with religion. The Irish Independence struggle is not even consciously present in sectarian minds. But then, neither is religion.

As researchers from Edinburgh's Queen Margaret University College have found, fans on both sides can chant 'Fenian' and 'Hun' all match long, and yet feel completely protected from allegations of sectarianism because they know there is absolutely no religious component to their behaviour.

Most genuinely religious adherents were long since deterred from attending live football by the amount of swearing they had to endure to watch the Beautiful Game. Only a tiny minority of 'Fenians' or 'Huns' have any interest in European history or knowledge of Ireland. Even fewer want to acknowledge that most members of the starkly divided, paramilitary groupings they will 'support forevermore' are doing their best to bury the hatchet and leave sectarianism in Ireland's past.

Nope – that's all too complicated.

Nowadays the average chanting Glaswegian is simply claiming membership of a tribe. His one. Part of whose *raison d'être* is to antagonise another tribe. Their one. It may get embellished with symbolism because even half-remembered points of religious distinction are less shameful than the real reason for the drinking, screaming, violence and hatred. Nothing.

Except 'us and them'.

Any original differences are long gone but the adrenalin rush and feeling of identity through intense loyalty and confrontation is still powerful.

Are the battle lines really drawn over religion, background or race? Probably not. The underlying problem is the absence of a larger, single, uncontentious, unifying Scottish identity. British and Irish. Scottish and British. Protestant and Catholic. And now Nationalist and Unionist.

Two sets of values have been operating in Scotland for so long that schism and confrontation seem natural, even necessary to help separate the sheep from the goats, us from them, family from strangers. The tendency to divide is like an instinct now – an instinct which makes no sense in such a small country.

Interviewing punters about sectarianism for a Radio Scotland series in Glasgow's East End some years back (neutrally dressed in purple), I visited a Celtic bar where the Protestant owner had to tolerate Scottish fans singing Republican songs whilst Scottish soldiers were being killed in Northern Ireland. 'Where was their loyalty to their ain folk?'

In another Celtic bar I asked if punters could tell Protestants from Catholics on sight. Of course they could…

'Prods are right wing – Tories, fascist even.'

'Catholics are socialist – there's Che Guevera tattooed on my arm.'

'Prods are just bad craic – they must have rubbish parties cos they've no decent songs, no tradition.'

Since this was all very good-natured, I invited the assembled drinkers to guess my religion.

'Well, you're a big woman – well fed. I'd say you're a Prod.'

'C'mon now, she's been game enough to wander in here talking about sectarianism. I'd say she's a Tim.'

When my name didn't offer any clues, there was one final assessment;

'Make-up, dyed hair and a phoney Coney [mock fur jacket] – you're a Prod.'

Correct – on the upbringing at least. It was hilarious banter about dangerously rigid stereotypes.

Both 'sides' in Glasgow have carved out entire personalities for the 'other,' while the rest of Scotland looks on. A few cup finals ago, victorious Hibs fans sang the entire repertoire of the Proclaimers. This is also Scotland. Joyful, exuberant and funny. This is the Scotland most Scots want to belong to – not the 33rd county of Ireland that's developed in the west of Scotland.

Sectarianism – like drink – is not the biggest problem in anyone's life, but it conveniently distracts attention from what is, and divides those who most need to make common cause. In 1935, *A Scottish Journey* by Edwin Muir was published and he observed:

> Glasgow is not Scotland at all... it is merely an expression of Industrialism, a process [which has] devastated whole tracts of countryside and sucked the life and youth out of the rest, which has set its mark on several generations in shrunken bodies and trivial or embittered minds.

Almost 80 years later, Glasgow is no easier to understand. Glaswegian men are dying from the effects of drink at twice the rate of everyone else. The rest of Scotland is more like the rest of the UK. But Glasgow is on a different level altogether – it's drinking to forget. I almost wrote Glasgow is in a different league – and that's half the trouble. A willingness to embrace excess is part of the culture. It still brings status – even if it also brings broken health. That downside is regarded as a small price to pay for a moment of action – away from the dreary, passivity of everyday experience. The worship of excess is very Celtic. By contrast, prudence and moderation is regarded as very British.

So it's hard for anyone to confront this worship of excess. Summarised succinctly in the BBC Scotland sitcom, *Chewin the Fat*: 'You've got tae drink.'

'More is more' might be the best way to encapsulate Glasgow culture with a 'grab life while you can' outlook developed over centuries of manual work in factories and shipyards. Those workplaces have largely closed, but the culture has not. Glaswegians are easily tempted to behave like powerless wage slaves for whom tomorrow may never come.

Why is that? As long as, time, money and attention is soaked up with empty reverence for an imperial past, it justifies the confrontational gallusness for which Glasgow is renowned. It's as if Scots fear that curbing the Glaswegian tendency to excess will turn the bold Weegies into the North British. And that will hopelessly weaken Scotland's cultural mix.

With Glasgow re-enacting the Battle of the Boyne on the terracing and Edinburgh streetscapes frozen in the aftermath of Culloden, it's astonishing that any distinct Scottish culture exists at all. And yet it does. Big time.

Britain is a state with a tax base, not a nation with a culture. Britain has a set of widely experienced administrative arrangements and the formal trappings of statehood (flag, currency, army, navy etc) but it's the constituent nations of Britain (England, Scotland, Wales and Northern Ireland) which have distinct cultures, histories, political cultures, languages, civic structures and (to varying degrees) distinct institutional frameworks in law, education, media and local government.

As Manuel Castells puts it:

> Nationalism, and nations, have a life of their own, independent from statehood, albeit embedded in cultural constructs and political projects.[6]

---

6   M. Castells, *The Power of Identity*, (Blackwells, 1997).

So Scotland commands emotional loyalty because it's a nation. Britain commands tax returns because it's a state. Neither Scotland nor England is a state – no matter how often the nation of England and the state of Britain are used interchangeably.

Indeed, as Michael Gardiner observes:

> England, a part of the UK, is a minor nation crippled by the idea of its own majority. [7]

It may sound messy. But as sociologist David McCrone observes, multination-state Britain is actually in good company:

> [There is] a plethora of political and cultural forms: stateless nations, nationless states, multinational states, shared nation-states, as well as a few – possibly only around 10 per cent – genuine nation-states in which the political and cultural realms are reasonably aligned. [8]

Britain is not a member of that ten per cent club. It consists of four stateless nations, not one nation state. And that's a vitally important distinction. Four nations stopped being states at different times in history – but they never stopped being nations exerting cultural clout. Indeed, as David McCrone has observed:

> Following the Union of 1707, Scotland was left with a deficit of politics and a surfeit of culture. [9]

Precisely. Thus many Scots consider themselves to have a British 'state' identity and a Scottish 'national' identity and are remarkably clear about the difference.

A team of Scottish academics led by Professor David McCrone has been surveying social attitudes in Great Britain on a regular basis since 1992, asking the same questions about identity and nationality. Over 21 years a consistent picture has emerged: three in four Scots consider themselves Scottish rather than British. Roughly the same striking result emerges from a more probing five-option question:

> Which of these best describes how you see yourself?
> Scottish not British; more Scottish than British; equally Scottish and British; more British than Scottish; British not Scottish.

7   M. Gardiner, *Modern Scottish Culture*, (Edinburgh, Edinburgh University Press, 2005).

8   D. McCrone, *Understanding Scotland*, (Routledge, 2001).

9   Ibid.

% by col.	Scotland 2006	England 2006	Wales 2007	N. Ireland 2007	Catalonia 2010	Flanders 2004	Quebec 2007
Only national	35	22	24	19	19	7	19
national > state	32	17	20	17	28	29	32
national = state	22	47	32	17	39	45	28
State > national	4	8	9	24	5	8	12
Only state	4	6	9	19	7	11	7
national: state*	8:1	3:1	2.5:1	1:1.2	4:1	2:1	3:1
Base Ns	1,456	2,431	884	1,160			

* Ratio of 'mainly national identity' i.e. Scottish not British and more Scottish than British (rows 1 and 2) compared to 'mainly state' i.e. British not Scottish and more British than Scottish (rows 4 and 5)

Figure 22: National identity in comparative context.

Figure 22 shows responses to that question from all the nations of the UK and further afield. The results are stunning. People living in Scotland are seven times more likely to feel 'more Scottish than British' than the other way round. The ratio in Wales is just two to one and in England identification is almost equal, with half explicitly stating their identity is equally English and British.[10]

David McCrone also compared Scottish identity with two other stateless nations and found national identity in Scotland markedly stronger than in French-speaking Quebec or amongst Catalans – even though 70 per cent of Catalans back independence from Spain.

How can we account for these striking differences? Anthony Barnett says:

> If you ask a Scot or a Welsh person about their Britishness, the question makes sense to them. They might say that they feel Scots first and British second. Or that they enjoy a dual identity as Welsh-British, with both parts being equal. Or they might say 'I'm definitely British first'. What they have in common is an understanding that there is a space between their nation and Britain, and they can assess the relationship between the two. The English, however, are more often baffled when asked how they relate their Englishness and

---

10 Ibid.

Britishness to each other. They often fail to understand how the two can be contrasted at all. Englishness and Britishness seem inseparable – like two sides of a coin, neither term has an independent existence from the other.[11]

This muddle may be acceptable in England – it's maddening in Scotland and only serves to accentuate the Scots perceptions of their national identity. Indeed since Mrs Thatcher and the abortive devolution referendum of 1979, Scottish feelings of solidarity towards other Scots have even transcended class differences as Figure 23 demonstrates.

% by col.	1979	1992	1997E	1997R	1999	2003	2006
Same class England	44	27	23	25	24	28	23
Opposite class Scotland	38	45	46	38	43	45	44

Notes:
1 Data are for people resident in Scotland.
2 %s do not add to 100 because other categories (e.g. 'no preference') are omitted.
3 Data for 'natives' (i.e. people born and currently living in Scotland) for 2003: 25%/49%; and for 2006, 22%/48% – so some small increase on 'opposite class Sc' for 'natives' compared with 'residents', but not a significant difference.
4 Data also available for England 2006 (residents): same class Sc: 23%/ opposite class Eng: 29%; no preference: 21%.

Figure 23: Who do you identify with most?

A similar survey of identity in England (2006) found respondents fairly evenly spread between those who identify most with the same class in Scotland (23 per cent), the opposite class in England (29 per cent) and no preference (21 per cent).

So Scottishness is more powerful than any other national or class identity – in contrast to every other part of the UK. The Scots feel extremely Scottish and yet a clear majority in every opinion poll wants to stay within Britain instead of opting for independence.

What should we make of that conundrum?

Until recently, key writers viewed the Scots dual identity as a source of confusion and weakness:

Scottish culture is characterised as split, divided, deformed. This

---

11 A. Barnett, *Our Constitutional Revolution* (London: Vintage, 1997).

is a not unfamiliar view of Scottish culture, epitomised by Walter Scott, that Scotland is divided between the 'heart' (representing the past, romance, 'civil society') and the 'head' (the present and future, reason, and, by dint of that, the British state).[12]

And yet across the world, nation-states – where head and heart combine – are the exception not the rule. Some degree of ambiguity in state/national identity is as normal as bi or tri-lingualism beyond our monoglot shores. In accepting and understanding this ambiguity, Scots may be surprisingly modern – or may be about to resolve the dilemma with further constitutional change.

As Cairns Craig points out:

> The fragmentation and division which made Scotland seem abnormal to an earlier part of the 20th century came to be the norm for much of the world's population. Bilingualism, biculturalism and the inheritance of a diversity of fragmented traditions were to be the source of creativity rather than its inhibition in the second half of the 20th century, and Scotland ceased to have to measure itself against the false 'norm', psychological as well as cultural, of the unified national tradition.[13]

This then, is the danger for the continuing Union. Britishness is a fairly unlovely cultural construct, just as Esperanto is a fairly unloved constructed language. It's nobody's top preference – but at least Esperanto is fair. Everyone must learn and hardly anyone has the undue advantage of being born a 'native speaker.' Britishness is different. It isn't neutral and it isn't fair. If there was was a carefully selected 'UK Greatest Hits' Robert Burns would surely be in the Top Ten and his poetry taught in every British school, as it has been for some time in Russia. Instead, modern Britishness largely means cultural Englishness and the preoccupations of the M25 cast widely across the whole UK. And Burns' 250th anniversary in 2009 went unmarked on network British TV and radio while Dickens' 200th anniversary merited an entire season. Was Burns not British?

The lazy conflation of the English nation and the British State will increasingly and disproportionately irk the Scots because we disproportionately notice and understand the difference. But a nation of five

---

12 Ibid.
13 C. Craig, *History of Scottish Literature* (Aberdeen: Aberdeen University Press, 1990).

million cannot force 55 million neighbours to show sustained interest in our distinctive cultural jewels – unless they become world famous like Andy Murray. Thus Scotland is constantly being 'rediscovered' by English TV presenters, gob-smacked and pleasantly surprised by the difference of the country they have been sent to explore – a valid reaction for coverage by a 'foreign' TV channel but hardly cricket for the British Broadcasting Corporation whose staff are meant to show some familiarity with all of these islands – not just the bit around London.

If 'British' culture was carefully composed of the best offerings from all four nations – a bit like the British Lions rugby squad – all UK citizens would know something of Britain's physical and cultural diversity and Burns' 250th anniversary would have had its moment in the sun. But that didn't happen because British culture isn't a distinct and consciously crafted umbrella fusing together the best of English, Scottish, Welsh and Irish cultures. It's often a tired, redundant restatement of Victorian Empire values concealed most of the time, like a shrivelled Wizard of Oz, behind the enormous bulk of its more energetic English proxy.

It could have been different. A federal or properly devolved British state based on parity, equality and mutual respect might have consciously created a synthetic Britishness based on the best work of all its constituent parts. The model was there in the heady (almost) devolutionary days of the '70s when *Nationwide* dominated peak-time viewing on BBC TV – a nightly news magazine programme (the equivalent of BBC1's *The One Show*) which brought reports from every part of the UK to everyone else. It featured a mixture of accents, stories and pre-occupations from all over the UK and exposed all viewers to that same mixture every night. Presumably *Nationwide* was anchored from London, but its feel was decidedly non-metropolitan. *Look North*, *Reporting Scotland*, *Scene around Six* and *Points West* all registered in my young mind along with their spectacular backdrops, accents and memorably flamboyant presenters. Today those 'regional' programmes still exist but broadcast only to themselves.

In the 1970s when Tory Ted Heath seemed to smile on the prospects of Scottish devolution, Britain's diversity was a cause for celebration, not eye-rolling exasperation. The Home Internationals allowed national football and rugby teams to establish surrogate pecking orders, and entertainment programmes like *It's a Knockout* pitted towns from all over Britain against one another every Saturday night. And then it all stopped.

The centralising English nationalist Margaret Thatcher won the election of 1979 – hot on the heels of the Scottish referendum debacle. Maggie's dismissive approach to a shared model of Britishness put an end to what conceivably might have become a more federal country. Instead, a 'winner takes all' Britain emerged, meaning England's sheer size would allow its values to trump all others for decades.

And that may have terminally unravelled Britishness.

According to David McCrone, the British state was built upon the three pillars of Protestantism, Imperialism and Unionism. After 1945 each began to crumble:

> Growing secularisation, but above all, the moral economy of the welfare state, transformed people's dependence on the Church. Demobilisation and the end of empire released the need for a standing army, and a military attachment to the state. Finally political Unionism lost its appeal to Scotland's middle classes, while there was less reason for workers to be thirled to the Conservative Party.[14]

In short the British State was crumbling before Maggie applied the tin lid by destroying the shared version of Britishness and the shared ownership of national resources Scots so earnestly supported. When she sold off Britain-wide institutions like British Rail, British Steel, the British Coal Board and British Gas and introduced privatisation to education and health, Mrs T shattered emotional ties and scuppered the post war deal that bound social democratic Scots to the British state. National, cultural identity north of the border was already cheerfully Scottish. With devolution state identity would become Scottish too. Since the days of Margaret Thatcher, Scots have been going through a slow process of disengagement – a bit like departing members of the Labour Party who once proclaimed 'we didn't leave the party, the party left us'.

It's ironic. The Scots' steadfast belief in a comprehensive welfare

---

14   D. McCrone, *Understanding Scotland* (Routledge, 2001).

state means we have become keepers of the flame – perhaps the only remaining 'true' believers in a British post war settlement which saw the Englishman Clement Atlee and the Welshman Aneurin Bevan deliver a welfare state conceived by the Scotsman Keir Hardie. That 'Best of British' settlement is ebbing away with each rightward lurch south of the border, each new privatisation of the English state and each victory by the Europhobic UKIP.

David Marquand once concluded: 'Shorn of empire, "Britain" had no meaning.'[15] Perhaps though, shorn of Empire, the 'old' concept of Britishness simply changed to mean something else. Immigrants from former colonies arrived to work and changed England's population profile and ethnic mix, prompting a new and urgent debate about Britishness centred on multi-culturalism. This debate about ethnic Britishness preoccupies England more than Scotland, where the ethnic population is ten to 15 times smaller. Effectively, in their conception of Britishness, the English have moved on.

So we have two partners in a territorial union established to run the shared machinery of a state, each updating their own versions of its shared culture.

The Scots are reassessing Britishness; by which we mean the Union with England.

The English are also reassessing Britishness; by which they mean the ethnic, multicultural challenge largely facing themselves.[16] We are talking at cross purposes except for those moments where the Scots force the old Union agenda on English partners who've otherwise forgotten the rules of the game (and lost the board).

Every day in almost every aspect of life, two sets of values are grinding away at each other – but only in Scotland. Like the juddering movements of two tectonic plates they disrupt business as usual, create

---

15 D. Marquand, *How united is the modern United Kingdom* (London: Routledge, 1995).

16 Now this is not to say the multicultural debate about Britishness is un-important to Scots. Far from it. The bananas thrown at black Rangers footballer Mark Walters were testimony to that. So too the murder of Firsat Dag, a Turkish asylum seeker stabbed to death in Glasgow in 2001. In 2006, three members of a Glasgow Asian gang were jailed for life for the racially motivated murder of white schoolboy, Kriss Donald and today the killers of Surjit Singh Chhokar – stabbed to death 15 years ago – have still to be brought to justice. Ethnicity and racism matter – but the size of Scotland's minority ethnic population was just two per cent in 2001 compared with 29 per cent per cent in Greater London and 20 per cent in the West Midlands Metropolitan area. That's a big difference. Historically there have been lower levels of immigration north of the border and a Scottish cross-party consensus arguing for more incomers to boost Scotland's flagging population. The British National Party has failed to win a single seat north of the border or save a single election deposit. Likewise the more moderate UKIP.

low level anxiety about the future, demand attention and consume energy.

But why only here?

Because here two distinct and powerful cultural traditions collide. On the one hand, Britishness is physically embodied in Scottish street-scapes, civic loyalties and 'National' cultural traditions. On the other, the enduring strength of Scottish institutions has given us Scots law, the Church of Scotland, Scottish Highers, the four year Scots degree and the tenement, as well as negative features like the 'Scottish Effect' in health. All have combined over centuries to create a backbone, a set of expectations, a quasi-state complete with its own 'Scottish way of doing things' – for better and for worse. And it is this tangible, institutionally supported and authentic Scottish culture that pinches every day it's forced into the increasingly ill-fitting shoe of Britishness.

Scots have also made themselves politically distinctive – not just through a devolved parliament with a proportional form of voting but also by developing a Nordic style social democratic cluster of parties instead of the Labour and Tory 'Old Firm' that still alternates in England. This has also produced a distinctive 'Scottish way of doing things' – a polarising national lens through which all other key political debates about the workplace, health and international relations are viewed.

Still, who can blame English folk for using British interchangeably? In population terms, eight times out of ten they are right.[17] Mind you, women have been similarly airbrushed from grammar, culture and history across the planet despite outnumbering men. Thirty-four million Canadians are regularly called Americans and 4.4 million Kiwis are confused every day with Australians. But nations that are also states can shrug it off. After all, they can reinflate squashed national identity with tangible symbols: passports, flags and national anthems. Scotland cannot.

Every small nation in bed with an elephant, as Ludovic Kennedy once described England, experiences a degree of disturbed sleep. There are ways for a small partner to avoid being crushed and Scotland has tried all of them.

---

17   The English population of 53.01 million in 2011 was 83.6% of the UK population of 62.74 million.

First, we have defended the elephant's 'right to roam' in the hope that currying favour or understanding the psyche of the bed's dominant force might improve the situation.

Second, we have tried to wake the elephant, electorally-speaking, for decades but no-one's noticed.

Third, we have tried ear plugs but it's hard not to be on the receiving end of London and British culture when BBC programmes and the most popular papers are largely produced south of the border.

Fourth, we have slunk off quietly to the spare room. But now we wonder why we should settle for permanent second best in a house partly financed by own oil income.

So finally, we are thinking of moving out. Such dramatic action, of course, runs counter to the other way Scots have survived within the UK – by learning to play it safe. We have become bi-cultural, learned to see ourselves as ithers see us and jettisoned – or learned to experience only in private – what isn't easily understood. You could call that the Scottish cringe, or a clever 'clandestine operation' or a cultural insurance policy with a fairly hefty premium. You could say that fluency in a second culture is as useful as fluency in a second language. Or you could say that therein lies madness – or at least the road to decline. In fact you could say Scotland's cultural dilemma arises from an inability to know which culture and whose cultural values we are meant to uphold, explore, learn about and value. Since no other part of the United Kingdom feels the pressure of two competing value systems quite like the Scots, it's possible that Britishness itself is most acutely experienced here, as an imposition Scots can neither shape nor control.

Real stories and cultures are playing second fiddle all over England, Scotland, Wales and Northern Ireland thanks to that cuckoo in the nest – Britishness.

Now to be crystal clear, none of this rejects the contribution of our closest neighbours, the English. According to research, the English are Scotland's largest ethnic minority (eight per cent of the population and 12 per cent if you count spouses) and the most successfully integrated. Unlike other minorities, the English don't live in all-English neighbourhoods and don't create St George's societies or sing 'Land of Hope and Glory'. Some send their children to private schools, but the vast majority send their children to local schools with local Scots. If they are church-goers they attend Scottish churches (there's even evidence that Episcopalians switch to the Kirk to fit in better).[18] And according to author Murray Watson in *Being English in Scotland*, the majority of English incomers – contrary to the stereotype – are not posh southerners, but working-class northerners. Indeed, English incomers have sometimes fought battles local Scots have hesitated to tackle. Dave Morris, the outspoken head of the Ramblers Association in Scotland, arrived in Aviemore from Wolverhampton 30 years ago:

> Back then, local people were being told how to vote by the laird. A fear of offending helped silence local dissent. It also explained why incomers were viewed as useful and potentially trouble-making at the same time – they weren't bound by the same local 'rules'.

Long-term English residents in Scotland are often aghast at the lack of support given to uniquely special bits of Scottish culture. The problem in Scotland is not 'Englishness', but the vast amount of cultural space given over to a relatively hollow, uninspiring and redundant Britishness which offends the Scots belief in the vigorous union that created the welfare state and the Scottish way of doing things, bolstered by our independent institutions and resurgent and diverse Scottish cultures.

If the vain attempt to marshal all diversity on these islands into one dominant narrative could finally be abandoned, each nation could plough the lion's share of its cultural cash first, foremost and unapologetically into its own culture(s) and its own understanding of world culture, in which the others may or may not play a part. Who knows, one day – if a heartfelt parity of esteem returns – a genuinely shared British culture may emerge.

In the meantime though, Scotland must re-order its priorities.

The problem is not the hardy English perennial – it's the shade-creating, soil-adapting and overgrown shrub called Britishness.

It's time for selective weeding in the interests of balance and support for home-grown species.

The hollyhocks will keep growing further south.

The little white rose of Scotland cannot.

18   Bill Miller and Asifa Hussain in *Multicultural Nationalism: Islamophobia, Anglophobia and Devolution*, OUP, 2006.

CONCLUSION

What Scotland Needs to Blossom

IDENTITY OR BAGGAGE? Scotland is currently on a quest for one, weighed down by the other.

It's high time we opened the heavy holdall to see what we've been lugging around. Put simply, it is disempowerment and mutual mistrust.

Centuries of exclusion, insecurity, exploitation, and betrayal – largely at the hands of our ain folk – are to blame. There have been glorious exceptions. There has been formidable resistance. There has always been huge potential and inexhaustible, cussed hope. And generally life today for the majority of Scots isn't bad. It just isn't as long, healthy, productive, reproductive, literate, wealthy, sustainable or creative as it could be – compared to like-sized neighbours and the vast wealth of our natural assets. That either bothers you, or it doesn't.

If it doesn't, congratulations for getting this far.

If it does, welcome to the growing band of Scots who feel stuck. And not just stuck within a stagnant UK. But stuck with the dead weight of mutual doubt.

Scotland can't move forward with this amount of baggage, but we can't let go either – because the unreformed, top-down structure of society reinforces our passivity and deep-seated fears every waking day.

Deep down we fear that Scots are somehow destined to be ill not healthy, couch potatoes not athletes, emigrants not pioneers and followers not leaders. Centuries of inequality are taking their toll. And we know it. Some Scots talk a good game but we've played second fiddle for too long to believe the propaganda. After all, we live in the shadow of giants. Our own mothers and fathers, grandmothers and grandfathers who endured conditions we can hardly imagine – heroes who still tower over this generation. If they could put up with their lives, what are we whimpering about? If their efforts failed to dislodge unfairness and inequality, what makes us think we'll succeed? And if their answer was to emigrate, what makes us think we can face down the odds and turn the ship around?

So we talk about other things – and sound like we mean business. We examine policies that work elsewhere in the sure and certain knowledge they will somehow not fit in here. Our malaise is too deep. Our self-destruct mechanism too strong. Our own goals too spectacular. Our leaders conceit of themselves too loftily distant from our own. Our poor, too poor. Our courage wanting. Our fondness for Big Men too entrenched. Our fear of Big Men too engrained.

Mebbes aye, mebbes naw.

Some of these fears are well-founded, but most are grandiosity – the self-importance of a nation that cannot face the fact it has big but fairly ordinary problems of inequality to solve. And yet because profound pessimism is rarely verbalised (sober), our negative self-talk goes unchecked and unchallenged – growing quietly in equal and opposite measure to the unverifiable claims of progress made by governments. We're perversely proud of it. Wha's like us?

We need change, yet we fear the grave-sounding, censorious-looking, finger-wagging fundamentalists on all sides. They don't sound like us. They suggest change could be easy and straightforward and we know it isn't. Otherwise why are things as they are? In the great inter-generational game of pass the parcel that is life, can it really be up to this generation to peel the final wrapper from what's 'ae been'? Can so much really happen on our watch? Are we up for it? Or will we keep our heads down and prevaricate?

Past form is not encouraging.

Scotland has become something of a pilot paradise specialising in one-offs, unworkable compromises, empty consultations, sticking plaster solutions, rubber-stamping and risk-averse policy – or rather policy which prefers the certainty of stagnation to the risk of success. We also do a pretty impressive line in exclusion, blame, judgement, personal abuse and media sensationalism. All conspire to nip progressive, adventurous possibilities in the bud and make sure our democracy defines progress in the weakest possible terms – rushing excitedly to the scene of accidents instead of isolating their recurrent source. So here we are: stuck.

Stuck with quasi-feudal land ownership because politicians fear a backlash if they apply even moderate land taxes. Stuck with the worst childcare in Northern Europe because politicians won't switch budgets to children from this generation of vocal adults. Stuck with educated women who can't join the workforce because of sky-high childcare costs. Stuck with unemployable boys thanks to chaotic early home environments. Stuck with rising bills for elderly care because service providers won't hand cash to communities. Stuck with 30 per cent turnouts at council elections because Europe's largest authorities mean 'local' is a hopelessly distant thing. Stuck with sky-high energy bills in the 'Saudi Arabia of renewable energy' because the land beneath the turbines belongs to lairds and the seabed belongs to those nice pin-striped gents at the Crown Estates Commission. Stuck with kids who don't know eggs come from hens. Stuck with density destroying low-rise city housing because no-one will champion tenements. Stuck with obesity and diabetes because politicians don't see the link between cooped up Scots and an inaccessible world. Stuck with the shortest life expectancies in Europe because of self-harming addictions, grief and powerlessness. Stuck in a 'stand there till we fix you' society because professionals don't trust Scots to heal themselves. Stuck with three times the jail population of neighbouring states despite similar crime rates because we have criminalised nuisance behaviour, because of record levels of drink and drug abuse, (despite pioneering moves on minimum alcohol pricing) and because of the hopelessness that arises from all of the above.

For jobsworths, mediating this stuckness is a worthwhile goal.

For Scotland, anything less than a jointly agreed plan for change is a colossal waste of time.

Of course in any unmanaged garden it always looks simpler to scythe away at the wilderness, spray some weed killer and plant easy to manage window boxes instead. Working to change the soil struc-ture, eliminate persistent weeds, provide shelter and support climb-ers and native species all takes more time, creates more work, dis-rupts flowering for a season or two and costs more in the short term. Anyone with the smallest patch of garden will know which approach really works. But Scots are out of touch with nature – the green stuff outside the door and the human stuff inside our communities, families and inside ourselves. So in general, short-term fixes suffice for prob-lems large and small.

A few days ago I had an enquiry from a senior Scottish politician about cycling and the shining example of Copenhagen. The Danish capital was as car-centric and congested as any Scottish city in the 1970s – now 37 per cent of the population goes to work or school every day by bike. Recently I visited Copenhagen, cycled about for four days and wrote an article detailing how the city made the transition – focussing on practical measures like bike-only bridges, cycle carriages on trains and the game-changing 'Copenhagen Lanes'.

After reading the three-page magazine feature the MSP got in touch. He had only one question. Not about the cost of Copenhagen's raised, separate bike lanes, the disruption to traffic during their installation, the number of accidents avoided or the way pedestrians feel having to negotiate streams of bikes to reach the kerb – all good questions for any politician preparing to advocate Copenhagen's excellent example. Just one question.

'Do they use cycle helmets?'

'Um... not really.'

'I've just spent the morning handing out free cycle helmets to kids to get them cycling to school. Surely wearing a cycle helmet must be better than not wearing one?'

In a second he managed to sum up all that's going wrong with Scotland. Well-meaning – certainly. Keen to see change – presumably. Yet attached to the merest fragment of a solution – unaccountably. Why?

In the 1970s when the oil crisis revealed Danes dependence on imported energy, their politicians jointly decided to keep oil and car prices high and invest heavily in wind energy, public transport, cycling and better city environments to discourage commuting in the first place. Copenhageners were given a menu of activities the council wanted to increase – cycling, public transport use, more inner-city living by families and more consumption of organic food. The council asked, 'What will it take to get you to do more (or less) of each?' Answers from the public provided the basis for a civic deal to achieve change. Thus by 2015, 90 per cent of Copenhageners should be able to walk to a park, a beach, a natural area or sea swimming pool in less than 15 minutes (60 per cent in 2012), 80 per cent of cyclists should feel safe cycling on city streets (58 per cent) and rubbish on streets should be removed within eight hours (currently 36 hours in some places). The public is engaged and up for it – the council must find the best ways to deliver.

As a result Copenhagen is going for gold – aiming to have the best urban environment of any capital city by 2015 and to become the world's first carbon neutral city by 2025. The sense of joint mission in the city is tangible – politicians may have hatched the plan, but citizens have reality-proofed and helped to deliver it. Mutual trust has allowed the boldest, most ambitious possible plan to be realised.

By contrast, mutual mistrust in Scotland is causing politicians to settle for sticking-plaster solutions partly because many taxation levers are not in the hands of the Scottish Government but also because there is profound fear of change which leaves us all prey to the effects of dogma, personal interest, prejudice, Establishment preference and knee-jerk hostility to 'the other side'.

Trust has allowed Nordic politicians (and people) to be so much bolder. Not just trust in government, but trust by the people in one another and in their shared capacity to run society well from the bottom up – with minimal central interference. It's worth repeating that Swedes earning less than £35k per annum pay no taxes to central government, get their energy from companies run (not for profit) by local councils and put their names down enthusiastically for high-quality, local council-run old folks homes. Norwegians read local papers, supported by central government, made from wood pulp produced by Finnish neighbours in the world's largest mutually owned forestry co-operatives. In Norway, it is illegal to make profit from education, in all the Nordics children attend affordable kindergarten (often outdoors) from the ages of one to six and in Finland the world's highest levels of school performance are largely attributable to the qualification level of teachers – even primary school teachers have Masters degrees and the profession itself chose to loup that high barrier.

But as David Cameron surveys this rich mix of shared, decentralised power, high taxes (though not much higher than the UK total) high standards for public services and relatively little 'opting out' by the wealthy – all the UK government wants to (partly) copy is the 'free school.' Even there the English version differs from the Swedish reality – their free schools are a recent departure from 100 per cent state provision of education and are wholly state-funded, not 'private' or allowed to select pupils by the ability to pay.

Nordic society is a different world – and a successful one, as their top places in every international league table of productivity, wellbeing, health and GDP tend to demonstrate. Of course there are scandals and upsets. But few on the catastrophic scale of Britain, whose long-run demise began when we decided to steal and then trade goods from colonised countries instead of continuing to create value ourselves. Without empires, the Nordics have had to develop other models. They have had to learn the value of co-operation and trust, while we burned off that essential commodity in the loadsamoney era just as we flared off gas from oil rigs.

So while we have had 'us versus them', a rampant market in every area of life and a disempowering, centralised state as the only bulwark against cut-throat competition, the Nordics have been able to resist the hollow temptation to Get Rich Quick and have performed rather better.

Of course it's helped to have the Nordic tradition of powerful, quasi-sovereign local government (in 2007 there were 270 Danish councils for 5.5 million people against 32 in same sized Scotland). It's helped to have had roughly a century of the horse-trading and compromise that comes with proportional representation, not the polarising, winner takes all mood swings of first past the post. It helps to have 'flat' management styles, one of the lowest income gaps between management and shop floor workers, a 'social contract' between employers and workers and high levels of workplace involvement. All these civic building blocks have helped the Nordics generate the highest levels of trust in the world and – getting back to bikes – public transport systems which actually work. Copenhageners have calculated that a ten per cent increase in cycling means a 9 million euros saving in health care costs. That's impressive. Here we pledge to have 15 per cent of all journeys by bicycle in 2020 (Edinburgh was at four per cent in 2012) and do little more than hand out a few free helmets to get there.

People are not stupid. They know Scottish roads are too dodgy to be made safe by wearing a cycle helmet. And the emphasis on tackling cyclists not road layouts or motorist behaviour tells would-be cyclists everything they need to know. Cars rule. The more helmets are handed out and the more onus for safety is placed on individuals, the less parents want their children to be out cycling at all.

More advanced societies know safety is built, not worn. Thus 80 per cent of Copenhageners say they would stop cycling if they had to wear helmets. When a Copenhagen architect came to talk about all of this to the Nordic Horizons group in the Scottish Parliament, I lent him my bicycle. Even though he was staying beside an area of cycle tracks and Edinburgh parkland, Soren didn't feel confident enough to cycle. 'Too many potholes, too close to traffic, too exposed', was his verdict.

Would a cycle helmet have made the blindest bit of difference to that? No.

I use this protracted cycling analogy only to demonstrate the dynamics of 'stuckness' across Scottish society. We are constantly producing 'cycle helmet' style temporary solutions to problems that require structural change. We should have been building up the stores of mutual trust and grass-roots capacity to pull a whole society free from the centrifugal force of what's ae been. But we haven't. So Scots struggle to really believe that rational people, with equal opportunities, early years support and local control will do reasonable and even impressive things with power where possible. Scots have long had a stronger conception of 'society' than our southern neighbours. But without the mutual trust and shared practice of democracy which are the building blocks of society, we're not ' living the dream'. Scotland has been running on empty for decades. We urgently need to top up. Instead Scottish politicians demonstrate their lack of faith in ordinary Scots with every centralising act, failure to empower, bottled decision, bound-to-fail compromise and displaced debate about something trivial.

Can independence alone change this stuckness? No it can't. Each politician or activist who insists that 'with one bound we shall be free,' diminishes belief in the independence proposition itself.

Taking control over all economic levers, making a statement to ourselves and to the world, taking responsibility and doing things 'our way' may indeed improve matters faster than staying in the increasingly regressive UK. But how much faster and what is 'doing things our way'?

Whatever the Great and Good have decreed?

Whatever isn't the way they do things south of the Border?

Whatever doesn't alarm the rich, powerful and landowning classes in whose interests one of the world's most unequal societies has slowly evolved?

It's not enough to say the choice will be made by the Scottish people. Of course it will. But such a response abdicates the responsibility that comes with leadership and best practice in the business of successful separation.

The Irish went from British rule to full independence very fast. No Irish citizen would go back – that's agreed and that's not the point. But every Irish citizen would have avoided the chaos and bloodshed of the Civil War if they could. Again, to be crystal clear, I'm not suggesting a drop of the red stuff will be spilt in the Scottish independence campaign. Not one drop.

But practice makes perfect. And our politicians are self-evidently not practising 'home rule' or genuine democracy in the bit of the pitch we already control. To progress further each member of the team called Scotland must have a touch of the ball – we must all move forward together. That cannot happen while political elites dominate, men speak for women, the middle classes speak for everyone, the central belt speaks for small town and rural Scotland, vested interests thrive, power is centralised, communities are left to sink or swim by their own voluntary efforts and the disabling virus of life-shortening poverty rips through some lives and every conscience.

Devolved Scotland is not promoting 'home rule' and independent-mindedness where it matters most and has been absent longest. In ourselves. In our communities. In the places where 90 per cent of our life choices are made. On home turf.

Holyrood – like Westminster – has been hogging the ball. Our politicians won't pass. Ordinary Scots have given up trying to show we want to play. In fact, we're not even sure we can any more. So we fail to appear at elections – and even that no-show is ignored while the most active players insist more space will remedy matters by letting them (sorry, us) play a better game.

Maybe it will. But these guys aren't using the pitch or the players they've already got. What's to say that will ever change?

Not every problem in Scotland is explained away by London mismanagement. We experienced unfairness and appalling inequality long before the Union. We are tolerating inequality now despite substantial devolved power. Until our political leaders tackle, pinpoint, or start to name the destructive dynamics at work in Scottish society, we will all be stuck with them. I realise the timing of the referendum was not exactly crafted. Doubtless the SNP wanted longer to demonstrate their competence. That's my point completely.

Instead they need to demonstrate OUR competence.

Scots need no more well-meaning proxies, smarter bureaucrats or distant saviours. If I'm not trusted to help run the place I call home, if it's better for the land to be owned by one absent Duke, if it's more efficient for local decisions to be taken on my behalf by one distant stranger, if it's fine to decide the future of my community over its head like an unconscious patient, dissected by volume house builders and privatised utilities, if it's okay for me to know my children will never, ever be able to afford homes near me, if the land I see from my window is endlessly derelict or hopelessly unaffordable, if my experience of being a parent is guilt-ridden and stressful because support to work will never, ever be affordable – if all of these realities are brushed under the carpet, then to be honest I will hardly care whether Supreme Power lies in Edinburgh, London, Brussels, Angela Merkel's kitchen, Beijing or Timbuktu.

I exaggerate for effect. Somewhat. Independence could change all of this or none of this, or some of this. I'll quite grant you it's hard to see how more of UK PLC holds the possibility of change.

So this is not to argue against a Yes vote. It is to say independence without empowerment is a recipe for no great change. It is to say there are other debates in Scotland as important as independence and their current exclusion doesn't simplify the case for constitutional change – it weakens it.

Certainly, Nordic nations like Iceland and Norway had longer periods of nation-building with substantial devolution before they 'took the plunge.' The Norwegians were indeed straight off the blocks when they appeared to have 'escaped' Danish control in 1814, writing their own radical constitution in five weeks flat. Instead Norway was offered a 'personal union' with the Swedish King which allowed them to grow as a democracy and tax-raising state. The Norwegians stubbornly insisted on a vote to decide (as if they had any real choice), formally abolished nobility and later challenged the King over the sovereignty of Parliament. Nor was this slow shaping of democratic muscle confined to parliamentarians. National heroes like the explorer, Fritjhof Nansen, composer Edvard Grieg, playwright Henrik Ibsen (especially in the early part of his career) and a clutch of influential artists helped devise a narrative around independence based on the honest, simple, nature-based idyll of the small independent Norwegian farmer or bonde. As one account has put it, 'Friluftsliv (living in nature) is the way home.'[1]

It was the time spent constructing solidarity and collective buy-in to this hardy, self-sufficient, nature-loving, equal (and admittedly romanticised) Norwegian identity that paid off in 1905 when a dispute over consular representation unexpectedly became the last straw in Swedish-Norwegian relations and a referendum on independence was demanded by a disbelieving Swedish King.

The cause was so popular that 368,208 Norwegians voted yes and just 184 against with a high turnout of 85 per cent. And that was just men. Women didn't have the vote until 1913 when Norway became the first independent country in the world to introduce universal suffrage, giving men and women equal democratic rights. And that was partly a result of action by suffragists in 1905 when – excluded from Norway's independence referendum – they conducted a poll amongst women and had 244,765 votes in favour within two weeks. The cause of independence in Norway was a measurably popular one – and that groundswell was enough to recruit even the Conservatives to an all-party independence campaign which hastened the end of union with Sweden. No separate nationalist party was needed to prosecute the cause.

All parties rapidly involved themselves in 'further nation building' and 'safeguarding the gains of independence' after 1905 – paving the way for the growth of the Labour Party, the avoidance of Russian or Finnish-style revolution, the evolution of a powerful social democracy and a preference for compromise and negotiation that has marked politics ever since. In 1945 Norway's political parties celebrated the end of German occupation by standing on the same shared manifesto. The job of building their new country didn't stop at the referendum finishing line.

It started far earlier and is still unfolding.

But the degree of preparation and involvement in civic life by all Norwegians made the job easier.

---

1   Faarlund and Jensen, 'Nature is the Way Home', USDA Forest Service Proceedings, 2007.

If nature and nurture shape the young – then the hand that rocks the cradle is vitally important. As with children, so with nations.

Alex Salmond and the SNP can only be midwives of Scottish independence, not mothers. No matter how much they want to deliver a new nation, it must be conceived, shaped, brought to life and nurtured by Scots. And not just the coalition of the willing that is the Yes campaign – but all Scots.

So the tough question is – are we in shape?

Have the political classes been building the public's democratic muscle, have we been extending ourselves, improving our democratic diet, sharing the load and spreading responsibility? The answer is evidently no. Or at least not within official structures.

The shameful 38 per cent turnout at local elections in 2011 was a sign that the vital signs of Scottish democracy are perilously weak. That's why ordinary Scots need more involvement in democratic life, given the scale of heaving lifting ahead – not less.

It's why we urgently need to become unstuck through unexpected breakthroughs, new perspectives, social progress – now not later. We should ideally have used, explored and improved every inch of our existing democratic space before demanding more. In the good/bad old days when Nadia Comaneci dominated Olympic gymnastics she had to use every inch of floor space to score a perfect ten. You have to admire the verve planned into that scoring system. It simply removed the idea of success within a small, private comfort zone.

Now to be fair, politics is messy, opportunities arise without warning and independence – like life – happens when you're making other plans. If the Second World War hadn't brought German occupation to Mother Denmark and an American airbase to Keflavik (along with promises of long term 'support'), Iceland might not have chosen to 'go it alone.' Indeed, without unplanned encounters between our parents, very few of us would be here. And yet.

The healthiest prelude to independence involves two processes – becoming unstuck from old ways and becoming convinced about the competence of the population. Neither is currently happening – at least not in a big, transparent and inclusive enough way.

Empowerment of all Scots is the only solution to the Scottish Effect, the Scottish Cringe, the Sick Man of Europe, No Mean City and the Empty Glen – and all these phenomena are as important to resolve as the constitutional question.

More revving the engine, more effort and more breast-beating by the influential few cannot compensate for the continuing failure to involve or empower the by-standing majority. Community effort in buyouts, community-led housing, voluntary effort in charities and self-help approaches to health show what's possible when Scots take the initiative. But the noxious fumes from this relentless machine of top-down, paternalistic governance minimises the spread of local achievement.

Do Scots believe in the capacity of our fellow men and women? If we don't, we can stop right here. If we do, we can rebuild Scotland from the ground up – because it cannot be transformed from the top down.

Retro-fitting skills onto broken teenagers doesn't help. Rushing to the scene of accidents doesn't find solutions. Nor does buying more sticking plaster. Heeding siren voices with persuasive models from more unequal societies than our own (like the United States) is no use. We do not need to get any better at temporary fixes. We need to get better at creating permanent, systemic solutions. So we need to learn from societies that operate without copious amounts of Band Aid or binder-twine.

That's not to say a new Scotland will be a carbon copy of Norway, Denmark or any other state. It's not possible, or desirable. In fact, better possibilities await a nation that comes late to the business of peaceful transformation – greater relative improvements can arise as soon as we acknowledge the downsides of our disempowering legacies. Ordinary Scots have traditionally owned, run and controlled less than ordinary folk in other neighbouring nations. Scots have therefore benefitted less from economic improvement and (shorn of the chance to invest in land, river, loch, house or even village hall ownership) we have had only one way to spend rising incomes since the war.

We have consumed it – whether on food, drink, cars, bling or the superficial, false-status conferring symbols of a nation whose people have little access to things of lasting value.

The Norwegians, by contrast, invest their cash in weekend huts, skis, ski-mobiles, excellent public transport and affordable heating. They invested their wealth because they owned their natural assets. We ate our wealth because we didn't.

It could still be otherwise. It must be.

We can turn and look at that stubborn bit of barbed wire on which we have become stuck. We could recognise lack of progress isn't our fault or really any individual's fault – it's the inevitable outcome of a political system. We are rushing towards constitutional change while inequality holds us back.

It's time to turn and study the problem because it isn't insurmountable. We must believe nurture not nature turns people sour – and nurture better right now. After that – and barring natural disasters – we can expect our own hardy wee blossoms to thrive like any others.

Scotland is currently snagged on the past, not the monster of our own nature – but fear of losing momentum stops us looking round.

And yet a cool, calm survey of the situation offers only hope. Adversity and official indifference may have created apathy towards authority – but adversity has also created connectedness, community and a voluntary skillset second to none. This unacknowledged capacity and these under-valued skills could make a seismic transformation to Scotland if they were at the heart of our democracy, not fighting constantly for credibility, funding and recognition – by right not occasional hand-out.

Despite having it beaten out of our parents, the Scots and Gaelic languages are still on our tongues and in our minds. With no official help and decades of obstruction, Allan Macrae and the Assynt crofters led the way and the people of Eigg transformed their little corners of the Hebrides to become internationally recognised models of rural regeneration. Despite their lack of academic credentials, the Greer-Pretswell ecology team in Perthshire has proved no part of Scotland needs to be written off as a barren desert or an empty glen. Glasgow has become the community-owned housing capital of the UK and dozens of tenant-run groups are ready to undertake whole community-making in the style of Phil Welsh and West Whitlawburn. Tommy Riley proved the poorest, sickest men in Drumchapel could heal themselves. And the internationally acclaimed obstetrician Mary Hepburn has showed how poverty can (and cannot) be shifted. The Scottish Effect can be tackled.

But the clock is ticking.

Tommy Riley, Phil Welsh, Charles McKean and Allan Macrae all died during the writing of this book – prematurely and much missed.

Like the little white rose of Scotland they survived hard times and official neglect.

Who would not be there when the clutter and debris of centuries is finally cleared and that hardy plant can finally blossom?

Bibliography

Aird, A. *Glimpses of old Glasgow*, Glasgow: Aird & Coghill, 1894

Begg, T. *Housing Policy in Scotland,* John Dodd, 1996

Checkland, S.G. *The Uppas Tree*, Glasgow, 1976

Christianson, J.R. 'Norway: A History from the Vikings to Our Own Times.' *Scandinavian Studies* 69.1, 1997

Crystal, D. *Language Death*, Cambridge University Press, Cambridge, 2002

Damer, S. *Glasgow: Going for a Song*, Lawrence & Wishart, London, 1990

Donaldson, J. *Husbandry Anatomised*, Edinburgh, 1697

Dickson, A. & Treble, J.H. *People and Society in Scotland III*, John Donald, 1992

Devine, T.M, *The Scottish Nation*, Allen Lane, 1999

Devine, T. M. *Farm Servants and Labour in Lowland Scotland*, John Donald, Edinburgh, 1984

Diamond, H. *Can you Get my Name in the Papers*, Neil Wilson Publishing, 1996

Dressler, C, *Eigg, the Story of an Island*, Birlinn, Edinburgh, 2007

Ferguson, T. *Scottish Social Welfare 1864–1914*, Edinburgh, 1958

Follesdal, J. *Norwegian Farms*, Rootsweb, Norway, 1998

Fraser, W.H. & Morris, R.J. *People and Society in Scotland*, John Donald, 1990

Green, D. ed. *Cobbett's Tour in Scotland*, Aberdeen University Press, Aberdeen, 1984

Hofstede, G. *Cultures and Organisations*, McGraw Hill, 1980

Hunter, J. *From the Low Tide of the Sea to the Highest Mountain Tops*, Islands Book Trust, 2012

Hunter, J. *The Making of the Crofting Community*, John Donald, 1976

Jack, I. *London Review of Books*, Vol 11, 1989

Johnston, T. *The History of the Working Classes in Scotland*, Forward Publishing Co., Glasgow, 1922

Jones, G. *A history of the Vikings*, Oxford University Press, Oxford, 1968

Johnson, S. & Boswell, J. *Journey to the Hebrides*, Canongate, Edinburgh, 1996

Kay, B. *The Mither Tongue*, Mainstream, Edinburgh, 1986

Knox, W.W. *Urban Housing in Scotland 1840–1940*, SCRAN online

McIlvanney, W. *Docherty*, Allen & Unwin, 1975

MacDonald, C.M.M. *Whaur Extremes Meet*, Birlinn, Edinburgh, 2009

McCormack, C. with Pallister, M. *The Wee Yellow Butterfly*, Argyll, 2009

McCrone, D. *Understanding Scotland*, Routledge, London, 2001

MacLean, C. *The Highlands*, Mainstream, Edinburgh, 2006

Miller, B. and Hussain, A. *Multicultural Nationalism – Islamophobia, Anglophobia and Devolution*, Oxford University Press, Oxford, 2006

MacKinnon, K. *Gaelic – A Past and Future Prospect*, The Saltire Society, 1991

McIntosh Gray, A. & Moffat, W. *A History of Scotland: Modern Times*, Oxford University Press, Oxford, 1999

McKean, C. *The Glasgow Story*, http://www.theglasgowstory.com/story.php?id=TGSEF10

McKean, C. *Fight Blight*, Littlehampton, England, 1977

Mitchison, R. *A History of Scotland*, Methuen, 1982

McIntosh, A. *Soil and Soul: People Versus Corporate Power*, Aurum Press, 2001

Muir, E. *A Scottish Journey*, Heinemann, Edinburgh, 1935

Mykland, K. Ed. Norges Historie, Bind 7, Gjennom Nødsår og krig, p. 221 (Oslo: J.W. Cappelens Forlag, A/S, 1979)

Østerud, O. *Agrarian Structure and Peasant Politics in Scandinavia*, Oxford University Press, Oxford, 1978

Robertson, J. *And the Land Lay Still*, Hamish Hamilton, 2010

Rodger, R. ed. *Scottish Housing in the Twentieth Century*, Continuum, 1989

Russell, J.B. 'Life in One Room, 1888': A Lecture delivered to the Park Parish Literary Institute, Glasgow, 27 February, Glasgow, 1888

Riddoch L, *Riddoch on the Outer Hebrides*, Luath Press, Edinburgh, 2007

Schama, S. *Landscape and Memory*, Harper Collins, London, 1995

Seaton, A. V. 'The History of Tourism in Scotland' in *Tourism in Scotland* by R. MacLellan and R. Smith, Thomson Business Press, 1998

Sherlock, H. *Cities are good for us*, Paladin, London, 1991

Smout, T.C. *A Century of the Scottish People 1830–1950*, Fontana, London, 1987

Smout, T.C. *A History of the Scottish People 1560–1830*, Fontana, London, 1987

Symington, J. *The Working Man's Home*, Edinburgh, 1866

Satsangi, M., Gallent N., Bevan M. *The Rural Housing Question*, Policy Press, 2010

Symons, J.C. *Arts and Artisans at Home and Abroad*, Edinburgh, 1839

Ward, C. and Hardy, D. *Arcadia for All: the Legacy of a Makeshift Landscape*, Mansell, London, 1984

Wightman, A. *The Poor Had No Lawyers*, Birlinn, Edinburgh, 2012

Wightman, A. *Who Owns Scotland*, Canongate, Edinburgh, 1996

Wilkinson, R. & Pickett, K. *The Spirit Level*, Penguin, London, 2010

Young, R. *Annie's Loo; the Govan origins of Scotland's Community based Housing Organisations*, Argyll, 2013

Index